D0316966

SELF-DEVELOPMENT IN ORGANIZATIONS

Books are to be returned on or before
the last date below.

SELF-DEVELOPMENT IN ORGANIZATIONS

Mike Pedler
John Burgoyne
Tom Boydell
Gloria Welshman

McGRAW-HILL BOOK COMPANY

London · New York · St Louis · San Francisco · Auckland
Bogotá · Caracus · Hamburg · Lisbon · Madrid · Mexico
Milan · Montreal · New Delhi · Panama · Paris · San Juan · São Paulo
Singapore · Sydney · Tokyo · Toronto

Published by
McGRAW-HILL Book Company (UK) Limited
Shoppenhangers Road, Maidenhead, Berkshire, SL6 2QL, England
Telephone 0628 23432
Fax 0628 35895

British Library Cataloguing in Publication Data

Self-development in organizations.
  1. Great Britain. Managers. Self-development
  I. Pedler, Mike
  658.409

  ISBN 0-07-707332-0

Library of Congress Cataloging-in-Publications Data

Self-development in organizations/Mike Pedler ... [et al.].
    p.   cm.
  Includes bibliographical references.

  ISBN 0-07-707332-0

  1. Employees—Training of. 2. Organizational change. 3. Self-
culture.   I. Pedler, Mike.
HF5549.5.S376   1990
658.3′124—dc20   90-5621

12345 PB 93210

Typeset by Times Graphics, Singapore
and printed and bound in Great Britain by Page Bros Ltd, Norwich

Contents

Contributors   vii
Preface   xi

Part I   The past: the historical perspective

1. A biography of self-development   3
   Mike Pedler
2. Self-development: from humanism to deconstruction   20
   Steve Fox

Part II   The present: current practices

3. Culture change through individual development: a story
   of the Life Business Workshop   39
   Stephen Merckx and Dennis Bumstead
4. Getting off the ground with self-development   54
   Sue Pritchard and Mike Nencini
5. Fit for the Future   67
   Sheila McLeod and Tom Jennings
6. Why personal development workshops?   84
   Peter Callender
7. Opening up learning in the Prudential   93
   Naomi Stanford
8. Learning resources centres   106
   Julie Dorrell
9. Open learning at W H Smith   114
   Bob Johnson
10. Corporate strategy and individual development in
    Hoechst UK   121
    Barry Allen
11. Management learning contracts: the training triangle   135
    George Boak and Peter Joy
12. Using personal construct psychology in self-development   146
    Fay Fransella and John Porter

Part III The future: challenges and questions

13. Organizational effectiveness and self-development: the
    essential tension   163
    Robert Adlam and Michael Plumridge
14. Your inner team: dealing with internal differences   176
    Jacky Underwood
15. The hot potato: a view of women's development   190
    Pauline Kidd and Sally Watson
16. Can opportunities ever be equal?   198
    Maggie Smith and Janice Leary
17. The learning community   208
    Roy Canning and Judith Martin
18. Using consultants to integrate management and
    organizational development   221
    Ita O'Donovan
19. Towards a working definition of a learning organization   234
    Margaret Attwood and Noel Beer
20. What price the learning organization in the public sector?   252
    John Edmonstone

Index   279

Contributors

Mike Pedler is a member of Sheffield Business School and visiting teaching Fellow at the department of management learning at Lancaster University. His main interests are in the fields of learner-centred management development, especially self-development and action learning approaches, and in the broader concept of the learning company. He is editor of *Management Education and Development* and a non-executive director of Transform.

John Burgoyne is professor in the department of management learning at the University of Lancaster. He was previously research director in the same department and also a lecturer in management development at the Manchester Business School. John has published, researched and consulted on managerial behaviour, management development policy, self-development, the learning process, career management and management competencies.

Tom Boydell is a member and director of Transform (Individual and Organizational Development Consultants) Ltd. He is actively involved in self-development approaches to management development and with applying the concepts of Total Quality.

Gloria Welshman works with Transform and is involved with biography work, self-development and women's development programmes.

Steve Fox is a lecturer in the department of management learning at Lancaster University.

Stephen Merckx works as an internal OD consultant with a particular interest in individual development and the performance of small senior management groups. His previous career, with ICI, has given him experience in production management, overhauls management, maintenance engineering, project management and safety.

Dennis Bumstead BA (Cambridge), PhD (MIT) runs Fordwell Management Consulting Ltd. He has been working in the field of self-development for twenty years and has consulted for ICI and other organizations.

Sue Pritchard and **Mike Nencini** are management development managers with Radio Rentals UK.

Sheila McLeod's twenty years with IBM have been spent as a line manager and as an educator of employees and customers. She now devotes part of her time to employee development training in IBM and leads courses for the voluntary sector and inner city management teams. She trained with the Centre for Transpersonal Psychology and works independently with individual and corporate clients on human development issues.

Tom Jennings is a management development manager with IBM UK.

Peter Callender is a management development consultant with Price Waterhouse. He was previously with the Stock Exchange.

Naomi Stanford is an educator and trainer with a particular interest in flexible, learner centred approaches to developing people in organizations. She is an Open University tutor and founder member of the Open Learning User Network.

Julie Dorrell is a consultant advising organizations interested in open and distance learning. She gives advice on appropriate schemes, costs involved, what suppliers to use and how to market initiatives internally.

Bob Johnson joined W H Smith in 1980 as management instructor and became training planning manager. He has been involved in the design, implementation and quality control of the company training plan and has had responsibility for designing and introducing open learning. In 1989 he joined OTSU Ltd., a training consultancy involved in the development of open learning.

Barry Allen is manpower planning and development manager at Hoechst UK Ltd.

George Boak is the programme manager for the Northern Regional Management Centre. He works with managers from a wide range of companies to improve their personal and interpersonal skills.

Peter Joy is a senior training officer involved in the development of managers at all levels in a large public company. He works with individuals and groups with an emphasis on self-development and self-management learning.

Fay Fransella and **John Porter** work from the Centre for Personal Construct Psychology in London.

Robert Adlam is a humanistic psychologists and group facilitator. He has worked in maximum security prisons and has directed the high-flyer self-development programme at the Police Staff College, Bramshill. He now works for Olivetti.

Michael Plumridge worked at the National Police Staff College, Bramshill and is now a tutor at Roffey Park Management College.

Jacky Underwood is a trainer and consultant in personal and management development, working with individuals and groups mainly from public service organizations. She brings to her work a combination of management and organizational theory grounded in practice and experience of bodymind healing techniques.

Pauline Kidd was employee development manager at STC Electronics Distribution.

Sally Watson works for Water Training, a company offering management development for the water industry.

Maggie Smith is director of Branching Out, a small consultancy in West Yorkshire specializing in the management of change. Trained as a counsellor and group worker, Maggie designs programmes in counselling skills, career transition and stress management for many organizations. She is the author of *The Best is Yet to Come—A Workbook for the Middle Years*.

Janice Leary is a partner in LIFE-ROOTS training and personal development consultancy. She works with individuals and groups on their development in a wide variety of settings. She has a special interest in self-development, biography work, creativity and bereavement.

Roy Canning works as a tutor and consultant at Roffey Park

Management College in West Sussex. His particular interests are in management development and developing the developers.

Judith Martin works as a tutor and consultant at Roffey Park Management College. She is interested in developing the developers and in equal opportunities.

Ita O'Donovan is a lecturer and consultant in public sector management at the School of Public Policy, University of Birmingham. She works mainly with British local government, overseas governments and institutions in the management development field.

Margaret Attwood is currently manager of organizational development for Mid Essex Health Authority. She also undertakes a range of consultancy work in management and organization development and in equal opportunities. She has written a variety of books and articles.

Noel Beer is an independent consultant.

John Edmonstone is an organization and manpower consultant on health care in the UK and abroad. He works with managers, professional staff and human resource specialists on a range of issues. He also teaches on a health care MBA programme.

Preface

Increasingly companies will only survive if they meet the needs of the individuals who serve in them; not just the question of payment, important as this may be, but people's true inner needs, which they may even be reluctant to express to themselves. (John Harvey-Jones (1987) quoted by Peter Callender in this book.)

When ex-industrialists of John Harvey-Jones's stature stress the meeting of inner needs as essential for organizational survival, it is not hard to understand why the fringe ideas of the 1960s and 1970s have gravitated to the mainstream of the 1980s and 1990s.

The idea of self-development has been moving centre stage as the limitations of instructional approaches to management development have become clearer. As a result the search has intensified for methods which engage the learner as active agent in her or his own development. Deciding what to learn, setting goals, choosing methods, and the times, places and extent of the learning to be undertaken become primary responsibilities of the learner. Instructors, deprived of their occupation, transform themselves into facilitators—enabling, encouraging, guiding, coaching and mentoring aspiring learners. Self-development makes the learner sovereign.

That sovereignty creates problems for the managing of people in work organizations. Democratic rights have been slow to come to the workplace. The employee lags far behind the citizen in terms of rights if not responsibilities. Work organizations, on the whole, are predominantly authoritarian in tone. A libertarian idea such as self-development creates all sorts of difficulties, philosophical and practical, as well as all sorts of new freedoms. As Adlam and Plumridge point out in this book, there is an essential tension between organizational effectiveness and self-development which they express as a basic predicament: 'How far can we, as a collective, demand the effort and energy of our constituent individuals without creating a disabling alienation from their personal and social needs?'

At a very practical level, people wanting to explore the idea of self-development in their organization often stumble at the very first step. How is it possible to give people the right to *choose* to be participants? (When in this company there is the unquestioned imperative of 'being sent on a course' by one's superiors.) People who have introduced self-development methods have first had to create the opportunity for people to escape this authoritarianism and to choose for themselves whether they wished to take part or not. Sometimes this has had to be done covertly: the company trainer as subversive holding an umbrella over the activity to shelter it. Where that freedom to choose to participate does not exist then self-development, in its full *by*-self and *of*-self aspects (Pedler and Boydell 1980: 165), can hardly exist either.

The working title for this book was 'Self-development at the Crossroads' and then in later discussions we couldn't remember which crossroads we had been referring to. However, one of the crossroads is formed by the ending of the coming of this idea into management education and development and the beginning of a new horizon, called here the 'learning company' or 'learning organization'. This new horizon extends the implications of this learner-empowering way of doing management development into the broader field of managing and developing the organization. The 'learning organization' is a utopia which not only meets the marketplace pressures of rapid response and collective learning from mistakes, but which also creates organizations fit to house the human spirit.

Using modern language we should call it a metaphor rather than a utopia—a star to steer by, not a place to arrive at. The book starts with the recent and longer-term tale of self-development. Self-development is revealed as the offspring of that optimist, humanism, whose lease may have run. In the middle part of the book there are few doubts to be found. The idea of self-development is treated with conviction, and well-tried methods to implement it are examined. Doubt and conviction are well mixed up at the close of the book where we can see that in discussing self-development in organizations we are returning to the dilemma posed for us, for example, by Chris Argyris over thirty years ago, of the inevitable conflict between healthy individuals and formal organization:

healthy individuals . . . agents who tend toward a mature state of psychological development (i.e. they are predisposed toward relative independence, activeness, use of important abilities) . . . are not congruent with the requirements of formal organization, which tends to require agents to work in situations where they are dependent, passive, and use and unimportant abilities . . . (1957: 233).

The contributors in the third part of this book are suggesting that we need to move in two directions simultaneously; into the inner space of the person and into the outer space of the organization and environment. We cannot take the self for granted, we must learn to manage ourselves, create order in ourselves, before we are fit to manage, to create order with others. We must learn to know and manage our 'inner team'. At the same time, as organization members we must take responsibility for the sort of environment we are creating and ensure that it is as fit for human beings as it can be. Following the path of self-development is not simply to take an inward turning, it is to go in and to go out. The clear implication is that organization will not be responsive, innovatory and self-renewing on the outside unless we are able to nurture and release the energy of those on the inside. This is the vision of the learning organization.

This book consists of chapters created from sessions offered at the third conference on 'Applying Self-development in Organizations' at the University of Lancaster in September 1988. (For papers from earlier conferences, see Pedler *et al.* 1988.) As befits the best marketplaces, our conference somewhat resembled a gaily coloured fair, with stallholders laying out their wares, hucksters calling up business and a few prophets. Offerers of sessions spoke to the general assembly before moving into elective workshops with their participants. A number of sessions were not pre-planned but sprang up from the conference process, with erstwhile participants making new offers. Word spread about some sessions and they were repeated once and even twice. Of other sessions little was heard or passed on.

Like managing, conferring is a performing art. The script is fairly straightforward and the art is in the acting out of the once and forever performance. The organization of this book cannot be thought to bear more than an occasional resemblance to that event. For the most part these chapters were written later, in response to our request for a record of the ideas and experience. Some chapters existed, more or less, before the event; some report the event and the workshop process as part of their message and some have been written after the conference in the light of experience.

The book is organized in three parts which reflect our sense of movement. Part I, the *past*, sets the context with an biography of the self-development idea and its place in a wider sweep of history which is at this very moment causing a change in our perceptions. Part II, the *present*, contains some accounts, most of them set in large commercial organizations, of some of the many differing forms which the self-development idea may take. Here there are stories, narratives, prescriptions and interesting methodologies. These are practical offerings to which you can respond—'I'll have some of that'—or not, and simply pass by. Part III, the *future*, contains challenges and questions. Here are not so much practical ideas as encouraging visions and disturbing dreams, pointers to the future.

Such was the plan. In practice it is not possible to separate out these three, so that the above distinctions are perhaps more in the nature of intent and flavour than of trade descriptions. The boundary between Parts II and III is hard to draw and there is some arbitrariness there, with plenty of challenges to existing practices in Part II, and interesting designs for current practice in Part III.

References

Argyris, C. (1957) *Personality and Organization*, Harper & Row, New York.

Pedler M. J. and T. H. Boydell (1980) 'Is all management development self-development?' in J. Beck and C. Cox (eds), *Advances in Management Education*, Wiley, London, pp. 165–96.

Pedler, M. J., J. G. Burgoyne and T. H. Boydell (1988) *Applying Self-development in Organizations*, Prentice-Hall, London.

Part I The past: the historical perspective

Introduction

This short first part of the book aims to provide an overview of self-development in the organizational context. It also attempts to place self-development within the broader sweep of the history of ideas. Although mainly concerned with history, Part I contains some pointers to the future. In Chapter 1 Mike Pedler gives a relatively narrow and recent account of the emergence of self-development in management education, while in Chapter 2 Steve Fox ranges over the centuries to sketch the origins of self-development's big sister—humanism.

Self-development is an optimistic creed which gives encouragement to managers and other people seeking a 'leg up' in their struggles to expand their horizons and to escape from limiting conditions. For some people, work organizations—the formerly benign institutions of life-long employment—have become restrictive and oppressive. Security is no longer enough for those who want to use their full energies and expand their potentials to see where they may go. For such people work is a primary ground for their self-development efforts and if we cannot organize to give such people the space they need then we will lose them in whole or part. For such people self-development is proving a powerful tool.

It is to this 'performative' aspect of things that Steve Fox addresses his deconstructive effort. This 'self-development' holds sway because of the cultural dominant of modernism. It is just another product 'commodified and packaged in low cost ways for mass consumption'. I shop therefore I am. A post-modern analysis throws doubt on the assumption of 'self' as the author of meaning. This 'self' is itself a cultural artefact.

Part I ends with some light. Self-development may become a cultural cul-de-sac unless we look for ways of being more socially responsible. Self-development becomes pathological only when we swing to the assertive individualism which would sometimes deny the very existence of society.

1
A biography of self-development
Mike Pedler

Introduction

This chapter is written by Mike Pedler for the collective Pedler, Burgoyne and Boydell. We jointly created the framework around which this chapter is written.

Biographies are written in the present and focus upon the past. Where they are of living things—people, groups, organizations or ideas—biographies may also have an important formative purpose. The understanding and acknowledging of the past, with the exploring of the present, can lead to a clearer vision of the alternative choices for the future. The idea of writing a biography of self-development comes at a time when the three of us—individually and collectively—are moving on. We have collaborated in exploring the notion of self-development for the last twelve years or so, each in his own way, but regularly joining together to share ideas, write, run conferences.

One of the features of biography work is the study of transitions. If there are 'laws' of biography then one is that sooner or later we all move on. Where have we come from? What have we done in this time? Where are we going next? These fundamental questions of human biography can also be applied to the development and maturing of an idea. Our account of self-development is rooted in our biographies, individual and collective; our lives in our time.

From the wider perspective, self-development comes from before our time and will continue. In the last twenty years it has emerged from the fringe in the 1960s to a position in the mainstream of ideas for working with managers on their development.

Ideas and learning

Before starting the narrative, a word on ideas and learning. Wherever ideas come from, we are the receivers, discoverers and interpreters of them. In their recently influential book, *In Search of Excellence*, Tom Peters and Robert Waterman remark (p. 117) that 'There's nothing new under the sun'–without acknowledging Ecclesiastes! But whether Peters and Waterman have really created something new with their 'bias for action'; 'close to the customer'; 'sticking to the knitting' notions for creating excellent organizations is a matter of some indifference in the managerial world. For the manager, seeking a new vision in a much-studied world described as 'hyper-competitive', 'turbulent', characterized by 'uncertainty', beset by 'megatrends' and so on, P&W's wisdom seems to have been gratefully received, manna from heaven. Whether P&W are original thinkers, or whether they are merely persuasive packagers of the already well-known, is of no consequence. What matters is the act of influence, the assistance to the imagination which might encourage and empower managers to take their next steps. For such purposes the ideas are perceived as hopeful, helpful and timely.

This does not mean, of course, that these are the only ideas around, nor that they are the best available. But, in an important sense, they are the 'right' ideas.

Learning is the word we give to that ultimately mysterious process whereby we make sense of ourselves in our situations. The way we are—our being—and what we do—our actions—are based upon whatever understandings we can manage in this process. Learning takes place when a person, with prior knowledge, beliefs and motivating purposes, is able to make sense, create meaning with the aid of an idea or ideas. That meaning does not exist in the book or teacher where the idea was found, for in the act of creating personal meaning it has become 'my idea', uniquely flavoured. It is only one of many ideas I might have made mine, and my choosing of it from those on offer cannot easily be predicted. My choosing of it is opportunistic in that I can do something with it. In choosing it, I transform more than the 'idea'; I transform myself and the world I live in.

In a critique of self-theorists, Ray Holland describes Carl Rogers' ideas: 'Thus client-centred therapy is modelled precisely on the man himself: its goal is a continuous process of movement away from the expectations and values of others toward self-determining, self-respecting (actualizing) choice' (Holland 1970: 70). Carl Rogers' ideas have been central to our self-development idea, yet Holland's criticism is that they are modelled on a man whose 'range of social experience is very limited' (p. 70). If

Holland's point is a valuable corrective to the delusion of the all-encompassing transcendental 'I', who can escape a narrow range of social experience? Ideas tend to come with names attached, only shedding them as they lose distinction in common sense. If learning is first a personal, meaning-making process, then such meanings will be biographically rooted.

This definition of learning underlies our idea of self-development and places it towards one end of the spectrum of learning theories in ultimately weighting human agency over social forming. In making this commitment we expose the limitations of the idea. How is it possible, in terms of human development, to choose agency over environment or heredity? A considered view might lead one to a pluralistic 'learning is always a product of unfolding inheritance, circumstances and individual striving acting together' or 'here what is called "learning" is mainly a matter of getting older; here a fortuitous conjunction of events; here, now here, there is real testimony to the action of the human spirit!'.

The idea of self-development emphasizes this 'third force' in human development—the action of individual will, agency, ego in influencing what we may be. It does not deny the influence of other factors, but chooses to focus upon the possibilities of self-direction. This is the political rather than the moral aspect of self-development. To the extent that the idea empowers managers and others in creating the lives and work organizations they would like to have, it flourishes mainly among the most endowed in the richly resourced Western world.

Thus there are not equal opportunities for self-development—throughout the world, nor throughout the United Kingdom, nor even throughout UK organizations currently hosting the idea. Self-development for all seems dependent upon all enjoying a rich environment, economically, socially and politically.

Past

Though we grappled with the ideas and practice of 'student-centred learning' from the early 1970s, our involvement with management self-development begins with our collaboration, starting in 1976, on what became *A Manager's Guide to Self-Development* (Pedler *et al.* 1978; 1986). At the same time we produced a map of the territory and an annotated bibliography.

The seeds of these books and of our understanding of the idea go back further. For Mike, experience as a tutor/organizer for the Worker's Educational Association established some ground rules. By tradition, WEA tutorial classes are self-organizing; they consult with the tutor on the syllabus; they elect a class secretary who manages the library and other administrative tasks and so on. During an Economics class in 1967, the 23-year-old tutor was questioned by a class member, the caretaker of the local secondary school, as to the definitive meaning of a particular concept. On hearing the response, the class member contrasted this with several others he had read and heard over the years, including that of Hugh Gaitskell, WEA tutor some thirty years before. Much was learned that evening, not all of it by the 'class members'.

Self-development means learners taking the freedom and responsibility for choosing what, when and how to develop. This implies the freedom not to develop particular skills or career directions at the behest of others; and the responsibility for the consequences of those decisions. At a time when the work world is changing more rapidly than ever before, people are being called upon to change roles, develop serial careers, swop outdated skills for new ones with increasing rapidity. John's research, with Roger Stuart, on managerial qualities was a key contribution here and formed the basis for the model of an effective manager in *A Manager's Guide.* Flexibility and adaptability in members is seen as a critical factor for the future well-being of organizations. Self-managed learning, in contrast to systematic training, is seen as one of the more promising ways of being able to create and maintain this 'learning habit': 'any effective system for management development must increase the managers' capacity and willingness to take control over and responsibility for events, and particularly for themselves and their own learning' (Pedler *et al.* 1978, 1986: 1).

Our first definition of self-development had two main dimensions: '*by*-self' and '*of*-self'. By-self refers to the dimension of learner control and self-direction, and is to do with empowering the learner and de-powering the teacher, trainer, expert or external authority. *Of*-self refers to the dimension of personal growth or self-actualization as a result of development. We were much influenced by the ideas of Maslow and Rogers here, by the T-group movement, and also with the unflagging efforts of a colleague, David Megginson, who was experientially researching some forty methods of personal development. A particular landmark here which firmly indicated the end of this 'systematic' phase was Tom's *Experiential Learning* (Boydell 1976).

Later we focused more on the word 'development', borrowing from many writers in various fields including Bateson, Piaget, Revans, Kohlberg, Loevinger, Bloom and especially Rudolf Steiner as interpreted by Lievegoed. (See especially Boydell 1982.) Development was a process occurring in a series of phases, each marked by a characteristic structure and values but which eventually ended in crisis heralding the next phase.

Each successive phase transformed yet encapsulated the earlier one and, however well managed, the moment of crisis is always experienced as shock or 'perturbation'. Development is a long cycle process extending over the lifetime; stages and ages are sometimes linked, and readiness to develop is a key principle. The ideas of 'inner/outer' and 'both . . . and . . .' are also core—the acquisition of managerial skill, for example, requires *both* an inner choosing and transformation *and* a changed outer performance (Pedler 1988: 5–10).

Development proceeds via the opposition of ideas, and it is often easier to trace the birth of a notion by examining the context in which it arises. The emergence of self-development in the 1970s, as an idea relevant to the education and training of managers in work organizations, can be seen in opposition to the then dominant methodology of 'systematic training'.

Systematic training was a response to the skills shortages experienced in industrialized countries in the boom years following post-war reconstruction. In Britain, the 1964 Industrial Training Act was a major turning point in the history of employee training and development in making a public enterprise to remedy the failings of the previous reliance upon individual employers. The Act proposed Industry Training Boards in all major sectors to create an adequate supply of trained 'manpower', especially in craft and operator grades. The approach was scientific/ analytic based upon detailed job, task, skill and needs analyses.

Qualified training officers specify training objectives for 'target populations' which follow standard syllabi on planned training programmes which are thoroughly reviewed and evaluated. As Boydell said at the time: 'the systematic analytical approach has been tried and proved very successful, and should be used wherever practical' (Boydell 1970: 3).

When applied to supervisory and management training, however, the systematic approach proved less impressive. Faced with the complexity, variety and generally 'unprogrammable' nature of managerial work, systematic training was far too prescriptive. While the programmes were well constructed and often enjoyable, the returning managers and supervisors rarely seemed to implement the 'lessons learned'. The 'Transfer of Training' problem, as it became known, led to a change of focus—upon the learner and the learning process rather than the trainer/training process focus of systematic training. In turn this led to 'learner-centred' designs such as action learning, self-development, and self-managed learning which used managers' work and life tasks as the primary vehicles for their development.

This historical or biographical construction suggests that where we are now depends upon past decisions and choices in the face of the perceived

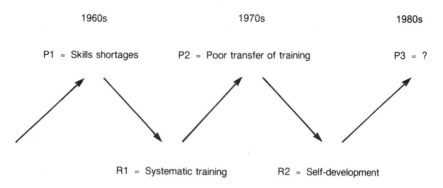

Figure 1.1   The evolution of self-development

problems of the time. Diagrammatically we can map the emergence of self-development as a response to an earlier problem (see Figure 1.1). This sequence is taken on later in this biography.

If the notion of self-development for managers is in some ways a discovery of the 1970s, this is but a reincarnation or re-emergence of a venerable idea. In 1938, Dale Carnegie's *How to Win Friends and Influence People* reached a wide audience of self-improvers and reflected the confidence of the North American 'free-enterprise' culture in much the same way that Samuel Smiles's *Self Help*, published in 1859, had symbolized the Victorian belief that material and moral uplift came through individual effort and enterprise. Lukes informs us that the word 'individualism' is a nineteenth-century word, originating about the time of the French Revolution; but also that some scholars hold that the New Testament made a great contribution to individualism with its conception of a direct relationship between God and the individual to balance the Old Testament view of the state (Israel) as the prime concern of God (Lukes 1973: 1, 45). The notion of human development towards enlightenment, oneness with God or the universe can be found in many of the world's religions and philosophies.

Present

The present reincarnation of self-development may have a wider significance than just being an appropriate methodology for management development. Writing in 1954, the biologist Julian Huxley suggests in his essay 'The evolutionary process' that human beings are becoming developed enough to be truly self-developing:

The present situation represents a highly remarkable point in human history in which the evolutionary process as now embodied in man has, for the first time, become aware of itself and has a dawning realisation of the possibilities of its future guidance and control. In other words, evolution is on the verge of becoming internalised, conscious and self-directing (Huxley 1954).

Thirty years later, Roger Harrison, a noted writer on self-directed learning and related topics, muses on the implications of 'New Age' thinking:

The term 'conscious evolution' refers to the idea that after millenia of evolution, we humans are on the verge of becoming aware of the transformative process in which we are involved. As we become aware, we can begin to participate voluntarily in our own evolution and that of the planet. We can influence the quality of life on earth through our thoughts and beliefs (Harrison 1983).

We shall have to wait for a little more history before we can evaluate fully the meaning of the current re-emergence of self-development. If the above views prove accurate then we are entering an age not only of conscious self-development and self-shaping, but also one in which we are beginning to feel empowered enough to influence the shape and future of our organizations and societies.

Managing ME

From our joint work in the 1970s, several strands of development can be distinguished. We conceived of the *Manager's Guide* as a 'user-friendly' set of ideas, instruments and devices to assist self-development as *managing yourself.* Initially we interpreted self-development somewhat literally as developing yourself on your own—it could be done in those odd moments, on the train or even in the bath. John's work at Esso Chemicals on a workbook for career planning and personal development is an outgrowth of this which seeks to integrate individual development with corporate planning (Germain 1988). The Resource Centres, Electronic University and other open and distance learning approaches are of this tradition (and of the older one of DIY self-education). Research indicates that lonely learning methods are difficult for most of us and that the success of open and distance learning packages in organizations depends crucially on the care taken with selection, briefing and, especially, the supporting of participants (Mann *et al.* 1987). When applied to self-development in the '*of*-self' sense, these methods are also limited by the palpable need we have for the ideas, feedback and companionship of other people. Like Dali's Autodidact, the lone self-developer lacks the social context of learning and can get lost, isolated, with narrow and distorted perceptions. Nevertheless, because of their cheapness and ubiquitousness, open and distance learning approaches have an important part to play in providing 'self-development opportunities for all'.

However, whatever the limits of learning by oneself, this is but one expression of the commitment to taking responsibility for self-development. Finding other people to help with one's self-development or just the opposite—finding personal space to be alone—is part of 'Managing ME'. Managing ME is the first step for the self-developer—unless I take charge of myself, how can I take charge of situations? Unless I can create order in myself, how can I contribute to creating order with others? Managing ME first is the key of self-empowerment and the empowerment of others.

The learning community

A second strand of development grows out of this first one. The need for support in self-development has long been recognized by therapeutic groups such as Weightwatchers, Alcoholics Anonymous and Synanon—a community for rehabilitating drug addicts—as well as in the experiential learning and T-groups. In organizational settings this support has been provided through quality circles, action learning sets, self-development groups and other forms of *Learning community* which bring together a small group of people 'as peers to meet personal learning needs primarily through a sharing of resources and skills offered by those present' (Pedler 1981: 68).

By going beyond the individual as a unit of organization for learning, the learning community idea creates a bridge between the isolated DIY self-developer and the organization. Although most writers who use the term imply that learning communities should be self-managing and self-directing, a continuing irony is that these designs are often known by the names of their originators. The truly self-designing learning community, that is, produced by the members present acting as peers and without leaders or facilitators, proves an elusive goal still. Such an ambition forms one of the avenues to the 'learning company', of which more below.

Differences at work

A third strand of work also operates in the wider setting of organization or society. This is the theme of *differences* which covers that wide range of social categories by which we divide ourselves, including class, race, gender, age, ability/disability. Each of these divides, and there are many others, creates a potential for 'top dog/underdog' social relations which are often implicit and unrecognized—especially, but not exclusively, by the 'top dogs'. The oppression of the difference, whatever it is—'being a man', 'being working class'—is often internalized by all concerned—it is in this sense that Tom, by birth male and middle-class, and at this time, middle-aged and able-bodied, could say that he only 'discovered' he was a man in his early forties (Boydell 1988).

We 'discovered' the area of differences on starting to offer self-development groups for managers. We found, on reflection unsurprisingly, that we were offering self-development groups for men. Mike and Tom were asked to help with a Manpower Services Commission funded project to create self-development groups for women managers. Later we were involved with 'Women and men as working colleagues' programmes at the Civil Service College. Working with this particular difference had profound effects on both of us. One thing which became clear was that before people could begin to act on their situation, they first had to bring it to consciousness, to pay attention to it. This process can be very painful, and may involve strong emotions such as fear, rage or grief, because we allow ourselves, perhaps for the first time, to see the social injustice and the extent to which we ourselves collude in it. If this 'perturbation' can be faced then, especially with the help of others similarly placed, the pain can be transformed into a clarity of vision, a determination to act and a joy of becoming.

Thus, the words 'oppression' and 'empowerment' are linked in a powerful process of development. Although we learned at school that black people in North America were liberated from slavery by the Civil War, it took the bus boycotts, school desegregation battles and civil rights marches of a hundred years later to achieve a measure of equality in citizenship. In our lifetime 'black' has become 'beautiful', 'rich', 'famous' and 'powerful'—words formerly reserved for whites. These struggles continue and will do so anywhere where we discriminate unfairly against people and where differences are not experienced as a source of variety, richness, creativity.

There is a link here between individual and social development. Development in individual people comes about through the emergence of differences—between you and me; expected and actual consequences; between thought and action. The discrimination and difference has to be noticed before the learning process of reflection, theory formulation and experimentation can follow. The aim of the learning process is to re-integrate the noted difference within the higher unity of the human being who, in so doing, becomes a more developed person. So, for example, if I see myself as a kind person and allow myself to become aware of my maliciousness, this will at first cause me pain, as it does violence to my self-image. If I can reach understanding, accept *both* the kindness *and* the malice in myself, accept and forgive myself, then I have developed from an earlier, now naive position, to a later, wiser one. Development is here a struggle to become aware of our 'shadow' selves and to integrate these into our acknowledged selves.

The differences theme also links self-development with learning company. As Lawrence and Lorsch pointed out, development in organizations proceeds via differentiation and integration; in differentiation the parts take on unique and autonomous characteristics, and in integration these diverse parts are unified and harmonized in a transformed whole (Lawrence and Lorsch 1967). Arthur Koestler made the same claim for all organisms, including individual persons, when he spoke of the 'Janus Effect—when we look inward we see ourselves as an autonomous whole yet when we look outwards we see ourselves as a dependent part. This basic polarity results in both a self-assertive tendency and an integrative tendency (Koestler 1975: 56). Working with differences requires us to embrace this 'both ... and ...' thinking and work with polarities to create development. If we are to create organizations which are flexible and adaptable, equally adept at cooperation and competition, able to be appropriately conservative in the face of opportunities or threats, able to change in good order with, or even in advance of, the circumstances, then we will need to know how to make the most of our differences. The white, able-bodied, male-managed, hierarchical, conflict-suppressing organization becomes less fitted for survival and development. To make use of differences and tap the fruits of diversity, we have to be able to manage the pain and denial of surfacing them and spread the time and resources to see the development process through.

The spiritual dimension

The fourth and final strand concerns the relationship of self-development and *spirituality*. When people are asked to think of important development events, they tend to come up with experiences which, however painful to start with, end up with positive outcomes. As a result of these experiences people feel more confident, have a wider view, are more self-aware. In the context of the person, development tends to mean a more fully functioning, more self-actualized person. Another way of describing this is to say that self-development involves the realization of the 'higher' and the redeeming of the 'lower' self (Pedler and Boydell 1986: 94–117). The ultimate end of the '*of*-self' dimension, as noted above, is oneness with some wider or higher unity. Whatever vision a person has of this unity is the spiritual dimension which Aldous Huxley found to be so widespread in human history as to be 'the Perennial Philosophy' (Huxley 1946).

The spiritual dimension is in some ways difficult to talk about in relation to management and organization development. The current state of affairs is, in this sense, largely material, concerning itself with external appearances rather than inner meanings. Formal education has been criticized for not educating people with regard to their emotions and feelings—a failing which the experiential learning movement seeks to remedy—and it rarely deals directly with matters of spirit. Yet we use the term often and value it—'It was a spirited performance', 'There is a good team spirit.' In such phrases, spirit seems to mean life and unity. The current stress upon developing appropriate 'organizational values' rather than detailed procedural rules as the 'guiding spirits' for people's actions and achieving adherence with the 'spirit' rather than just the 'letter' of the law, is clearly linked. So, as human beings we are body, soul *and* spirit, and in organizing we work with all these three aspects of people and collectivities. A 'whole-person' or 'whole-organization' approach to development is therefore in part a spiritual quest.

Future

Where are we going? The foregoing implies a larger stage for self-development than just an approach to the learning of individual managers. Yet, if individuals are not empowered, then none of the rest can come about. The problem–response sequence begun earlier in this chapter can be continued beyond R2 (self-development), which, it was hypothesized, was a response to the 'transfer of training' problem (P2) (see Figure 1.2). Once we have some facility with the idea and method of self-development, the next problem or issue begins to appear. We know now a good deal about how to empower the individual learner; given the will and the resources we can do it. Then we come to see that working at an individual level is not sufficient. What is the point of having resourceful, empowered learners if our current conceptions and enactments of 'organization' are too restrictive, constraining and limited to use this potential? Leaders may say 'we learn from our mistakes here' or 'we reward initiative' but unless that same leader can demonstrate that she too admits her mistakes and learns from them, no follower will have the confidence and belief to make the effort. If a likely person somewhere in the body of the organization does it their way and the weight of precedence, entrenched attitudes and 'we've always done it this way' is

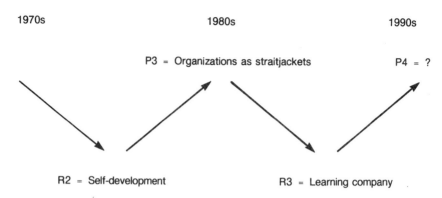

Figure 1.2   The evolution of learning company

brought down upon his or her head then there will be few 'intrapreneurs' in that neck of the woods.

Learning company

'Learning company' seems an appropriate metaphor for the organization which is fitted to house the self-developer. As ever this new idea has a history—Donald Schon called for them back in his 1970 Reith Lectures: 'we must invent and develop institutions which are "learning systems", that is to say, systems capable of bringing about their own continuing transformation' (Schon 1971: 30). The learning company is not just a company that runs lots of courses or which offers all sort of opportunities for its people to learn; it is one which has the capability of self-transformation. Although we have known this for twenty years, there are few examples of the idea in practice. Writing with Argyris in 1978, Schon admits failure in finding an organization which regularly engages in 'double loop learning'—learning which changes current operating assumptions, norms and values (Argyris and Schon 1978: 312). Ten years earlier Revans offered his model of how to bring about this desired state in his little known (1969) paper 'The enterprise as a learning system' (Revans 1982: 283–5). These are but two of those who acted as harbingers of the idea and they no doubt stood on the shoulders of earlier natural scientists like Huxley and Gregory Bateson who pointed in this direction. Now there are clear signs that the notion has reached the mainstream: 'The excellent companies are learning companies' (Peters and Waterman 1982: 110).

The Learning Company idea is one of our current joint preoccupations, and we feel ourselves to be at the beginning of understanding what it is and how it can be applied. We have developed some ideas about the key dimensions of such a development and are continuing work on these (Pedler *et al.* 1988; 1989). Around this central theme there are other related ideas such as John's ladder of management development maturity (Burgoyne 1988). Through this metaphor of learning company we aim to link the individual and organizational levels of self-development. Our concern is therefore both with the individual taking responsibility for his or her own learning and with creating organizations fit for such people. At the moment this seems an awesome task—the structures, hierarchies and career patterns of organizations appear designed to control rather than to enable and facilitate individual efforts and energy. To make this move requires us radically to change our ideas of what organizations are and therefore to change our efforts from seeking to manage 'complex machines' via attempts to 'structure' jobs, careers, departments, hierarchies of control, towards an emerging view of organizations as focused energy, powered by self-developing people, continually changing shape and direction.

'Futurism' is as prey to light-headedness as 'historicism' is to leaden-footedness. To look forward means to work with uncertainty, with vague shapes, colours, melodies. The learning company is a theme we shall be hearing more of—but how, and what will it look like? What problems will it create? For, following the logic of Figure 1.2, R3 (learning company) will lead to P4—the next problem.

Other themes that we should expect to hear more of—and which are represented in this book—include open and distance learning, with an increasing emphasis upon equal opportunities in learning to make the 'open' more than just a slogan; 'management development' for everyone in the organization—that is the 'goodies' which 'management development' practice has created becoming available to all organizational members who will be increasingly 'Managing ME' as well as managing others including colleagues, clients, customers and competitors; and, perhaps, 'spiritual' development.

A hunch we have is that P4 may have something to do with spiritual and ethical development. The effects of creating 'learning companies' can only be imagined but we should not suppose that, because they look attractive from our present perspective, they will not have a 'shadow' side. We can learn better to exploit and destory as well as create and build. Any company can be a 'learning company' in theory—whether they are in business to save lives or to kill people; but could the latter easily be dubbed a 'good company'? The 'good company' creates and accepts responsibility for quality in an ever-widening constituency—quality service for customers, quality of working life for members, quality of business performance for owners and quality of social responsibility for community and society. Such a company will be morally strong enough to engage in the struggle to 'manage for mutual advantage'—seeking to make ethical decisions about priorities, weighing profit against environmental impact; public service against members' well-being (Morris 1987: 103–15).

The limits to growth

In the future we may not view self-development as approvingly as we do now. The self-assertive, DIY aspect has become a topical sub-text of what is currently known as 'Thatcherism'; which scoffs at notions of 'community' and 'public service' and exalts individualism and helping yourself. From one perspective, the humanistic, empowering-people mission of self-development may represent a profound delusion. Post-modernism asks the question 'Are you being conned?', e.g. by self-development. This question has arisen in all three of us, but perhaps most in John who remarked: 'My intellectual doubts have coincided with my mid-life crisis!'

The post-modern analysis is hard to grasp but appears to distrust notions of rationality, truth and progress. Such a stance clearly challenges this chapter with its persuasive account of the biography of an idea. Perhaps our current era is so egocentric that not to believe in the central significance of one's life (and self development) is to negate ourselves and our individuality (Burrell 1989: 61). Steve Fox explores post-modernist ideas in the next chapter, posing such de-constructionist questions as 'What is self-development without the self and without the development?'

The irritating effect of such questions is to render suspect some of the solid ground upon which self-development (or any other idea) stands. Without the 'self'—an implied unity which we take for granted; without 'development'—which we think of as a good thing—where are we? A constructive response to this irritating question is that perhaps those of us who practise self-development, and encourage others in this, lose sight of the context, become selfish or arrogate more than we should to our own efforts. Like 'self-made men who worship their makers' we not only lose sight of others and their predicament, we lose a sense of our own precariousness.

Living as I do in a society that sanctions individualism, free will and self-assertion, I imagine that I am the architect of my present and future self. But what if this 'self', this 'development' is illusory—laid into me by early training? The ideas of 'learning community' and 'learning company' offer a way of going beyond the cult of the individual but only perhaps so that I can acquire a larger stage? Marx and Freud pointed out how prone we humans are to 'false consciousness' and how likely we are to be deluded by the actions of our own 'invisible' ego defences. Habermas has suggested the idea of 'discourse'—collaborative dialogue with others who may be similarly deluded (which Revans has enshrined in the Action Learning Set)—as a way out. It may be.

Doubt must remain. In respect of self-development, one paradox is thus: self-development empowers people, makes them aware of their condition and encourages them to act upon it and transform it *but* it is a cheaper and more effective way of fostering the self-development of people in organizations. The 'training' budget can be cut, and, to all the other responsibilities people have, can be added that of being responsible for keeping up with the world. In this scenario, self-development is a Trojan horse wheeled in by power merchants who well recognize its potential for encouraging 'self-immolation for the good of others' in the words of Andrew Ure, a nineteenth-century advocate of economic freedom and, among other things, child labour (Anthony 1977: 59). Self-developers do it on the way to work and even on holiday. They work harder, thinking they are self-developing, they don't need supervision. Suckers!

We can balance this depressing scenario with a more optimistic one—that self-developers are less likely to put up with poor conditions, exploitation and so on.

To take a second, and last, approach to the limits of self-development, what is the applicability of self-development ideas to 'world development' that is, to the development of poor people in poor countries? Is it just a convenient ideology for richly resourced folk? This question presses for a number of reasons. Prominent among them is our tardy but growing understanding of the 'one-world' interdependence of all nations—cutting down trees to rear cattle to supply McDonald's may be changing the climate for all of us; discharging waste into the sea is poisoning all our fish. Another is the obvious parallel between the lessons of development work in rich and poor countries. Creating vision at the top and power at the bottom; putting experts on tap and not on top; putting people first; emphasizing equal opportunities for women and oppressed minorities; recognizing the crucial importance of local participation; using appropriate technologies; learning from mistakes; the need for education and training—might apply to 'cultural change' in a major Western business corporation, although in fact these headings were taken from a book of development projects in poor countries (Panos Institute 1987).

This should not surprise us. To help us with our own self-development we have been nourished by ideas developed in poor countries. An obvious example is that of Paulo Freire whose adult literacy work in Brazil helped him to develop his ideas of 'liberating education'. This involves using the language of the people, learning by posing problems, through dialogue with others and acting to throw off oppression to transform the world and our own reality (Freire 1972). A part of the future might be giving something back to help others with their development.

References

Anthony, P. D. (1977) *The Ideology of Work*, Tavistock, London.

Argyris, C. and D. A. Schon (1978) *Organizational Learning: A Theory in Action Approach*, Addison Wesley, Reading, Mass.

Boydell T. H. (1970) *A Guide to Job Analysis*, BACIE, London.

—— (1976) *Experiential Learning*, Manchester Monograph, Dept. of Adult Education, University of Manchester.

—— (1982) 'Development', *Management Education and Development*, **13**, 1, Spring, 10–32.

—— (1988) 'Transformations for men?' in M. J. Pedler, J. G. Burgoyne and T. H. Boydell (eds), *Applying Self-development in Organizations*, Prentice-Hall, Hemel Hempstead, pp. 136–46.

—— and M. J. Pedler (1979) *Self-development Bibliography*, MCB, Bradford.

Burgoyne J. G. (1988) 'Management development for the individual and the organization, *Personnel Management*, June, 40–4.

—— and R. Stuart (1976) 'The nature, use and acquisition of managerial skills and other attributes', *Personnel Review*, **5**, 4, 19–29.

—— T. H. Boydell and M. J. Pedler (1978) *Self-development; theory and applications for practitioners*, Association of Teachers in Management, London.

Burrell, G. (1989) 'Post-modernism: threat or opportunity', in M. C. Jackson, P. Keys and S. A. Cropper, *Operational Research and the Social Sciences*, Plenum Press, New York, pp. 59–64.

Freire, P (1972) *Pedagogy of the Oppressed*, Penguin, Harmondsworth.

Germain, C. (1988) 'Integrated career planning' in M. J. Pedler, J. G. Burgoyne and T. H. Boydell (eds), *Applying Self-development in Organizations*, Prentice-Hall, Hemel Hempstead, pp. 195–207.

Harrison, R. (1983) 'Strategies for a new age', *Human Resource Management*, **22** 3, Fall, 209–35.

Holland, R. (1970) *Self and Social Context*, Macmillan, London.

Huxley, A (1946) *The Perennial Philosophy*, Chatto & Windus, London.

Huxley, J. (1954) 'The evolutionary process' in Routledge and Kegan Paul, London.

Koestler, A. (1975) *The Ghost in the Machine*, Pan, London.

Lawrence, P. R. and J. W. Lorsch (1967) 'Differentiation and integration in complex organizations', *Administrative Science Quarterly*, **12**, 1–17.

Lukes, S. (1973) *Individualism*, Blackwell, Oxford.

Mann, S. J. *et al.* (1987) *The Effective Design and Delivery of Open and Distance Learning for Management Education*, Centre for the Study of Management Learning, University of Lancaster.

Morris, J. (1987) 'Good company', *Management Education and Development*, **18**(2), Summer, 103–15.

Panos Institute (1987) *Towards Sustainable Development*, London.

Pedler, M. J. (1981) 'Developing the learning community' in T. H. Boydell and M. J. Pedler (eds) *Management Self-development: Concepts and Practices*, Gower, Farnborough.

—— (1988) 'Self-development and work organizations' in M. J. Pedler, J. G. Burgoyne and T. H. Boydell (eds) *Applying Self-development in Organizations*, Prentice-Hall, Hemel Hempstead, pp. 1–19.

—— and T. H. Boydell (1986) *Managing Yourself*, Collins/Fontana, London.

——, T. H. Boydell and J. G. Burgoyne (1988) *Learning Company: Final Project Report*, Training Agency, Sheffield.

——, T. H. Boydell and J. G. Burgoyne (1989) 'Towards the learning company', *Management Education & Development*, **20**(1), Spring.

——, J. G. Burgoyne and T. H. Boydell (1978; 1986) *A Manager's Guide to Self-Development*, McGraw-Hill, Maidenhead.

Peters, T. J. and R. H. Waterman (1982) *In Search of Excellence*, Harper & Row, New York.

Revans, R. W. (1982) *The Origins and Growth of Action Learning*, Chartwell Bratt, Bromley.

Schon, D. A. (1971) *Beyond the Stable State*, Random House, New York.

2
Self-development: from humanism to deconstruction
Steve Fox

Overview

This chapter begins by questioning the nature of the self and finds that this is dependent largely on culture. Culture, however, is constantly changing, even though strands of continuity can be found. Humanism, culminating in modernism, is seen to have replaced the Christian world-view, placing humanity instead of God at the heart of the meaning of life. Deconstruction challenges humanism, threatening to replace humanity as the creator of meaning with language itself, which takes on an autonomous life of its own, of which human consciousness may be just an epiphenomenon. Implications are drawn for self-development and for management development in post-modern times.

Introduction

What is the self? Where can we start to unravel the beginnings of the concept; or would such unravellings be irrelevant to what everyone automatically knows already about selves? You know yourself, I know myself, we may or may not have met but our basic presupposition is that other selves are just like ourselves. We know what to expect about each other just as we know what to expect about the world out there, which we both presume is generally the same for me as it is for you, apart that is from our specific personal circumstances of biography, career, present employment, where we live and other particulars.

But underneath these common-sense notions of self-hood—which are after all good enough to get by with ordinarily in our everyday life—perhaps we can also recognize that the self, as a general experience of selfhood common, say, to a generation or a locality, for instance a nation or region, may also be a thing that changes. As we ourselves have changed and will change over a lifetime, 'the self' as a general experience has changed and will change over the decades, centuries, millenia, and from place to place. The ancient Greeks and Romans probably did experience their selfhood differently to us, and differently again to the ancient Chinese and the present-day Chinese and so on. Following this tack of thinking we might imagine, in a frustratingly difficult-to-grasp kind of way, how may diverse ways of experiencing the self there have been and are still and will be. And how impossible it is for us to project ourselves properly into other generations' and cultures' experience of selfhood.

And so we might concede that the question 'what is the self?' is something of a conundrum, for we are aware of the cultural relativity of the experience of selfhood. What is more, when we go on to ask what is self-development?, again we are faced with cultural relativity; for self-development for modern Tibetan monks, or modern Western business people, modern Japanese business people, twelfth-century Christian theologians and seventeenth-century Western scientists are unlikely to be all that similar, even though it is possible.

Despite such difficulties, in this chapter I would like to take conventional Western understandings of self-development and to look back within the humanistic traditions of Western learning to examine the roots of self-development as it is now popularly understood. Also I would like to examine how these understandings are now being questioned and challenged by what Jacques Derrida calls 'deconstruction'. Deconstruction presents, I will argue, a revised understanding of the self, an understanding central to the emergent post-modern cultural experience and modes of learning. But to show what I mean by post-modernism I must first talk of modernism and to do that I must first talk of humanism. And to do that let me examine a relatively recent approach to management self-development which I will then argue is the product of the humanistic tradition which deconstruction challenges.

This approach was set out by Pedler, Burgoyne and Boydell (1978) and based on the following premise:

that any effective system for management development must increase the managers' capacity and willingness to take control over and responsibility *for events*, and particularly *for themselves* and their own learning (p. 3; my emphasis).

In addition to this premise they add:

we define self-development as personal development, with the manager talking primary responsibility for her or his own learning and for choosing the means to achieve this (p. 4).

They also suggest the following to be further legitimate meanings and purposes of self-development:

- career development and advancement;
- improving performance in an existing job;
- development certain specific qualities or skills;
- achieving potential—self-actualization (p. 4).

As the first quote most clearly brings out, management self-development is concerned simultaneously with two aspects of the self, namely its control over and responsibility *for events* and for *the self itself.* The 'out-there' and the 'in-here' of experience we might say. These two aspects are echoed in the subsequent quotes: 'personal development' is a matter of both the manager's internal learning process and the manager's choice of means for facilitating this—the 'means' being external to the self in many cases; for instance, resources such as books, experts, institutions, courses, colleagues and so on. And again in the third quote we find a double emphasis on the self itself—'self-actualization' and developing 'specific qualities or skills'—and on externalities such as job performance and career advancement.

To sum up, self-development in this approach emphasizes self-mastery of the self itself (the in-here emotional, cognitive, intuitive sensory and other learning processes) and mastery of events in the 'out-there' world of events, business, politics, educational design, other people and more—i.e. the whole environment outside the singular self.

Now these two aspects of self-development (mastery of the inner and the outer) go back a long way within the educational and cultural traditions of Western humanism, culminating in the project of modernism. As such they are all deeply challenged by a post-modern critique such as deconstruction.

The idea of a cultural dominant

To understand the challenge of deconstruction let us consider first the idea in wide circulation of a 'cultural dominant' by which I mean that at most points in Western history there may be different forms of cultural experience and expression but nonetheless one form is dominant. We talk, for example, of the Romantic period which arguably began with the writings of Rousseau and subsequently came to dominate Western culture. At the time Rousseau began to write, Neo-Classicism was in fact dominant but in a sense 'dead'. Against the Neo-Classicist cultural dominant Rousseau and others in different spheres of culture (e.g. Beethoven in music and Wordsworth in poetry) innovatively rebelled and produced in time a new cultural dominant, that is, modes of expression and experience governed by different assumptions and different rules.

Such shifts in cultural expression and experience alter human consciousness of self and the world. Rousseau and the romantics in general idealized nature and humanity's relation to it in a fresh way; almost a pantheistic way (but not quite, for pantheism was originally a cultural product of the Roman world hundreds of years previously).

The idea of a cultural dominant is similar to Kuhn's (1962) idea of scientific 'paradigms' which are like miniature cultural dominants within specialized scientific communities. Thus in physics the paradigm of Newtonian mechanics, which saw the universe as if it were a huge predictable clock slowly winding down, eventually gave way to the new paradigm implicit in Einstein's general theory of relativity.

In the world of business and marketing, the idea of product life-cycle, which is tied to the ideas of market penetration, share and saturation, is an explicit recognition that the ways goods and services are designed—as cultural objects as well as functional ones—will become outmoded (functionalism itself is a cultural dominant/paradigm emerging in architecture, the social sciences and the arts during this century).

In the present, every business marketing strategy struggles to fashion new images, new designs, new concepts and packages in a thoroughly modern acceleration of cultural change. Previously, however, cultural change has a less popularistic character, since it is only in the last one hundred years that mass production, mass education and mass-media have produced a mass or popular culture. Previously there was a wide gap between high culture appreciated by the Western educated elite and the culture of ordinary people. In the modern period industrialization enabled new art forms with a wider appeal and the commodification of the artefacts of previous high culture. William Morris and the arts and crafts movement, for example, began to make a commonplace thing like wallpaper or cloth designs for curtains into an artistic accomplishment, capable of mass production and sale. And now we can all have a good-quality portrait of the Mona Lisa in our front room courtesy of Athena or other high-street chains specializing in low price imitation 'high cultural' objects. In the same period Penguin books and Everyman put high literature on sale to a mass market.

The modern period has commodified and packaged in low-cost ways for mass consumption the high cultural forms of previous centuries in painting, music (records, cassettes and Radio 3) and literature. It has also spawned a proliferation of new artistic technologies from photography, to cinema, to television, to screen-printing, to hiphop and electronically synthesized machine music. And many of them are increasingly aimed not at a small, educated, cultivated elite but at a mass market of Western consumers.

Modernism, as a cultural dominant, is therefore characterized not by a unity across all the cultural capitals of Europe and across all the media of expression—literature, painting, music—as was the case with Romanticism or Neo-Classicism in the past, but by fragmentation and disunity, because in every sphere of human experience and expression innovations are constantly being sought, marketed to saturation, dropped and replaced by the new.

It is difficult for us now to realize the differences modernism has made to Western understanding of the self and the world. For although, as Habermas has pointed out, modernism is an extension of the Enlightenment and hence of humanism, it is different chiefly in terms of the speed with which it is transforming our everyday experience of selfhood. High culture changed very slowly in the past and scarcely touched directly the ordinary people except through the first thoroughly modern bureaucratic organization in the West, namely the Church.

In the following section we will briefly examine the interweaving and opposition between Christianity and humanism in order to come back to the question of modernity and the post-modern and the implications for self-development.

Christianity and humanism

It is hard for us in the West to conceive a world without telecommunications, TV, newspapers, rapid transport by air and rail and all the other products of international industrialization and organization. In the medieval world from about the eleventh to the seventeenth centuries the major international bureaucracy with its head office in Rome was the Church. As the historian of the seventeenth century, Christopher Hill (1955: 16–17) described it:

It guided all the movements of men from baptism to the burial service and was the gateway to that life to come in which all men fervently believed. The church educated children; in the village parishes—where the mass of the people was illiterate—the parson's sermon was the main source of information on current events and problems, of guidance on economic conduct. The parish itself was an important unit of local government, collecting and doling out such pittances as the poor received. The church controlled men's feelings and told them what to believe, provided them with entertainment and shows. It took the place of news and propaganda services now covered by many different and more efficient institutions—the press, the BBC, the cinema, the club and so forth. That is why men took notes of sermons; it is also why the government often told preachers exactly what to preach.

The Church produced many of the cultural ground rules for the conduct of everyday life. No doubt it was sometimes manipulated by the secular powers of local kings and powerful noble families, and indeed many of its own bishops and popes took a practioner interest in secular politics as well as their more spiritual concerns. However, if we read accounts of the changing doctrinal positions of the Church—as far back as the twelfth-century dispute between Anselm and Roscellinus on which should take priority, God's revelation or human reason (through which revelation must be interpreted), down to the disputes among the reformers like Luther, Zwingli and Calvin in the sixteenth century on matters like transubstantiation, baptism, predestination and freewill—it is clear that such theological disputes and controversies had pressing implications for the educated believer in those times. These *were* the burning issues of the day, not just life but eternal life depended upon their settlement. Throughout the Middle Ages enormous human energy, ingenuity and creative thinking in Western Europe were devoted to such issues.

Apart from these disputes arising within the Christian faith there was also a competing secular high culture which began with the Italian Renaissance in the Florence of the Medici family. The Italian Renaissance preceded that of northern Europe by about a century. Italian nobility saw themselves as the spiritual heirs of the Roman Empire in which it was common for the secular aristocracy to be highly educated and cultivated, whereas in northern Europe education and culture were the province of the Church and disdained by the feudal nobility.

In 1348 the University of Florence was founded and its students were as likely to be studying the 'new learning', that is classics from the Graeco-Roman world rediscovered after the Dark Ages, as Christian theology. For example, one of the first expressions of this kind of humanistic education and culture was Vergerio's (1349–1420) exposition of Quintillian's *Education of an Orator* and his own *On the Manners of a Gentleman and on Liberal Studies* (Boyd 1961: 162–3).

The latter work had been written for the guidance of the lord of Padua and became very popular and influential in the following two centuries, summing up, as it did, the aim and methods of humanistic education. Like Quintillian twelve centuries previously it insisted upon: 'the value of an all-round education for the man of affairs, and the same recognition of the need to adapt the subjects to be learned to the individual bent and to the age of the pupil' (ibid.).

Vergerio, however, combined Quintillian's ideas with the Christian conception of life, and in the generation following, Vittorino of Feltre (1378–1446), who has been called 'the first modern school master', put into educational practice the former's views on education.

His school (called 'The House of Joy'—La Gioisa) catered largely for the children of the lord of Mantua his patron and those of other noble families plus poor scholars of promise. In 'La Gioisa' Latin and Greek classics were studied alongside music, astronomy, geometry and arithmetic. In addition there was a strict regime of bodily discipline via games and exercises and finally throughout the whole, the Christian spirit was cultivated via daily devotions and the living personality and religious practice of the schoolmaster. Thus, in this first school of humanistic education, the 'whole man'—(mind, body and spirit) was subject to intensive training.

In this short account of the origins of humanism we can see themes echoed in present-day understandings of self-development. For there is the twin emphasis again on the 'inner' and the 'outer'. Education was a preparation for future 'men of affairs' not simply for fine theological and ecclesiastical discussions. The world of events out there was the reason why the secular noble families wanted to train their children, so that they would have the knowledge and skill to defend their interests either in the courts or in battle. At the same time there was a recognition of individual bent and the preferences of learners as well as a disciplinary religious training of the spirit.

As the centuries passed, however, humanism came into conflict with Christianity. Scientists like Galileo (1564–1642) came across facts that were unpalatable to the Church of Rome. Galileo was condemned twice by the Inquisition for maintaining that the Earth revolves around the Sun and is not the centre of the universe. On the second occasion he recanted, promising never again to maintain that the Earth revolves or rotates (Russell 1946: 520). The Inquisition managed to end the development of science in Italy for several centuries.

Galileo died in the same year that Newton (1642–1727) was born, and by this time northern Europe had experienced the Protestant Reformation, and the grip of the Roman Catholic Church over learning, education and culture was considerably weakened. Newton and his colleagues founded the Royal Society and developed a new form of knowledge production different from revelation or reason applied to scholastic arguments: namely the power of 'experimental method'. This 'new science' was most strongly advocated in Bacon's (1605) book *The*

Advancement of Learning which begins with a scathing attack on the Schoolmen of European theology and philosophy:

Here therefore is the first distemper of learning, when men study words and not matter . . . for words are but the images of matter; and except they have life of reason and invention, to fall in love with them is all one as to fall in love with a picture (Bacon 1973: 25)

As experimental methods slowly produced results and assisted the Industrial Revolution, secular scientific education became less and less linked to the Church. New universities were founded by states rather than by the authority of the Church of Rome, unlike ancient universities such as Paris. Practical knowledge based on sensory experience, experimentation and empiricism, became as important, if not more so, than Christian revelation or rhetorical argument and the armchair theorizing of the scholastics and earlier philosophers.

The effect of humanism was to replace God's supreme position in the Christian cultural dominant or world view with 'man's' supreme position in the humanistic cultural dominant or world view. The declining international power of the Church of Rome coincided with the emergence of national identities and states as the case of Luther's Germany illustrates. As the authority of the Church in the sphere of knowledge declined, the authority of the kings and aristocracies of Europe declined in the sphere of secular power. America threw off the authority of the English monarchy, in France the Revolution replaced the monarchy with a republic and in our own century the Russian tsars and Chinese emperors have both been replaced by Communist states.

The European Enlightenment emerged with the seventeenth-century scientific revolution and with industrialization gave rise to what we have earlier called modernism. In modernism, as the high point of humanism, it seems that the old hierarchies have been overturned. Man replaces God. The masses replace kings. Human mastery of nature via science, technology and industry is at a maximum and human self-mastery in the existential world without God is also at a high point: man is the ultimate author of human meanings. Self-development is a thoroughly humanistic movement for increasing everyone's 'capacity and willingness to take control over and responsibility *for events,* and particularly for *themselves* and their own learning' (Pedler *et al.* 1978: 3).

Deconstruction, however, presents a revised understanding of the self and its relation to events in the world. Potentially deconstruction is as threatening to Western humanism as Galileo's observations were to the Christian cultural dominant. With humanism, God, as the origins of meaning, was removed. With deconstruction, humanity, as the origin of meaning, is removed. This time there is no neat reversal, no revolution by which man supplanted God and the masses supplanted the monarchies. Deconstruction does not replace one hierarchy with another—in breaking down hierarchical order it does not create a new master-order or meta-order. Rather hierarchy, mastery and order are diffused—the air is let out of them so to speak and the effect may be experienced as unnervingly sickening—'all that is solid melts into air'—or as playfully pleasurable, as the following section describes.

Deconstruction

Humanism attacked the origin, it cast doubt upon God's revelation, upon God's authority, it perceived between the world of God and the written text of the Bible the interpretive interference of the Bible's human authors. Liberal theology eventually replaced earlier fundamentalist dogmas or convictions; in the more extreme words of Nietzsche: 'God is dead', that is, God had began to be seen as a social construction rather than the origin of the true meaning of the Universe. As humanism spread, overturning the old order, writers like Rousseau and other romanticists began to hanker after lost origins of primal innocence. In the absence of God humanism began the cult of nature worship and numerous expressions of longing for lost origins and innocence emerged.

Modernity brought alienation and brought antidotes such as the arts and crafts movement of Morris, Ruskin and the pre-Raphaelites. More recently in the most rapid period of industrial expansion and functional instrumentalism namely the 1960s, the hippy movements emphasized self-knowledge and expression, and again a return to nature. Mastery over events out there and over the self itself are the twin themes of humanistic self-development. In the period of modernism both impulses are at the extreme. The question is whether post-modernity offers any alternative. Post-modernity is often seen in two ways, firstly, as a throwback to a golden age of unalienated pre-modern times and secondly as that which succeeds modernism—that is, a kind of super-modernism, modernism accelerated and in its nascent state constantly, freshly emerging; faster than ever, more fragmented than ever.

But this very diversity and fragmentation in Western culture has spawned a widespread understanding within the modern cultural dominant about the cultural relativity of things—of most things: art, politics, business, music, holidays and more. Everything now is a matter of interpretation, absolute authority went with God and in the post-war period even 'Western Man' has begun to see itself in perspective and to recognize alternatives ('After Japan', for example). And this is where deconstruction comes in, for deconstruction is simply a way of reading.

And the text does not have to be marks on a page, it can be any form of symbols. For just as Claude Levi-Strauss the anthropologist could apply the structuralist linguistic theory of Saussure to pre-literate society's systems of symbols such as kinship patterns and taboos, so it is possible to apply Derrida's deconstruction not just to text but to other patterns of symbols.

Derrida's deconstructive way of reading is not, however, just one reading among many other equally possible ones; it is a way of reading which overturns, without setting up a new hierarchy, the assumptions of mastery over self and events implicit in humanism. 'For Derrida, *writing (in its extended sense)* is at once the source of all cultural activity and the dangerous knowledge of its own constitution which culture must always repress' (Norris 1982: 32; my emphasis).

Writing has a key significance for Derrida because in the Western traditions of thought writing is always seen as secondary to speech. Speech is the closest thing we have to the pre-articulate origin of the self's human experience. How do we experience the self without words? Clearly we cannot answer even if we know. How do we experience things out there without words? Again we cannot answer even if we know. In the Western tradition speech has primacy over writing; once things are written down they are somehow alien to what the author meant—they take on a life of their own.

Throughout the Western logocentric tradition (as Derrida calls it in order to emphasize the 'spoken word': Logos) there has been an overriding concern for the original authorial intention, the words behind the text, the meaning behind the words, in the presence of the self. During the Christian cultural dominant this Western fixation is evident in all the endless theological debates of the Schoolmen and scholastics as they tried to articulate what God meant by the close textual analysis of the Bible. Numerous distinguished theologians from Aquinas to Luther and Calvin periodically re-read and reinterpreted the whole of scripture in a way which was arguably more consistent and therefore truer to God's originary meaning.

Writing or text was blamed for the mistakes and misunderstandings preserved over the centuries. If only one could get to the presence of the originator of the words that were written then one would have the true meaning. Written words were untrustworthy, hence in the Christian tradition—particularly after the Lutheran reformation—the emphasis was upon the believer's *personal* experience of the *presence* of Jesus Christ, as a way of avoiding the pitfalls of mere cognitive faith based on an understanding of slippery texts.

With the rise of humanism and secular knowledge, writing had to become increasingly precise, especially as science came to depend on a precise correspondence between the elements of a propositional sentence and, say, the motions of planets or the relations between gases represented by some equation. So again writing was seen as secondary to the mind or presence of the scientist or human expert, whose words and living presence were far more trustworthy than mere writing which could so easily be misinterpreted.

As Bacon put it: 'words are but the images of matter' (1973: 25) and should not be studied *per se*. The empirical scientist had to attempt to study matter or nature in the raw not through the dissembling images of writing.

Humanism replaced a logocentric concern for working out what God had really meant all along—the preoccupation of a thousand years of Western theologians—with a logocentric concern for working out what each other really meant. And throughout, writing was seen as the spoken word's inferior. The presence of the author—a masterful self with authority over his/her own meaning was of central importance. Writing is therefore repressed by Western culture. Rousseau, for example, (among many others from Plato onward) in his interminable *Confessions* frequently repeats himself with minor changes of meaning often berating the written word's inadequacy for saying precisely what he meant in his long attempt to bare his soul honestly for the reader. In Rousseau's *Confessions* it is Rousseau, the man, who is honest and writing is blamed for all the problems and deceits. Derrida reads Rousseau deconstructively (Derrida 1974) pointing out that Rousseau's 'text cannot mean what it says, or literally say what it means'. Wherever Rousseau advocates a return to Nature or to speech he must do so nonetheless *through* the duplicitous vehicle of writing. Rousseau's return to Nature is itself a highly cultivated move. The origin cannot be returned to. As Norris puts it: 'What emerges is the fact that language, once it passes beyond the stage of a primitive cry, is "always already" inhabited by writing' (Norris 1982: 36).

Deconstruction is a way of reading which highlights the inescapable contradictions implicit in any text which argues for a direct return to origins, to speech and to primal self-awareness. The self itself as an authentic author of its own meaning cannot be reached therefore. Language and writing always invade the attempt. And writing or language are both external to the self's meaning—either spoken after the fact or written down distant from the author. Derrida shows us how very often what we understand to be human meaning is actually detached from any original self-presence or author. In the symbols we read in everyday life from words on pages to the kinds of cars different people drive we discern meanings free-floating and cut-off from their original author's intention. I certainly have little masterful control over the way you make meaning by reading this chapter. Even if we were face to face we could never ultimately understand each other's meaning.

This is no grounds for despair, for we all manage to get by in practice. Derrida's point is that we continue acting as if we are selves with definite personal meanings yet if we apply a deconstructive analysis the actual grounds for that presupposition can not be found. All we have is a pre-articulate assertion of our selfhood. The more Derrida explores the relation between the inner meaning (the presence of some self) and the outer symbol (your words, or your car, for example) the more the basic hierarchy breaks down. The inner meaning is not necessarily prior to the words uttered or written, nor necessarily superior. We cannot say which came first. Another way of putting this is to say that deconstruction breaks with hierarchy without setting up a new hierarchy. In logocentricism the hierarchy is:

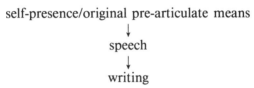

$$\text{self-presence/original pre-articulate means}$$
$$\downarrow$$
$$\text{speech}$$
$$\downarrow$$
$$\text{writing}$$

In this figure speech is secondary to self-presence which provides original meaning. Writing is even more supplementary still: it is secondary to speech, two stages removed from the origin. Speech tends to distort the original meaning and writing distorts it event further. In this hierarchy the human self as originator of meaning is clearly superior to speech and writing (two varieties of language). Derrida's deconstructive reading of Westen thought finds this hierarchy implicit from Plato down to the romantics and existentialists. He points out, however, that this hierarchy always promotes dissatisfaction with writing, in the most extreme case, because it tends to ossify the original meaning and to distort it in 'dead letters'. But he goes on to point out that without writing and speech we have no access at all to the pre-articulate original meaning of some self present. We are wholly dependent on language, in its written and spoken conventions, not only to convey or transport meaning from A to B but to 'mean' anything in the first place. Thus in a radical sense, 'meaning' no longer originates in self-presence, but in language (written and spoken conventions) which is by its nature outside the self-presence of the individual subject. In this sense we—our experience of self-hood and self-presence—are written as we write.

Deconstruction reverses the hierarchy of Western logocentricism:

However, it does not stop there: it challenges the idea of hierarchy *per se.* Rather than simply replacing one hierarchy with another, it points out that both ways are equally possible, but that if we accept that it is undecidable which way predominates then what is lost is the idea of an *origin.*

To capture this undecidability Derrida coins the word differance (spelt with an 'a'), which ambiguously carries simultaneously the twin meanings of to *differ* in spatial terms and to *defer* in temporal terms. Differance cannot capture the undecidability Derrida is referring to. Paradox cannot be pinned down. Deconstruction opens a way of understanding the self which does not buy into thousands of years of privileging the idea of a self as the author of meaning—neither the presence of God nor the presence of Man guarantees meaning. Meaning is a product of symbols which have a life of their own beyond our capacity to master them. Selfhood is understood therefore in a radically different way; the self is written as we write, it is not a point of origin but a by-product of writing. In an interminable, undecidable way the external world inhabits the internal world: there is no outside of the text, once we leave the pre-articulate origin—if there is one. (Compare Cooper 1989.)

The human self, like Nietzsche's God, is dead, that is, through deconstruction we can see that the inner self is as much a product of our language as it is the author or master of that language. Deconstruction breaks down our binary modes of thinking making it impossible to contemplate the internal separate from the external—each inhabits and invades the other, changing our experience of the self itself and events out there. Deconstruction can be seen as thoroughly Taoistic because opposites inhabit each other (see Figure 2.1) and the world of action out there becomes inseparable from the self-experience in here. As Lao Tzu writes:

> Without stirring abroad
> One can know the whole world;
> Without looking out of the window
> One can see the way of heaven
> The further one goes

> The less one knows
> Therefore the sage knows without having to stir
> Identifies without having to see
> Accomplishes without having to act.
> *(Tao Te Ching*, XLVII).

Such passages are not advocating slothful indolence, but they commend a different way of being. Deconstruction too suggests a way of being in the world which does not constantly seek to master meaning, language, nature, people, natural resources and is not mastered either. It challenges us to think about authenticity, original means, self-actualization differently: to stop reaching for the rock bottom, for the most honest self-knowledge, and to stop reaching for the stars via the technology of human progress. Deconstructive self-development is without the traditional humanistic understanding of the self and without the traditional view of development (in both senses of economic progress and self-actualization). Paradoxically in stopping reaching for the limits we may find them.

What implications follow for the practice of management development?

Figure 2.1   The Yin–Yang of Taoism

The first proposal has an organizational focus: rather than promoting a language and corporate strategy for global domination and mastery, deconstructive management development might emphasize a *symbiosis* between the organization and all its environments. The organization as an extension of a number of exploitative, aggressive corporate egos might spend more time researching the marketplace, consulting the customer, watching what happens to its corporate waste and pursuing genuine joint ventures; rather than—or as well as—asset-stripping takeovers, understanding world-wide social, political and culture currents including religions and arts. In other words 'learning organizations' might attempt to understand more about the complex ways they participate as citizens in the global village, not simply to focus on the bottom line. This does not mean ignoring the bottom line; it does mean examining more creative ways of improving it than traditional methods such as acquisition and divestment games in the name of diversification or 'defining the business we are in'. One of the businesses that all organizations are in is making meaning, not only through their advertising campaigns and customer-care programmes, but in the kind of deals they make and the kind of demands these put on their managers and their ways of life.

Managerial ways of life are still little understood, even though managers are frequently at the entrepreneurial frontiers of the moral dilemmas of the times, scientific advances, establishment of style, taste, fashion, conceptions of ideal beauty and more. That managerial life is stressful and is the subject of some studies on stress is not surprising, but in general managers do not take themselves seriously enough. Managers' ways of life, and the tensions to which they must seek new ways of handling, need to be understood in the rest of society as well as among managerial populations themselves.

A second proposal has a managerial focus: deconstructive management development might enable individual managers to make connections between their own individual actions and the meanings by which their lives are governed. In a post-modern world where culture fragments and differentiation abounds, organizations decentralize and small bands of intrapreneurs sell their services within and between companies. Managers are becoming more autonomous and in a sense isolated; a Hobbesian war of all against all might result in a marketplace of guerilla warfare. In such a post-modern context managers constantly need to learn new fighting techniques, ways to produce faster, think faster, perform faster. But they also need to understand the 'bigger picture', not only because that will help them to find or carve out new niches to colonize, but also to help them produce integrative devices and ways of working which are individually profitable without adding up to collective destruction.

References

Bacon, F. (1973) *The Advancement of Learning,* ed. G Kitchen, Dent, London.

Boyd, W. (1961) *The History of Western Education*, Adam and Charles Black, London.

Cooper, R. (1989) 'Modernism, postmodernism and organizational analysis 3: the contribution of Jacques Derrida', *Organizational Studies*, forthcoming.

Derrida, J. (1974) *Of Grammatology*, trans. G. Chakravorty Spirak, John Hopkins, University Press, Baltimore.

Hill, C. (1955) *The English Revolution in 1640,* Lawrence and Wishart, London.

Kuhn, T. (1962) *The Structure of Scientific Revolutions,* University of Chicago Press, Chicago, Ill.

Lao Tzu (1963) *Tao Te Ching*, trans. D. C. Lau, Penguin, Harmondsworth.

Norris, C. (1982) *Deconstruction: Theory and Practice*, Methuen, London.

Pedler, M., J. Burgoyne and T. Boydell (1978) *A Manager's Guide to Self Development*, McGraw-Hill, London.

Russell, B. (1946; 1979) *History of Western Philosophy*, 2nd edn, Unwin Paperbacks, London.

Part II The present: current practices

Introduction

After the airy speculations of Part I, some readers will be relieved to reach the solid ground of experience and example. Part II contains ten chapters on the current practice of self-development in mainly large commercial organizations. The household names of ICI, IBM, Radio Rentals, the Prudential and W H Smith can all be found here among others. In some of these organizations self-development remains a minority pursuit, both in terms of numbers and of centrality to company philosophy and practice. In others the idea of self-development seems to have penetrated to the heart of policies for business and people development. These contributions make it plain that self-development is an idea in good currency.

Closer inspection reveals a wide variety of interpretations. Chapters 3, 4, 5, 6 and 12 stay close to the personal-development pole, while varying in the extent to which they stress the business impact of such personal development. While all these contributions are concerned with helping people and organizations become 'fit for the future', the approach here is of a fairly loose fit. A close connection between the person and business is not required. Chapters 7, 8, 9, 10 and 11 on the whole go for a closer fit of self-development with organizational needs. There are three examples of the use of open and distance learning here from the retail and financial sectors. Chapters 10 and 11 offer macro and micro examples of how self-development may be harnessed with corporate or managerial objectives. Here the fit between individual and organization is explicitly negotiated.

Part II offers a variety of answers to the questions 'What is self-development?' and 'How can it be used to help individuals and organizations?' Take your pick.

3
Culture change through individual development: a story of the Life Business Workshop

Stephen Merckx and Dennis Bumstead

Why are a dozen or so senior executives from leading British companies wielding scissors and Sellotape, surrounded by a sea of cuttings from magazines? What is the connection between this unusual activity and concerns about the need for British companies to perform better? And why is it that many senior managers have a general feeling of dissatisfaction and a need to take stock, to review their lives and their career direction? How does their participation in the Life Business Workshop relate to these questions?

The answer to all these questions can be found in a story about Phil. Phil is a fictitious participant in one of a continuous programme of workshops which have been running for the past ten years. Fictitious Phil has many of the characteristics of the middle or senior manager from large British companies who have participated in these workshops. By British standards Phil's company is successful, showing satisfactory profits, reasonable growth and considerable ability to accommodate change and introduce new technology. But Phil and his colleagues are aware that there are competitors, particularly in Japan, Europe and the USA, which are ahead in terms of the main performance indicators, profit per employee, return on investment, introduction of new products, and so on.

But the story starts many years ago when Phil was still at school. He was a clever child and had a loving and supportive family. He did well at school both in his studies, and in sports and other extramural activities. He went on to a highly respected British university where he worked and played hard and earned a good degree. In his final year he was interviewed by a number of well-known companies and accepted a tempting offer with a good salary, an interesting job and the prospect of rapid promotion.

Phil did well, his job was lucrative. He worked hard and he was rewarded with promotion. As he progressed he acquired a bigger salary, more responsibility, a bigger desk, an executive car and a lot of status. He had also acquired a wife and children, an appetite for cigarettes, a large house, and an enhanced waistline. Life was good.

But time passed and Phil has been working for the same company for twenty years. Promotions had given Phil a variety of experiences including technical and marketing roles and some time overseas. Now he was a senior manager with responsibility for a large number of subordinates, some of them graduates from university just as he had been twenty years before.

Yet somehow things were different. Although the ambitions of his early years had been satisfied he was aware that it was unlikely that he would ever make it to become a director. Although he was a senior manager he did not have the freedom he had imagined went with such a job. He had to work very hard and nearly always took a briefcase home where he dealt with a daily stream of reports and letters. He had little time for exercise or leisure and he was increasingly aware that his health was suffering. He had become irritable and sometimes took it out on his wife and children. Yes, he had plenty of money, but life was not much fun any more.

So the day when he bumped into Ian stands out in his memory. Ian had talked about the Life Business Workshop, 'An opportunity to take stock of your life and career,' he had said. Ian had described how the workshop was specifically for middle and senior managers who feel that they are at a crossroads along the road of life. He had talked about an analogy with business management processes of reviewing, analysis and planning. Phil had been intrigued. He had said to Ian 'Why don't we have lunch together one day next week and then you can tell me more about it?' And so they did.

'I want to know all about this workshop,' said Phil, 'and what it can do to help me. But tell me why our company is supporting this activity in the first place. It seems to me that this workshop is all about me and my job and my life. I am already doing a big job. I have been on lots of training courses and I know all I need to know in order to keep on top of things. Why should the company support my taking time away from the job on this workshop thing?'

Ian explained that for someone in Phil's position his effectiveness depends heavily on how he feels about himself and his job. Any mismatch which may exist between the individual and the job is a potential source of dissatisfaction, frustration, or stress and can lead to a shortfall in performance. The mismatch may be in the area of ambition, competence, culture, attitude to life, the role of the job, relationships with others and so on. Although it is unlikely that a perfect match can ever be achieved, any serious differences need to be addressed if an employee is to perform really well. Ian said that the dissatisfaction and frustration which Phil had said he was feeling are commonplace throughout most large organizations.

'There are so many intelligent, skilled and capable people who are not happy with their jobs but who go on doing what they are doing because they expect work to be like that. How often have you heard people say "I only go to work for the money. I cannot wait for the weekend to come round." Or how many people will introduce a grouse with "I don't know why *they* don't . . ." and then go on to list many problems which are expected to be solved by the company, the government, their boss, in fact anyone other than themselves. These are only symptoms of the same sort of problem.'

'The problem is that many people have an expectation of the organization in which they work that it will look after them hand and foot, look after their grouses and grumbles, look after their careers, ensure that they are happy and satisfied. The reality is that except for a very small number of high-flyers the world is not like that. If individuals are to achieve a state of development and satisfaction in their lives, both at work and outside work, the odds are greatly improved if they take control of things themselves. And what is more, when they do this, as well as being of benefit to them it is also greatly to the benefit of the organizations in which they work. The outcome is a major stride to achieving what others have called "the learning organization". Or, using different words, if the outcomes of this workshop for a single individual can be disseminated through an organization, then what takes place is no less than a major culture change, a change in the way things get done, a change in attitudes in which the performance improvement in the whole organization is greater than the sum of the improved contributions of all its employees.'

'So to come round to the answer to your question, Phil,' said Ian, 'there are three different reasons why the company supports these workshops.' And he went on to explain the main objectives of the Life Business Workshop shown here in Box 1.

Box 1 The objectives of Life Business Workshops

1. To provide space, time and a process to enable employees of companies to address issues around their own lives including job, career, home, family, friends, health and hobbies.
2. To improve the performance of individuals at work through a raised level of purposefulness and personal energy.
3. To bring about a major change of culture by progressive extension of the processes and principles of the workshop to the whole organization.

'It is not a "quick fix". Like all change processes which involve human behaviour it takes time and requires sustained effort. But all our experience over ten years confirms our belief that it is worth while. All the feedback from previous participants says that this is a thoroughly worthwhile programme both for individuals and for organizations.'

'OK,' said Phil, 'so you have explained to me why the company should be supporting this activity and I'm beginning to understand that. But say a bit more about what I will get from it.'

'Well, you know how any company puts considerable effort into gathering data about its performance, analysing its market, planning its future,' said Ian. 'Well, in very simple terms the output of that process is a strategic plan, a plan covering its major businesses and customers, its research, its support functions, in fact, every part of the organization for some years ahead.' He went on to say that very few people ever think systematically about where they are going. They just muddle through from day to day, from year to year, reacting to what happens without any sense of long-term goals. He explained that the workshop provides a framework for participants to look at their own 'businesses', 'customers' and 'markets', to examine the balance in their personal energy, their strengths and weaknesses, the opportunities and threats around them and to draw up a personal life plan.

'I had never thought of it like that,' said Phil. 'When you come to think of it, it makes sense to invest a few days in order to try to make the most of the rest of your life. But tell me a bit more about the workshop itself.'

'OK,' said Ian, 'but first of all I want to tell you about a few very important ground rules.'

Ian went on to explain that it is important that participation in the workshop be voluntary.

'Nobody goes to the workshops because they are sent by their boss,' he said. 'The last way to bring about any change is to tell someone that they must do something,' and he went on to support this statement with experience with other events. 'Another ground rule,' he said, 'is that there is an unwritten contract of confidentiality around the workshop. Obviously anyone who takes part in the Life Business Workshop is likely to want to talk about his or her own job, career or home life. It is important that participants should be able to talk about aspects of their life both within work or outside it without the fear that their personal feelings will be shared with their employer or neighbour. But don't get the impression that this is a T group. There is no pressure on any participant to open up any part of their lives which they do not wish to share. Clearly the more that participants share in the workshop the more they are likely to get out of it, but that's as far as it goes. But that particular lesson applies to so many sides to life, doesn't it?' He went on to expand on the ground rules for the workshop which are summarized in Box 2.

Box 2   Ground rules for Life Business Workshops

1. Attendance is voluntary.
2. It is not a T Group—there is no pressure for participants to tell all.
3. It is confidential:
    (a) no feedback to company;
    (b) topics related to organization and business are kept confidential within syndicates;
    (c) personal matters treated in confidence.
4. No two individuals who have a close work relationship are placed in the same workshop unless by mutual agreement.

'OK,' said Phil. 'All that sounds pretty sensible. I like the sound of those ground rules. I wish they applied to some of the other events I have been to. How do you ensure that everyone understands them?'

Ian answered by explaining that potential participants are encouraged to talk to previous participants and/or workshop staff ahead of the workshop. Occasionally an applicant is advised not to attend or it is suggested that he postpone his attendance. 'Sometimes I can sense that an individual is coming for the wrong reasons,' he said. 'Sometimes I know or discover that one chap works very closely with another applicant. If they both came to the same workshop there is a good chance that they would inhibit one another. Under those circumstances it would be a mistake to have both of them attend the same workshop.'

'But now I want to tell you about the structure and process of the workshop.'

Ian went on to describe how the workshop is structured. Day 1 is devoted to a review. The principal business analogy is with compiling the annual report of a company. The concept of personal energy is used to draw up a personal 'balance sheet'. Day 1 is called 'The Annual Report'. Day 2 is devoted to examining personal attributes. Just as a company carries out an analysis of its market strengths, weaknesses, opportunities and threats (SWOT analysis), participants use a series of exercises in order to develop a better understanding of how they stand in their own life market. Day 2 is called 'The Market Report'.

Day 3 is all about planning. Using information gathered from the exercises in Days 1 and 2 participants first look at the options open to them, identify their principal 'business areas', draw up a plan and carry out a feasibility study. Day 3 is called 'The Planning Report'.

Then comes a two-month interval. 'This,' said Ian, 'is a period in which participants gather more data, test their plan on the most important people in their lives, and start to put it into practice.' The two-month interval is an integral part of the workshop and it is called 'Market Testing'.

Finally, as far as the workshop is concerned comes the 'Plus One' day. It is the day when participants, having done their market testing, come back to do some additional exercises and draw up a plan which will influence the direction of their future lives.

Ian summarized all he had said like this:

Stage 1	1 day	Annual Report
Stage 2	1 day	Market Report
Stage 3	1 day	Planning Report
Stage 4	2 months	Market Testing
Stage 5	1 day	Review

'But let me explain the process we use in the workshop,' said Ian. 'The whole workshop is built around a programme of exercises. It would be impossible to describe them all to you, but each exercise is designed to help participants gain an insight on information or experience which on the whole is already inside them. Have you come across the idea of left brain and right brain?' he asked.

'You mean,' said Phil, 'that idea that the left side of the brain is the intellectual, analytical side, and that the right side is the intuitive, artistic side?'

'That's right,' said Ian. 'Well, in the Life Business Workshop some of the exercises are aimed at the left side of the brain. Businessmen are familiar with that kind of activity, particularly if they work in technologically based organizations, because that is the sort of thing they are doing all the time, gathering information, classifying it, analysing it and then drawing conclusions from the analysis and using that as a basis for making decisions. Essentially the process is about *thinking* and *doing*. It works very well.'

'But the trouble is,' said Ian, 'that it is not the only thing that works well and many of us in business do not allow ourselves to use the important right side of the brain. As you say, this is the side of the brain which we are told is the artistic side. It is associated with creativity, imagination, emotion, colour, music, shapes, intuition and so on. The processes associated with the right side of the brain are much more to do with *feelings*. If we couple the thinking, feeling and doing we have a much better chance of achieving a better balance in our lives. For this reason a number of the exercises in the Life Business Workshop are designed to engage the right side of the brain.'

'Now you are beginning to worry me,' said Phil. 'I have heard about some of these way-out activities they get up to in some places, I have seen them on TV. You are not telling me that you use any of that sort of thing, because if you do it is not for me.'

'Don't worry,' laughed Ian. 'The exercises which we use are straightforward and our previous participants, including directors, engineers, research chemists and marketing people have managed to make very good use of them.'

Ian went on to explain that nearly all the exercises follow a similar pattern in that participants are given a simple task which usually requires that they work on their own for a short time. This is then followed by some pair working or sharing in a syndicate. Typically syndicates are made up of five or six individuals and each syndicate will be led by an experienced staff member. 'In the course of the workshop,' said Ian, 'the members of a syndicate get to know each other very well and develop a tremendous sense of mutual trust. They often make arrangements to meet up again after the workshop to continue with a process of ongoing support for each others' change programmes.'

Phil and Ian continued to talk about the workshop until lunch was finished and they had drunk a second cup of coffee. Phil explained to Ian how he felt about things; how, although he was successful in career terms and how everyone around him made the same assessment, it felt quite different inside. 'I think I really will have to make the space in my timetable to come to the workshop. It won't be easy but then it never will be. And if a few days' organized thinking can help to make things even a little better then it will be a thoroughly worthwhile investment.'

So Ian made a note of Phil's wishes and sent him the information about the arrangements for the next two workshops. Phil chose to attend one which was to be held in about three months' time, when he could make the space in his diary without too much disruption. Shortly before the workshop Ian sent him a letter confirming the arrangements.

These arrangements suited Phil. The workshop was held in a small, comfortable hotel, where the food was good and where it was easy for the whole group to work. He found that he got on well with the other participants, particularly as he got to know them better as time progressed. It was refreshing to be in a group of people from different companies, men and women who were employed in a wide variety of different jobs. But he quickly realized that he was not alone. The other participants had similar problems to his. He found that he was able to help other participants by sharing some of his own experiences and realized that he was picking up all sorts of ideas from the others. Some of them were quite simple ideas which it was easy to apply to his own life. Other ideas, he discovered, would mean to be tested and fell more into what he would call options. The process was challenging and testing at times, but he also found that it led him to see his own situation from a new perspective. He was beginning to revisit his values, the values which he had had when he was a student and before he plunged into his career and his domestic responsibilities. By the end of three days he felt tired but pleased that he had produced a plan for himself and was starting to feel more positive than he had for ages about life in general. Somewhat to his surprise he found that a good deal of his plan focused on his family and home, his health and hobbies, as well as aspects of his career and the way he did his job.

Examining the plan which he had written for himself at the end of the first three days of the Life Business Workshop left Phil with mixed feelings. He felt quite proud of it; it looked challenging but achievable. At the same time he felt disappointed that he had not produced something like this ten years earlier. The plan seemed to give a real purpose to his life in a way which he realised had been missing for a long time.

His plan was divided into three 'business areas'. These were:

1. job and career,
2. family,

3.   health and hobbies.

The workshop had led him to realize that his sense of dissatisfaction was not just centred on his job but was very much to do with the interaction between his job and his life away from work. While he had been very surprised when he first noticed how much of his plan was concerned with life away from the office, when he reflected further he became aware that what happened at work often affected how he felt and behaved at home. Similarly the way he spent his leisure time had a strong effect on his performance at work. So although he had identified three different business areas Phil realized that they all interacted on each other.

Each of Phil's 'business areas' comprised a programme of activities which covered a twelve-month period. The twelve months had been divided up so that the first group of actions and activities were those which he expected to complete before the Life Business Workshop follow-up day in two months' time. The next group of actions and activities were those which he expected to have completed between the follow-up day and before six months from the first part of the workshop. The remainder would occupy the second six months of the year.

Phil had set himself some tough targets and he knew that they would not be easy to achieve. He was afraid that he might possibly let himself down. Having heard some of what the other members of the workshop had planned for themselves he was aware that they had also set themselves some difficult objectives and was anxious not to perform any less well than them.

Phil's plan was very much focused on 'actions' rather than 'directions' because he had recognized that this was his preferred planning style. Some of the other participants in the workshop were much happier with a directional approach to planning but he knew that this would not work well for him.

So Phil came away from the first three days of the workshop with a number of new friends, a plan for the next twelve months of his life, a bag full of mixed emotions and the knowledge that in two months' time the group would meet up again in order to check up on the progress made and to review their personal plans. In the two months that followed Phil worked hard on his own plan. He was anxious to talk with his wife about a lot of the things which had come out of the workshop. She was interested and supportive, although privately she was also somewhat sceptical. Much of what Phil had learned from the workshop she felt she had been quietly observing for years. But if the workshop could help him to achieve a better balance in his life then it would make things better for her too, and for the rest of the family. Phil also needed to talk to his boss but he needed to work out a few things first and to choose a good time to do that. He had also undertaken to do a little reading and to meet up with one of the other workshop participants. In fact, along with all the other things which were featured in his plan, Phil was going to find it extremely difficult to fit everything in, particularly as his desk and his diary were both very full, after having been away from the office for three days.

Two months went by very, very quickly and when the follow-up day came round Phil hardly felt ready. Although he had looked at his plan a number of times and he knew that he had done a number of things listed in it, he felt that he really had not done as much as he had committed himself to do. But when he got out the plan again on the day before the follow-up day he was pleasantly surprised to find that he could tick off most things, and had made some progress with many of the others.

Phil enjoyed the follow-up day. It was good to meet up with the same group again and to hear how they had got on with their own plans. The process was similar to the first part of the workshop. Again, there were exercises which provided some supporting data, and, again, the work in syndicates enabled participants to help each other. He was surprised at the amount of progress which nearly every participant had made and he felt good about his own achievements. The day enabled him to review his own plan in the light of his experience in the first two months and as a result of what had emerged from discussions with his wife, his boss and a number of other people. By the end of the follow-up day he was confident that the plan he had put together for the next twelve months was realistic and achievable. It still felt ambitious but now it was tested and had the support of others who were a part of his life. He felt that he had made considerable progress and was anxious to get on with things. At the same time he recognized that he would continue to need help with the execution of his plan. He was pleased that most of the group agreed to meet up informally six months later. He also arranged to have lunch with one of the other participants once in a while in order to help to keep things moving.

Twelve months later Phil had one of his occasional meetings with Ian. 'I've been thinking,' said Phil, 'about the workshop I went on a year ago and everything that's happened since then. I thought at the time it was one of the most valuable development events I had been to, but I'm even more convinced now than I was then.'

'Well, I can see a big change in you, Phil,' said Ian, 'but I'd be pleased to hear what you have to say. Why don't we have a pint and a sandwich together at lunchtime?'

In a corner of the bar at their local Phil described some of the achievements and changes which had featured in his life in the twelve months since the Life Business Workshop.

'I really don't know quite where to begin,' said Phil, 'because so much has happened.'

'I'll tell you one thing before you start,' said Ian. 'It most certainly did not just happen. I am certain that you made it happen. You did it. It was part of your plan.'

'Yes, I suppose you are right,' replied Phil, 'because nearly everything which has happened was part of my plan. But all the same a lot of it seems to have happened without a great deal of effort from me.'

Phil then went on to describe the story of the past year, how he had talked to his boss of his feelings about his current job and the many reasons why he wished to broaden his experience in a new field. He had obtained some help and had suggested that a career move into a technical development role would suit him. He explained the sequence of events which had led to just such a move taking place. He had been in the new job now for four months and had got to know his new staff and the work of the department. The job suited him particularly well and Phil was enjoying himself enormously. He felt that his personal productivity at work was better than it had every been.

'Do you know, Ian, I hardly ever take work home these days. Somehow I seem to be able to get it all done at the office. One of the things I learned at that workshop was that if I got my life more into balance the energy generated in my life outside work would improve my output at work. The new job is almost a bonus because I find it so stimulating that I have energy to spare on my hobbies as well.'

Phil went on to say that he and his wife were leading a much more active social life. 'We go out to the theatre and to concerts quite often and we entertain our friends at home pretty regularly. I used to hate dinner parties, you know. I always felt so tired and it seemed such a struggle to be at all sociable. But these days I wonder what the problem was. And these days I manage to find time to play golf too. And do you know I have given up smoking! I never thought I could do it.'

Phil went on to explain how he had achieved most of the things that he had listed on the plan from the Life Business Workshop and had prepared a new plan for the next twelve months. 'There are a few things I have had to bring forward from the last plan, but not many. I'm still not as good as I would wish at writing letters, and I have been meaning to get involved in a few things to help out the vicar at our parish church.' Phil was clearly overflowing with energy, much happier than he had been a year before, and he looked fitter, more relaxed.

'You know, Ian, I feel I have got so much from this workshop. Does it always have such a great impact?'

'Well, I do have to say that you seem to have derived a particular benefit from the workshop,' answered Ian. 'On the whole because of the pre-workshop screening which we do we've managed to avoid the sort of disaster which might take place if someone who was totally unsuited were to attend. Clearly some individuals come to the workshop and take away a general message that there is not much wrong with the present balance in their lives. Mind you, even that can be an important positive message. Occasionally we have had a participant who may need help of a different kind, such as that provided by a professional in counselling. These individuals if we fail to spot them in advance of the workshop tend to get little from the process, but the process is so supportive that I am confident that there is a negligible risk of doing any damage to such individuals. And of course there are some people who put together plans but then fail to make much progress with implementing them. But on the whole most of the participants in the workshop get something positive from it and after ten years it still has a high rating in the organizations where it has been used.'

'Yes, I think that matches with some general impressions I picked up from the participants in the workshop I attended,' said Phil, 'There is something else I have been wanting to ask you. When we originally talked about the Life Business Workshop you said something about culture change. You said that one objective of the Life Business Workshop was to bring about a change in the culture of the organization. I can see what the workshop has done for me, but I am less clear how it has contributed to changing the culture.'

'That would be a very easy question to answer,' said Ian, 'if culture was something which could be measured like profit or output or raw material efficiency. You can only measure culture change by looking at the changes in the way the organization is managed. If I think back a few years managers appointed people to fill vacancies simply on the basis of the best person available. It was only a small number of graduate high fliers who had a career mapped out for them. People expected to get moved about a bit but it really depended on the boss. The system was really set up to sustain the business and if the needs and aspirations of individuals were satisfied then it was a happy coincidence. If you look about now you will see all sorts of processes which recognize the needs of individuals. A very few of them were in place before, but the way those are now used, and put alongside all the other processes, I believe we can see all the symptoms of a very major cultural change.' He went on to describe a lot of indicators of cultural change within the organization and expanded on each one (see Box 3).

Box 3   Indicators of cultural change throughout the whole organization:

1. Development workshops will be available at regular intervals.
2. Effective personal reviews will take account of performance in the job as well as the wishes of individuals.
3. Individuals will have training plans to improve their performance in their current job and to anticipate future development.
4. Open learning will be freely accessible.
5. Secondments will take place into other jobs and other organizations.
6. Transfers and promotions will be open to any individual with appropriate skills, qualifications and competency.
7. The processes for recruitment and selection will comprehensively assess individual attributes and every individual will understand the reasons for the outcome of the process.
8. Line managers' performance will be assessed in part on their contribution to developing their subordinates.
9. Further education will be available where it is appropriate to the career development of selected individuals.
10. Early retirement will be a negotiable option for all employees.
11. There will be effective processes in place to match career plans to the needs of both the organization and individual employees.

'And you relate all this to the Life Business Workshop?' queried Phil.

'Yes,' said Ian, 'I am confident that the workshop was the foundation on which most of these new processes were built. You see, when senior staff attend an event like the Life Business Workshop and get something from it they want to open up similar sorts of opportunities for their subordinates. At the very minimum they do not resist when such developmental initiatives are introduced. So in the last few years there are all sorts of new things happening which allow the purposeful, self-driven development of individuals to be synchronized with the development of the organization as a whole. The things I am talking about include development events similar to the Life Business Workshop for more junior levels of staff, the introduction of open learning, better career planning, the use of secondments both inside and outside the organization in order to broaden experience, improved selection processes, access to further education for employees, improved processes for releasing employees before normal retirement age and so on. A most important part of all this is the better recognition of individuals' aspirations in the routine appraisal system, and the support given to preparing personal training plans and following them through.' Ian went on to list a number of other processes which support what others have called a learning organization.

'Yes, I see what you mean,' commented Phil. 'I have noticed all of these things happening round me but I had not seen them as a coherent whole before now.'

'There is still a long way to go,' said Ian. 'I shall only start to relax when I see all of these things happening throughout the organization at every level, in every department and section. I suspect that even then it will require a lot of effort to keep it going. It is so much easier to ignore individuals and to treat them all as a sort of aggregate, a resource of more or less competent people with more or less identical skills. We can only achieve excellence by providing processes which release the energy and resourcefulness of every one of our employees. We must then continue to put effort into maintaining an environment which will sustain or improve on this culture.'

'Ah, now I see the connection,' said Phil. 'My attendance at the Life Business Workshop not only did an enormous amount for me personally but it enabled me to support this new regime by being open to all of the processes you describe and encouraging others to support them too. And because there are now quite a few of my colleagues who have been through the workshop there is now a nucleus of people who understand what this is all about.'

So Phil went home satisfied with the more balanced life he had planned for himself and with an understanding of how it not only made him feel good but contributed to the future success of the company. Ian went home confident that the organization's culture had moved one more notch in the right direction, and wondered where the next move would be.

Somewhere in the next few weeks another group of senior executives, men and women from leading British companies, will be crawling around on the floor with magazines, scissors and Sellotape. They will be taking part in another Life Business Workshop. They will be addressing issues which have contributed to a general feeling of dissatisfaction which they share with many of their colleagues and the outcome of their participation in this activity will be greater individual performance and a further shift in the culture of their organizations.

Please note: the concept of Life Business was originated by John Eckblad. The first workshops were run for ICI and Shell in 1979. A number of other companies, particularly BP, have taken part more recently. The workshops are supplied by the Fordwell Management Consultancy, 31 Mount View Road, London N4 4SS (Tel: 081-348 7742).

4
Getting off the ground with self-development
Sue Pritchard and Mike Nencini

Introduction

The Lancaster conference gave us the opportunity to celebrate some anniversaries. It was especially good to do so as most of those people, significant to our 'getting off the ground', were present.

In September 1986, two years prior to the conference, Sue was introduced to some concepts of self-development. Margaret Attwood, a colleague in the Health Service, told her about the North East London Polytechnic (NELP) Diploma in Management by Self-Managed Learning, which Sue subsequently undertook and completed. Sue's tutor on the NELP programme, Alan Mossman, introduced her to Mike at the 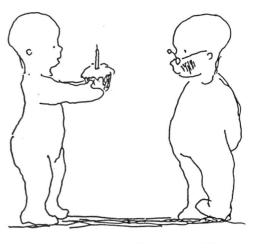 1987 self-development conference in Blackpool, following which she joined Radio Rentals in August 1987.

Mike has been part of Radio Rentals since 1968. He was appointed company training and development manager in early 1985. This was a time of radical change in the organization. In the year that followed he set up the central training department to cope with a massive influx of new managers at first line level, who required training in basic management techniques.

By late 1986, it was clear that further organizational change was necessary—a move toward decentralization—and Mike was instrumental in the visioning and change process. This gave him impetus to undertake a fundamental review of the training function and a search in the wider world for directions, ideas and concepts which were congruent with the newly espoused corporate culture. It was this search which found and connected with, among others, Mike Pedler, who

was doing some pioneering work at the Thorn EMI group development centre with self-development groups.

The third member of the conference workshop was Hedley Bowen, a regional manager in the south-west division of Radio Rentals and an early supporter of the self-development initiative. Mike introduced Sue and Hedley to Mike Pedler who then became part of our journey towards getting off the ground with self-development in Radio Rentals.

This may seem to be a convoluted introduction but it is important to us because it illustrates the long, uncertain journey we made towards getting started. It also illustrates the interconnectedness of the many strands in our own development which brought us to where we are.

The chapter, then, describes the journey we made towards getting off the ground. In describing this we will give you some history of Radio

Rentals and some of the processes we used to start self-development groups in our organization.

A short history of Radio Rentals

Radio Rentals came into being in 1930 renting radios. The company was based on the premise that it provided a way of affording what was, at that time, an expensive and unreliable item, backed up by technical service. Radio Rentals expanded in the 1950s with the rental of television receivers, which supported the original premise. During the next two decades, particularly in the 1970s, with the advent of colour television, the rental sector boomed. It is common historical lore in the company to look back on the days when 'customers queued round the corner to rent televisions and waited six weeks for delivery'.

In this climate the company evolved a culture in which management focused their attention on existing customers, providing them with technically first-class service. Primarily, it was an introspective, paternalistic organization, in which customers flocked through the showroom doors and the key managerial skills were concerned with managing the infrastructure that supported the servicing of these customers. Progress was sustained by technical innovation which left the challenge of change mainly with the development of the technical workforce, managers being relatively unaffected. Furthermore Radio Rentals was a highly profitable organization, with little impetus for primary structural change for at least three decades.

All this changed in the early 1980s. Following the video boom, our core products—television and video—became relatively much cheaper and more reliable, and the competition from retailers increased dramatically. As our traditional strengths in the marketplace diminished, the company strove to maximize market share and to reclaim lost markets. In addition Thorn EMI, who had acquired Radio Rentals in the late 1960s, required a revitalized, more streamlined and cost-effective management and an increased level of contribution to group profits.

Thorn EMI itself was undergoing major personnel and structural change to rationalize its business portfolio, and, following adjustments to management at the rental/retail sector level, some far-reaching organizational changes took place throughout Radio Rentals. Senior management focused on corporate regeneration and embarked on a process in which they attempted to describe shared visions of the future, corporate directions and corporate values.

In 1985, an internal restructure had swept away a whole layer of traditional middle management. This was followed by a second wave of management reorganization in 1987, during which another tier of managers was lost. Much was learnt from the earlier change and this time the company began to work through an organizational transformation process designed to make the company more 'strategically-led, market-focused, customer-oriented, people-driven and able to produce super league profits'. A new company mission emerged together with a set of role models describing behaviours and processes upon which the restructured company would be built.

Clearly, this period was traumatic for those working within it, and is characterized by uncertainty and turmoil, especially at middle and junior management level. There was an understanding that the regeneration of the company relied on the skills and will of those managers who worked closest to the customers—many of whom were the people most affected by the organizational changes.

Change in the training and development function

This process fundamentally affected Mike's thinking about the values and beliefs underpinning the development of people, and reinforced a long-held, instinctive belief that people should have more responsibility and control for their own development. He also had a discomfort with the role of the trainer as an expert, and a strong feeling that more could be achieved in the company, by operating with working groups and individuals in a less structured, more facilitative manner.

In the drive towards decentralizing decision-making out into the organization—nearer the customer—changes had also impacted on the central service functions, including the training and development function. Historically, training in Radio Rentals had been of very high quality and held in high esteem by managers within and outside the organization. Training and development was primarily organized by a central training department and focused on the enhancement of technical and managerial skills; for example, selling skills, recruitment skills, interpersonal skills, etc.

However, it was apparent that if we were asking managers to work and manage in an increasingly complex environment then the 'skills' that would be important and valued were of a different quality to those traditionally emphasized. There was much talk throughout the organization of managers needing to become more creative, more self-reliant, more independent, more innovative, more challenging, more market-aware, more autonomous, more responsible and so on. These 'meta' skills, clearly, could not be 'taught' in the way managerial skills had been taught in the past.

Further, it was decided that, in accord with organizational direction, the training function should also be located closer to the customer. Consequently, as part of the second organization, Mike led the devolution of the training and development function to the six divisions in Radio Rentals. Sue was the first management development manager appointed to the new divisional post.

So, there were two clear organizational impetuses around the issue of self-development: a strong organizational need for transformation to meet the demands of the new markets coupled with a corresponding awareness that the key factor in achieving this centred around the abilities of junior and middle managers, and secondly, a belief that training and development must work congruently with the proposed corporate culture.

New directions

The first stage of the journey towards getting off the ground, then, was a long and often tortuous period for some. It was a period of rapid and far-reaching change in which traditional and accepted beliefs and values were questioned and challenged, a period when conventional solutions were found to be moribund and new processes were sought to fill the gap.

does it hurt, then ?

only when you're getting somewhere

The second stage of the journey is about exploring new paths and directions which would prove to be most valuable in moving towards the company vision and in supporting business strategy.

As we mentioned earlier, there were fairly clear criteria around the sort of directions we could take. Our own values (and, indeed, those expressed by the company in its mission statement) led us towards open, participative styles of working, demonstrating respect for the skills and abilities of our fellow employees. While the majority of people shared these values, their belief in the company's will to prove these values through action was shaken through the restructuring. So, our efforts at revisiting and reinforcing them were treated with some scepticism.

The starting point came late in 1987, when Sue held a management development strategy meeting with the senior management team in the south-west division. The meeting was about reviewing training practice and planning for the future, but at the same time she wanted to establish overtly a style of working with these senior managers which would enable movement forward. The meeting followed a fairly common self-development model, i.e.:

Where have we come from?
Where are we now?
Where do we want to get to?
How will we know if we're getting there?
How do we get there?

It was clear from the views expressed at the meeting that the analysis of the organizational culture and practice was close to that which had been offered by top management working on organization development centrally.

That is, these managers believed that historic solutions were no longer valid and that new approaches were necessary. They believed that Radio Rentals needed to empower managers to act creatively, independently, with shared knowledge and shared accountability. They agreed that they required new skills and qualities from their staff—ones which hadn't previously been required—and that traditional skills were being superseded by the changing nature of the business.

They recognized that orthodox training methods, while valuable at certain times, were not sufficient to help create and sustain the new organization. When the training function had been located centrally there had been a small menu of off-the-job, off-the-peg programmes on offer including: interpersonal skills training, recruitment and selection, and performance review. While the training was participative in style, the nature and responsibilities of the central resource meant that it was extremely difficult to produce tailored programmes or to develop new courses, as the training team had to cover the entire country training new managers in basic managerial skills. This system also suffered problems with the effective transfer of skills into the work environment, lacking commitment and involvement from may established line managers who largely failed to follow up off-the-job events. The senior management group were clear that they did not want to replicate this training provision.

So, we looked at our vision of the ideal training culture and identified these common themes.

1. Organizational and environmental needs mean that we must enable our managers to be more creative, able to solve a wide range of complex problems and more able to cope with rapid change, uncertainty and ambiguity. The training culture must reflect and support this.

2. Development should be ongoing and focused on the person, with key support coming primarily from operational managers, backed up and facilitated by the training staff.

3. Responsibility for a person's own training and development should be invested in the individual to encourage ownership and commitment to reinforce the vision in point 1.

4. Commitment to the above would be explicit at all levels in the division.

The senior management team were enthusiastic towards this approach and all agreed to work with Sue as trainers/facilitators on a programme identified as being of pressing importance.

This programme was offered to showroom sales managers and gave them an opportunity to explore both the practical and personal issues involved in running a commercial unit. Furthermore, because the programmes were facilitated by senior managers, there was an opportunity to discuss and share thinking about the business.

These programmes proved to be successful and gave us our first indicator that the division might take on the principles of self-development. The facilitators enjoyed the loose, sharing process as much as the learners. All the participants identified the process of this programme, more than the content, to be one of the key aids to their learning.

The upshot of this series of programmes was a call of 'more of this, please!' from both first-line managers and the senior management facilitators.

A month after the end of this series of programmes, we held a meeting to review the effectiveness of the courses with a working group of senior managers. Feedback was clear that a more wholistic and individualized approach had been valuable and that all levels of management had been able to learn. It also gave the lie to the notion that training was something that experts had to do and instead it encouraged the sharing, open, supportive environment which is consistent with our own training vision and the company mission statement.

Self-managed learning groups

It was at this meeting that the concept of self-managed learning groups was introduced. This approach seemed to fit with the specification for future training directions and the principles were readily accepted by the working group—with the proviso that they would participate in a similar process too!

The next stage of our journey was to offer the process to the whole division. As a way forward, we enlisted the help of Mike Pedler and Nigel Kemp, a development executive at the Thorn EMI Home Electronics International Development Centre.

With their help we designed a process which would enable those people interested in participating, to find out more about the activity of self-development before committing themselves.

We called this the 'contract day', during which people could decide whether or not to 'contract' or opt in to the process.

Prior to running the contract day, information was circulated to all managers outlining the principles behind self-managed learning groups. It was a simple A4 sheet which said, basically, we offer you time, space and resources for you to work on your own development needs, with the support of a group of fellow managers.

At the same time Sue canvassed those managers who had facilitated groups on the previous courses about their willingness to facilitate a self-managed learning group—depending upon the number coming forward to participate.

The contract day was held in June 1988, and half of the managerial staff in the division attended. After introductions, the day ran using self-development models as far as possible. That is, we worked mainly in small groups on questions such as:

- 'What have been the key development events in my own life?'
- 'What do I want out of a process such as this?'

During the day we also stressed the connection between the values and principles underlying self-development and the company mission and direction.

At the end of the day, people had the opportunity to ask questions to clarify their thinking. Finally, they were asked to submit their names by the end of July, should they want to participate. With this approach we emphasized the element of choice and personal responsibility.

By the end of the July names for 16 participants and 8 potential set advisers had been received. It was decided to run with 2 groups and 4 set advisers initially, maybe starting more should the demand arise later in the year.

Set advisers

In September we held a two-day set-advisers' workshop. The aim of this was to enable potential set advisers to work on the way that we, and they, wished to operate. This workshop was facilitated by Mike Pedler and Nigel Kemp. However, during these two days it became apparent that the process we, as set advisers, wanted was not a simple 'how to facilitate' but more an occasion to work on our own development in relation to set advising. So, out of that came another self-development group.

It seemed to us that the facilitators' group was, and is, of real importance to the strength of the whole initiative. The issues being shared and worked on are often basic to our relationships with the organization. There are also personal concerns to be dealt with, commonly to do with working alongside people in areas of high emotion, and the fear of releasing 'uncontrollable' feelings which may hurt or even 'damage the individual'.

The act of facilitating has brought many deeply held beliefs and values to consciousness and, as a consequence, challenged working practices in the wider company world. Of course, working with first-line managers and others in a self-development group also provides a different perspective than the one often gained from the everyday 'manager and managed' relationship, and can cause some dissonance. Group members also appear more sensitized to signals and messages radiating through the corporate atmosphere, particularly those which seem to contradict newer ways of working.

Frequently these conflicts are crystallized in short- versus long-term debates, with the self-development approach at the long-term end of the spectrum, whereas some key management decisions and actions are located at the other. This can lead to speculation such as 'Does the company really mean us to be involved in this work?'

Our meeting gives the opportunity to reflect upon and share our own thoughts and feelings from the groups. Of course group confidences are protected absolutely, but facilitators do need access to a supportive, challenging environment, where they can explore and learn from their personal experiences of self-development, and the reactions of colleagues (and others) to their involvement in this kind of development activity.

The facilitator group is therefore essential in providing time, space and support for these kind of issues to be worked through and allow the removal of blockages to effective set advising and personal development. The other two groups started in November, each facilitated by two set advisers and have met ten times at the date of writing this. Although it is still early days, feedback is positive with managers commenting on increased confidence and contribution from participants in their work role.

Postscript

Since the Lancaster conference, things have moved apace.

Mike has been involved in spreading interest in the self-development approach through the divisional training and development manager network. Two other divisions have 'got off the ground' and one, or both of us have been involved in contracting days in those divisions.

Interestingly, the routes to entry into self-development groups have been varied. In one case, a group of managers who started on the path of more structured development—a 'summer school'—found the process of interactive learning interesting, challenging and productive. At the prescribed 'end' of the event the group asked if they could continue the relationship, but take responsibility for their own direction. The organization has responded by engaging in a 'mini contracting day' to ensure mutual understanding and agree ground rules for support.

In another case larger groups of managers attended an outdoor development event over the period of a week. Once again the common strand was a revelation around the power and potential of a group of people to help one another's learning, once they develop some trust, openness and the will to share. The desire to build upon this experience has been the fuel for forming more groups. Altogether there are eleven groups in existence throughout the company, albeit in various stages of development and guises.

In all these cases we have engaged in workshops for set advisers prior to the self-development groups forming.

We still have a long way to go! Much of the activity to date has been carried through with the encouragement and energy of a small group of like-minded people with shared values and beliefs. There are sceptics, particularly those who question the shorter-term direct payoffs for the business, and have a need for tight structure and control. Part of our vision for the future is to reach a wider audience, involving more and more managers in the process of self-development. We are strengthened in this endeavour by the climate in Thorn EMI, where considerable emphasis is placed on the idea of learning sets as a process for management development.

The long-term prosperity of our organization is clearly dependent not only on the ability of individuals to grow and develop, but also the capability to share these experiences so that collective learning takes place. We believe the process of self-managed learning must be internalized; in this way the richness of organizational activity will provide a wealth of potential for development and participation. Taking full advantage of these opportunities should, in turn, lead to an understanding of the learning process and the development of the organization—a kind of 'double loop' learning wherein conventional wisdom is continually questioned and challenged to enable the company to transform itself. This, then is our challenge for the future.

Our journey towards getting off the ground has been a long one, but, in our view, this is one of the keys to success. It has been about finding routes that recognize where we have come from, where we are and the fit with where we want to get to. It has been an organic and dynamic journey—not without trauma, and one which has been about learning to learn in order to grow both personally and as an organization.

5
Fit for the Future
Sheila McLeod and Tom Jennings

Introduction

We want to share our experience of pioneering some unorthodox approaches to personal development training in a large, high-technology organization. We will explore the implications of changing organizational and personal boundaries and explain how we turned our vision into a practical reality.

This chapter describes the organizational needs and the history of personal development training within IBM United Kingdom and lists what we believe are the critical success factors for trainers who are innovators. We will give a taste of the programme 'Fit for the Future' (FFF), giving examples of how over 300 participants have responded, and discuss how we are approaching the evaluation and measurement of its effectiveness in terms of added value for IBM.

FFF in context

Fit for the Future is one of a number of personal development training courses in IBM UK. All the courses share the common aim of increased understanding of oneself and of others. This aim is approached by different types of training: group exercises with peer feedback; group exercises with feedback from managers as observers; and individual, introspective exercises with a peer group as support. FFF is the prime example of the latter type and is seen as the highest level of personal development in IBM; participants would normally have done some previous training of the other types.

The purpose of personal development courses is to increase the effectiveness of the employee, both now and in the future, regardless of the particular job in the company. The training is therefore in a different category from the greater part of education in IBM. Personal development courses are cross-functional, made up of 12 to 18 peers but strangers, 4–5 day residential, and run by skilled facilitators. They are generally considered to be voluntary, on offer to the employee through the manager, and are regularly oversubscribed. The majority of attendees are professionals rather than managers; managers are more likely to have done personal development courses prior to their appointment and have little time subsequently for training other than the standard management development courses.

How does IBM justify personal development training? That is, how do we make the leap from personal insight to increased effectiveness at work? IBM's corporate goal in employee relations is 'Respect for the individual'. The right and the opportunity for each individual employee to make the most of his or her abilities is fundamental, and personal development courses are seen, by participants and by senior management, as one way of fulfilling that ideal.

But personal development training is also expected to meet business needs, needs which will change though the corporate goals remain the same. Examples of current business needs are:

- *the flexible employee*—able and willing to change jobs and to retrain;
- *the creative employee*—able and encouraged to think beyond apparent boundaries;
- *the healthy employee*—with a balanced, rather than stressed, approach to increased responsibility.

Increased understanding of oneself means more confidence, more personal control; knowing one's strengths and values means one can make the most of change; being aware of one's attitudes opens the possibility of deciding to change those attitudes.

This still does not explain why a first-line manager will willingly do without the services of a valued employee for a week and indeed will make a case to ensure allocation of a scarce place on a course for the employee. An analysis of these cases indicates that 30 per cent of the reasons given relate to the future development of the employee's career. That leaves 70 per cent relating to improved performance in the current job. Here one can make the case that it is through better understanding of oneself, and of human behaviour, that the employee can make the greatest use of his or her technical and business skills training and experience. So it is that managers most often give reasons for personal development training as improved communications, better ability to work with others, building confidence, and assertiveness, or re-assessment of strengths/weaknesses and personal goals.

Critical success factors

How do you turn vision into practical reality? We were well aware that within our own organization there are myths, legends, and some true stories of what has happened when a trainer or consultant has pushed at the training boundaries and disregarded the organizational implications of their actions.

In designing Fit for the Future we had distilled a wide range of knowledge and techniques into simple lifemanship skills that could be acquired in four days. These included *gestalt* work, personal construct theory, guided affective imagery, Chinese philosophy, psychosynthesis, and using the right-hand side of the brain. The use of such techniques raises concern that personal development training can overstep the boundary into unsolicited therapeutic interventions. Where does the organization's role end and the individual's private personal domain begin?

We believed that pushing out boundaries without threatening the individual or the organization would become one of the most valuable ways in which we could support IBM's need to develop people who can physically and psychologically meet the pressure of continued technological development, frequent organizational change, and the information explosion.

So how do you win and maintain organizational commitment to a programme that many managers would regard as a rather dubious initiative coming from what they perceive as a 'feely-feely' group? We drew upon our marketing experience and applied the same disciplines to 'selling' Fit for the Future to IBM as we would have done in a valued customer situation. We knew we were looking for commitment to an ongoing programme with recognizable benefits, and not just seeking agreement to run one pilot as an exciting experiment.

We identified the critical success factors as:

- relating FFF to the business needs;
- finding a committed sponsor;
- avoiding high risk;
- winning line management support;
- running a successful pilot;
- assessing organizational benefits;
- integrating FFF into the education curriculum.

How did we go about applying our marketing experience? First we needed a committed sponsor who had clearly defined needs. As we had both worked in the market support function earlier in our careers we had close links with, and a good understanding of, the systems engineering (SE) function who provide specialized technical support for the sales force. In 1985/86 the function was facing the major challenge of how to accelerate the development of a young and vigorous group to meet the complexity of the current business environment. Nearly one-third of the group had joined IBM since 1980; the majority as graduate recruits. We knew that the director of systems engineering was looking at ways in which personal development could be accelerated to meet the growing demands of the business.

We were already closely involved in two established programmes which were well-regarded by systems engineering line management and had a very good working relationship with the SE careers development manager who reported to the director. They were both people of vision who were keen to explore new approaches, yet at the same time they would not sponsor a programme that could be perceived as high risk for the participants or without benefits for the organization. They agreed to a pilot course which we ran in January 1986. The pilot was successful and during that year we ran a total of five courses for 52 systems engineers. We were severely challenged by one or two SE managers during that first year and were glad that we had support at a high level.

A successful pilot opens the way to further courses. We had seen many highly paid and highly experienced external consultants denied the opportunity of further programmes because their pilot had 'failed'. We knew that we would not get it absolutely right first time; we also knew that there would be no second chance if it were perceived as unsuccessful. We knew from our systems implementation backgrounds that you are courting failure if you run your pilot in an uncontrolled way in a hostile environment. So, with the help of the SE careers manager, we hand-picked 12 systems engineers who represented our target group. Women are well represented in the SE force and we were able to invite 6 men and 6 women. The inevitable cancellations occurred and we ran the pilot with 5 men and 4 women.

The SE careers manager introduced the course and facilitated a course review session on the final day. This encouraged a sense of ownership, it belonged to their function, they were not trainers' guinea pigs. The feedback was objective, mature and constructive, which enabled us to make amendments to the programme before offering it to people with longer service and experience or a different range of expectations. It was particularly important to us that participants felt safe and not under any pressure to participate in any sessions which made them feel unduly uncomfortable. The course had a specific design which we believed would preserve a sense of security and safety; the changes we made did not affect this fundamental approach.

Design considerations

We have between us almost forty years of extramural activity which extends from astrology to Zen, plus the personal experience of how so many of these approaches, techniques and practices can lead to self-knowledge, insight, personal awareness, expression of potential, transformation, joy, love. We also know that increased awareness often brings to the surface problems and dilemmas regarding commitment to relationships with an individual, a group, or an organization. We have met many 'course junkies' who seem to be on the self-development circuit; forever transcending but with little evidence of actualizing. We have seen consultants (with a vision that we share in principle) fall by the wayside because the organization felt anxious about what they were doing. We were aware that it was extremely important to select approaches that we believed would be acceptable in a business environment. We risked discussing the I Ching—the Chinese book of wisdom—which we knew would raise highly controversial issues; but as it is generally unknown to most of our participants they enter the discussion without the prejudices, assumptions, and attitudes a subject such as astrology might raise.

We have belief in all the approaches we are able to offer and had to be careful not to be carried away by personal enthusiasm resulting from our own particular awareness experiences. We know that being too evangelical can diminish credibility and invite hostility. In designing the course we had to continually consider the question 'Where are they coming from?' The majority of our participants are focusing their energy into career and home and do not spend their time among people who are avidly seeking the meaning of life or sampling yet the next offering which promises the key to empowerment and contentment. We decided we needed a gentle movement from the known to the unknown so as not to generate unnecessary anxiety; yet at the same time we needed to create a climate of change and ambiguity in which participants could experience and experiment with their own responses to the unknown and unpredictable.

Fit for the Future takes four days, starting after lunch on the first day and finishing at teatime on the fourth day. The decision not to use the whole week was driven by the fact that we orginally 'sold' the concept to the systems engineers who need to maintain customer contact and are reluctant to be away from the business for too long. This has advantages for the trainers who are not continually fighting the intrusion of urgent calls on the internal telephone network and the participants' need to get to a computer terminal to handle their electronic mail. Participants tend to put their house in order on the Monday, attend the course from Tuesday until Friday, and have the weekend to reflect on their experience before returning to the demands of the job.

Moving from the known to the unknown had implications in respect of process as well as content. Completing an inventory and discussing the results in the full group would be a familiar experience; one of our prerequisites is that participants must have attended at least one training course which develops interpersonal skills in a group environment. On the other hand, lying on the floor and being guided on a daydream which can put you in touch with deep inner feelings is a very new experience for most IBMers. For some people this is quite threatening, so setting some ground rules is very important. The overall aim of the course is 'To enable you to live with change and ambiguity in a creative and innovative way, so that you can respond responsibly and appropriately in whatever circumstances you find yourself'. Responding responsibly may mean saying 'No, that is not for me', so right from the beginning we make it clear that no one has to participate in any session which feels personally unsafe. We invite them to talk to us on an individual basis if they have any concerns. Some people are reluctant to make their feelings known, so we have to be continually on the alert, watching body language, listening for what is implied rather than overtly stated, and maintaining an overall guardianship of the process. This takes up a lot of mental and emotional energy!

We originally worked as a team of two with 12 participants and have now increased the class size to 15. We found that a group of 17 was too large, even with 3 trainers. Ideally we would like to have 3 trainers for a group of 15 participants. This gives the trainers some personal time for reflection, consolidation, and regeneration. There is also more of their time available for one-to-one sessions.

Technical training is highly structured and many IBMers feel threatened by a course that appears to have no structure. While encouraging fantasy, imagination, and creativity, it was essential that we also provided the security of structure. The use of inventories, the provision of handouts and a framework of timekeeping gives a sense of security to those who need it. We need to be reminded of Kolb's learning styles; not everyone takes an immediate delight in active experimentation! The programme unfolds daily and deliberately alternates between the familiar and the unfamiliar, trainer input and group discussion, being active and being reflective, 'left-hemisphere' activities and 'right-hemisphere' activities. Personal construct psychology made us so aware of the need to balance 'loosening' with 'tightening'. When flying hot-air balloons there is a need to carry sandbags to help you remain safely grounded.

With the exception of a few energy-raising games which take no more than ten minutes each, we have not built any physical activity sessions into the course, mainly because of time constraints. We know that many participants would prefer to have more physical activity or outdoor sessions. However, it does come as a surprise that the collage exercise is so deeply relaxing. From this develops an awareness that re-creation can also come from more passive activities. We too are always amazed by the way participants exclude the outside world and retreat into the childlike fascination of cutting and pasting their very own unique creation.

Course content

On the first day, an input from the trainer about the function of the brain hemispheres establishes a model for use on the course. The fundamental design of the course is one of working on personal insight through both logic and intuition, through exercising both the left and right hemispheres of the brain. Many participants are already familiar with this concept and have been trained in Tony Buzan's mindmapping techniques.

The reference to 'left-hemisphere' activity and 'right-hemisphere' activity provides a language to help explore understanding of the opposites that we choose to describe as 'logic' and 'intuition'. Working with personal constructs, participants become more aware of the limitations of language when we try to describe personal feelings and experiences.

To get most benefit from the course we ask participants to do three things:

1. to be open to new ideas, avoiding the extremes of mindless rejection or unthinking acceptance;
2. to balance logic and intuition, using the model of the left and right hemispheres of the brain;
3. to look inwards and so understand their strengths, values and options.

Fit for the Future is like an archaeological dig in which participants unearth shards, fragments of their selves, which can gradually be assembled into a coherent pattern. We will only describe a few of the fourteen ways the course offers for searching for these fragments.

The personal introduction is an example of this approach. Instead of just saying who they are and what they do, a familiar routine for breaking the ice, participants produce two drawings. In one they present their ideal vehicle. Among these there are, as you might expect, a high proportion of fast cars, space bubbles, magic carpets and leisure boats, although we have had less conventional things, including a flying brass bed-stead—themes of freedom, space, safety, comfort, rising above it all, effortlessness. In the other drawing they show their current situation and may see themselves on roller coasters (travelling at breakneck speed), on a pogo stick (a lot of effort to get nowhere) or proceeding at a steady pace in a sturdy farmcart (sometimes a bit boring).

To begin the shard collection participants comment on their drawings. We now use a tape recorder to catch their words so that important attitudes and preferences can be noted. This is more reliable than trainers' notes and does catch the highly relevant throw-away comments or slips of the tongue that are often of key importance. There is no 'person in a white coat' to provide interpretations; we hand back a transcript the next day and emphasize from the start that what the participant perceives as 'meaningful' is what should go into the shard collection in the form of Post-it notes that decorate a sheet of flipchart paper that becomes their personal storyboard.

From the visual of the introductions we go to Meredith Belbin's teamwork inventory. This has echoes in other personnel development courses, but the emphasis here is not on gaining experience of working in a team, but on identifying the type of team role or roles an individual may be drawn to. Later in the week we introduce the strengths deployment inventory developed by Elias Porter to explore underlying values. These more 'structured' approaches always raises the question 'How objective are we in answering a series of questions?' Does the rational left hemisphere take over? To test this we follow with a guided daydream in which participants are invited to free the imagination and go on a journey of inner exploration.

Both guided imagery and the I Ching are strange, and often contro-versial techniques. It is these two sessions which have raised the most questions about what we are offering. As experienced practitioners of both these disciplines we now understand how to work with the powerful emotional reactions these often provoke. This needs to be done without provoking pain or leaving unfinished business. On the last day we return to these sessions and offer the options of doing some further work on the material that has been raised. Participants get an opportunity to consult and test out the I Ching and to use active imagination to go a stage beyond the guided imaging so that the full power of the creative imagination can be safely released to carry forward a chosen theme.

Why do we introduce such an unusual subject as the I Ching? Here is an entire philosophy of unceasing change that is so applicable to the aim of Fit for the Future. It is a philosophy which is significant to a quarter of the world's population and which is claimed by the Japanese to underlie their economic success. But the real challenge to the Westerner and participant in our course is the method of consulting the I Ching. How can our logical left hemisphere deal with the notion that there can be meaning in the fall of coins? Many come to see the I Ching with its emphasis on the interconnectedness of all things, as a way to let their right hemisphere participate in the decision-making process.

After each session participants systematically collect information which is meaningful for them and add these fragments to their personal storyboard. How do they start to make sense of all this information? The 'core process' exercise is often a culmination point when the shards begin to form a pattern. It is a driving force that underlies and connects the activities in a person's life in which there is a consciousness of being in harmony with his or her true self. It manifests itself at all stages, and can slip out of reach at any stage.

To arrive at this core process participants review periods of their lives, such as from childhood to adolescence, their twenties and thirties. They describe the highlights, the moments of peace and contentment, times when they felt at one with the world, revealing as they go why these were so important to them and what contributed to their satisfaction.

At the next stage, with the assistance of two other participants, they single out words and phrases that have recurred in the narrative. Finally, prompted and encouraged by their companions, they strive for a phrase or sentence that summarizes their fundamental motivation. The insight when achieved, and many participants achieve it, may not seem very spectacular to the outsider, but to the person concerned it can have a Eureka-like impact. In many cases it helps resolve confusion about motivation that may go back many years.

One participant, who had a spread of interests and abilities, recognized that he was most fulfilled when they were evenly distributed between work and the wider community. His core statement was simply 'fully utilizing my skills for the good of the communities in which I live and work'. Another, keenly ambitious and whose record demonstrated a will to reach to the top in whatever activity she was engaged but who foresaw potential conflict with demands of her family, understood that she needed 'to excel while preserving traditional values'.

On the last morning of the course the archaeologists get to work on their flipcharts which are now covered with Post-it notes, drawings, comments, insights—the classroom has grown into an exhibition of graffiti! Patterns emerge, redundant information is discharded, it is now time to consolidate and plan for re-entry into 'the real world'. Will anything change?

Measurement and evaluation

What happens as a result of attending Fit for the Future? How do we know it works? IBM follows a procedure called Systems Approach to Education which has four levels of measurement and evaluation.

The first level of evaluation is the end-of-course assessment form. To the question 'How would you rate the overall programme as an interesting educational and developmental experience?' Fit for the Future consistently rates among the top personal development courses (this rating is however sometimes referred to as 'the happiness factor'). The second question 'To what extend do you think this experience will enable you to do a better job?' tended to be rated lower relative to other courses until the question was changed to '... a better job—now or in the future?'. Indeed Fit for the Future participants added their own comments beside the original question to the effect that the benefit was related more to their career development than necessarily to their current job.

There is a comments box at the end of the assessment form and 90 per cent of Fit for the Future participants take the trouble to write something in this box (compared to 70 per cent for other personal development courses). These comments are predominantly positive and praise the course as 'thought-provoking and useful', 'well-balanced', 'best course in my 20 years in IBM'; or the trainers with words as 'supportive', 'understanding', 'knowledgeable', 'committed'. Or the comments are more personal, either about the insight gained as 'a revelation', 'understand my needs', 'enabled me to look inward in a meaningful and positive way'; or the ways it may help as 'better decisions', 'greater awareness of others', 'able to sort out my goals', 'will probably change my life!'.

Critical comments are currently 12 per cent of the total, but earlier they were as much as 30 per cent, relating particularly to the number of participants and whether there was sufficient time or trainer resource to do justice to the material. We took notice, not to change the numbers or the duration, but in how we could put across the concepts more effectively.

The second level calls for testing participants immediately before and after a course. This has not yet been attempted for Fit for the Future, but it could be done to measure learning, as increased knowledge of oneself or to look for a change of attitude as a result of the course.

There is evaluation at the third level of 'Has it made any difference back in the workplace?', and this is tested at about 9–12 months after the course by inviting the participants to return for a three-day follow-up. The principal purpose of the follow-up is to allow participants to take further the personal work they commenced on Fit for the Future, to allow them to build on the investment they and the organization have already made in learning new ways and techniques of looking at themselves. At the same time it is an opportunity for IBM to find out what, if anything, has changed since Fit for the Future.

The comments made by participants on Fit for the Future follow-up about personal change since the original course fall into two categories. Either the change is outward and active—'I am doing something different'—or the change is inward in terms of 'I understand myself more'. The ratio is 5:3 and the analysis is based on a total of 120 comments from 83 participants.

The first category 'outer change' then divides into four sub-categories which can be headed as follows with examples:

Taking charge

- More control, more performance.
- I am saying 'no', stopping to think first.
- More confident in taking decision.
- Channelling my energies.
- Stopped trying to be something I am not.
- Stopped doing things, am making choices.
- More challenging, more authoritative.
- Less head in the clouds.

Less stress—more effectiveness

- Greater flexibility in response, less flap and more calm.
- More productive since not spending energy on anxiety.
- More relaxed, less wary, thereby more effective.
- A framework to handle the unexpected.
- Allows me to do the job more effectively, with less wear and tear.
- Have got something to help when things get tough or energy low.

Better working relationships

- Changed my ways of working with others.
- More confidence in my ability to help others.
- Radiate more in the office, more helpful.
- More flexible in group situations through understanding differences.
- Not imposing on others in order to improve myself.
- More tolerant through understanding what is going on.
- More patience with customers and greater understanding of their views.

More creative

- New ways of thinking.
- Can respond intuitively when needed.
- More aware of my bright ideas.
- Intuition and logic—working together.
- Letting go of frustration has let the creativity through.

The other principal category of 'inner change' divides into two groups of comments:

Understanding and acceptance

- Comfortable about the things I found out about myself.
- More acceptance of myself.
- Stronger sense of self.
- Accept my need for proper home/work relationship.
- Understanding my beliefs and how they run me.
- My self-image has changed—more in line with the reality the course allowed me to see, which has meant greater self-confidence.

An evolving process

- Did not in itself produce sudden change, rather increased awareness and the desire to keep going.
- A continuing process, of value to work.
- Have dealt with some undesirable aspects, necessary for change.
- The darker bits have become clearer.
- Ever since the course I have had the desire to change, but slow and steady.
- Am I honest with myself?
- Do not know what I want to achieve, but I now know the elements.
- Starting to come up with some answers.
- Taking a pickaxe to the wall.

There are of course some comments which express concern and these are most often ones of frustration that nothing has changed, either in the environment or in one's self, and a few regarding unsuccessful attempts to change.

It would require a control group to test whether this degree of change noted on the follow-up is any greater for Fit for the Future participants than the employee population as a whole. However we are aware of many participants who have told us about making specific job changes following Fit for the Future and who ascribe some credit to the course. In some cases considerable credit:

- I have changed jobs and it was FFF that made me bold enough to say I wanted to change.
- I was getting nowhere fast at the time of FFF; I have a new job with loads of opportunity.
- Two new jobs since FFF—happened as a direct result of my attendance.
- The fact that I can now actually do the work I wanted, I will say that FFF helped me to get this job.

The course may have enabled the participant to sort out career direction or confirm and improve the current job:

- FFF caused me to realize that I did not have the opportunities I should have in my job—I have done something about it.
- The opportunity to sit back and take stock, to *really* think about personal priorities and objectives. I thought I had become jaded with my current job and wanted a move—I now know that was not the real problem, FFF helped to define the problem and address it.
- With the benefit of the analysis I did on FFF I now know the job I want to do.
- Helped clarify my career direction.

Yes, there have been some participants who have left IBM. Like the other job changes or decisions mentioned above the action seems to have been a focused, purposeful step rather than something imposed. Nor are changes necessarily job related, though they may have indirect benefits to the work:

- I actually did something I said I would on FFF. I now have my certificate as a gymnastics teacher.
- On FFF my core statement (as a result of the core-process exercise) was 'a new day dawning'. In the year since there has been great change in every sphere of my life—my nickname at home is 'sunshine'.

- One of my wishes on FFF (three-wishes exercise) was to enjoy my family more. I had an idea, tried it out, and things have really picked up for the first time in years.
- I have put IBM in its place!

Finally, two general comments from the follow-up:

- I find myself constantly thinking of the things we discovered on FFF and am now applying them to the situations I find myself in.
- All these changes! Thank God I did FFF.

What difference does Fit for the Future make to the bottom line? At this fourth level of measurement and evaluation, it is not easy to apply the results of a relatively small programme to the business results of a big organization. However we have some straws in the wind:

- Of the nine professionals on the first Fit for the Future course, one has left IBM and seven others have since been promoted to manager.
- In 1988, of 12 sales representatives who attended FFF, 3 were subsequently named Sales Representative of the Month (which at least disproves the old adage that successful sales people are too busy to attend courses).

There have been a number of spontaneous and unsolicited comments from managers of participants, which stem from some noticeable behaviour thought to be as a result of the course, and powerful enough to cause the manager to wish to acknowledge it:

- Changes are now considered, then entered into wholeheartedly, bringing the rest of the department along with him. I believe that FFF awoke something in this man.
- —— is full of new-to-her thoughts and ideas that will do her good (even if they give me/IBM some work to do!).
- I don't know what you did, but the effect has been electric!

It is worth noting the apparent contribution of FFF to the development of the careers of women in IBM. IBM recognizes the increasing contribution of women and the value of taking action to accelerate that contribution. Currently women make up 18 per cent of the professional workforce and 30 per cent of FFF participants are women. Perhaps of more significance, 70 per cent of all participants choose to attend the follow-up course, but 92 per cent of the women come back. What is the value? According to one female professional: 'I don't have to sacrifice anything, it does work; I am confident and am getting recognition.' There are also signs of a support network developing among female FFF participants.

Hints and tips

The exercises used in Fit for the Future are based in the humanistic tradition of working on oneself with a little help from friends, of finding the meaning in a process for oneself, of working in a small support group. This will be new thinking for many who have the notion that to find out about oneself involves being the private client of someone who will provide the answers. We have found it essential to get this message across—in the pre-course information, in the introduction at the beginning of the course, and again prior to some of the exercises. Otherwise problems, such as the following, do arise:

'What are your (the trainers) qualifications to run this course?' Usually unsaid but lurking in the thoughts of some is the concern that IBM is using 'amateur psychologists'. We make it very clear that the kinds of activities in Fit for the Future are not those which require an 'analyst', are inherently 'safe' in themselves, and that the trainers need to be experienced only in running the process and helping the participant to handle anything which may result.

Some participants feel uneasy about being questioned about their life by other participants, as in the core-process exercise. They think it would be alright if done by 'the experts', the trainers. To counter this we now provide a handout of the process and then make frequent checks during the exercise to ensure that participants stick to the guidelines. With a little guidance anyone can pick up and use the techniques effectively and have the added benefit of feeling that they have done something to help.

A related problem is simply that of talking about oneself, one's life. There are still some participants who are surprised and concerned to find that some exercises involve talking about themselves in a way they never before associated with work. So it needs to be clear from the start that there will be no pressure, that they may opt out of a particular exercise. At the same time they are encouraged to give it a try. It often happens that, for example in the core process, after the procedure has been demonstrated, maybe only five of the fifteen participants will be keen to be the person being questioned. This is fine as we work in triads, and the others can be involved in questioning, listening, note-taking, and helping to pull it together at the end. After this first round invariably others are reassured, both about the process and the safety of talking about themselves, and go on to achieve their own core statement.

There are occasions when a trainer will work with an individual for a short period, perhaps helping to deal with a puzzling aspect of their guided imagery, helping to clarify an I Ching reading, or helping to fit together the 'shards' at the end of the course. It is always on offer to the participants to see a trainer privately but it is also made clear that it is optional; the trainers are a resource but so are the other participants. After the course we are pleased to have queries or see former participants casually, but our time available to help in further work is limited to the follow-up course.

There are some aspects of the course that participants, with different learning styles, will never agree upon: 'The course should be a full week'; 'It could be done in three days'; 'The pace is too slow'; 'We needed more time'; 'More explanation before the exercise'; 'Get on with it!'

It is important to state the purpose of each exercise, but how much rational explanation does one attempt for what is a non-rational process, such as introducing a meditation technique? Our experience is that it is probably impossible to convince the doubters, but the attempt to do so may end up frustrating the others who are keen to try it. Also it is best to let participants know at the beginning that it is unlikely that every exercise will work for them. At best an exercise will produce a flash of insight, a real 'Ah-ha!'; at worst the reaction will be 'So what?'

Be wary of the participant who sets out to 'protect' the group—'I don't think we should be doing this.' Rather than defend, use the power of the group. There will always be some who are ready to try and who see risk as acceptable; therefore 'What do others feel about this?' is a good response. Then challenge the 'protector' to state his or her own personal concerns and be sympathetic to those concerns.

A final hint: we use the candidate selection process to ensure that we always have at least 4–5 women on each course. The trainer team is also always mixed. Our experience is that women are usually more willing to try an 'intuitive' approach which in turn makes it 'OK' for the men to go along, to express themselves more openly. A good example is in the collage exercise—it is a little difficult to imagine an all-male group sitting on the floor cutting out and pasting with the same enthusiam that we get on Fit for the Future.

Conclusions

Fit for the Future is now firmly established in IBM UK training, to a degree we would not have dared think about when we started it. It seems that the number of courses will continue to increase—as word gets around the demand grows. The range of its applicability is wide and we get the

IBMers with twenty years' service who *want* to sort out their careers and themselves. We are seeing that the need to step back and reassess happens at a number of stages during working life. Participants do question their relationship with IBM in a way that we suspect does not happen in the formal appraisal and counselling process—too risky perhaps? As participants have typically commented, 'This is bound to be valuable for both me and IBM in the long run.'

From what managers are telling us we believe the concept of Fit for the Future is a sound one.

Having seen the results of sending two senior engineers on the course, said one, I am intrigued! I feel that as managers of people we spend all our time looking after the health of our people, our customers and our business targets but we neglect to look after ourselves. We maintain and build on our management skills through courses, seminars and forums, but I strongly feel that we can benefit from taking time to look into ourselves to see what sort of person lies beneath all the management skills.

Recommended reading

Assagioli, Roberto (1973) *Psychosynthesis*, Turnstone Books, London.

Bannister, D. and Fay Fransella (1971) *Inquiring Man*, Penguin, Harmondsworth.

Dunnett, Gavin (ed.) (1988) *Working with People: Clinical Uses of Personal Construct Psychology*, Routledge & Kegan Paul, London.

Ferrucci, Piero *What We May Be*, Turnstone Books, London.

Gawain, Shakti (1978) *Creative Visualization*, Whatever Publishing Inc., Mill Valley, Ca.

Gendlin, Eugene *Focussing*, Bantam New Age Books, New York.

Jung, C. G. *Synchronicity: An Acausal Connecting Principle*, Routledge & Kegan Paul, London.

Ornstein, Robert E. (1975) *The Psychology of Consciousness*, Pelican Books, Harmondsworth.

Progoff, Ira *The Symbolic and the Real*, Element, Shaftesbury.

Russell, Peter *The Brain Book*, Routledge & Kegan Paul, London.

Shone, Ronald (1984) *Creative Visualization*, Thorsons, Wellingborough.

Wilhelm, Richard (1983) *The I Ching*, Routledge & Kegan Paul, London.

6
Why personal development workshops?
Peter Callender

Introduction

This chapter looks at the following questions:

- What is personal development?
- Why personal development?
- Who is it for?
- Why do organizations sponsor personal development workshops?
- How do we organize workshops?
- What are we as management developers doing?
- Where next?

Clearly each of these questions could sponsor a paper on their own. I will therefore be brief, and exhaustive answers to each of these questions will not be attempted!

The objective of this chapter is to raise awareness of some of the complex issues around personal development. And to ask what action we, as developers, should take?

What is personal development?

Personal development is a process which enables individuals to generate their own strategies for the future. Personal development can be applied to any aspect of our lives, for example: our health or our career, our fitness or our wealth or our families and friends or our intellectual development. To develop these examples a little further: personal development for some of our colleagues has included running a half marathon in under 90 minutes, completing an Open University business course and landscaping a garden from scratch. What is the key to all of these activities is that the individual has chosen to pursue a specific activity which has helped the individual to develop new strengths and/or overcome past weaknesses.

John Harvey-Jones made an excellent reference to personal development in his book *Making It Happen* (1987: 249, para. 3):

Increasingly companies will only survive if they meet the needs of the individuals who serve in them; not just the question of payment, important as this may be, but people's true inner needs, which they may even be reluctant to express to themselves. People want jobs which have continual interest, and enable them to grow personally.

Why personal development?

Figure 6.1 summarizes some of the forces currently driving personal development.

The 'New Order' organizational climate has been characterized as:

- an enterprise culture;
- market-focused;
- subject to highly paced change;
- requiring new styles of leadership.

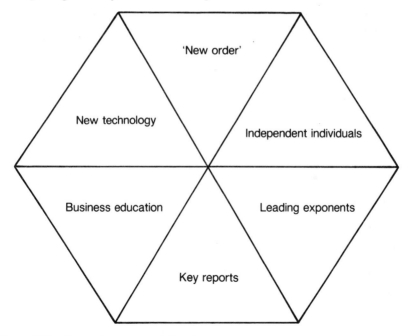

Figure 6.1 Forces for personal development

If we look at a reference to this: Handy (1989: 72) talks about the 'shamrock' organization. He describes this as comprising three sectors: the professional core who work long hours for high salaries, contractors who carry out non-essential work on a consultancy or contractual basis and, third, the flexible workforce who may be part-time or temporary but who enable organizations to manage periods of peak demand.

Other recent work by Peters (1988: 377) and Brown (1988: 243) contain similar evidence to Handy's. We can suggest that there is an increasing awareness that many organizations are experiencing rapidly paced change. One way of summarizing this is to refer to a 'New Order'.

The phrase 'independent individuals' captures the rise of the knowledge worker and an increasing level of specialists of all kinds. With the rolling back of the welfare state, the development of private medicine and personal pensions, the affluent individual gains more independence. Similarly her career may depend more on her profession than the organizations she is employed by.

There are several leading exponents of personal development, who have written some helpful textbooks on personal development as well as acted as missionaries through their research, consultancy work and inputs at seminars.

Besides these exponents, two reports which were produced in 1987 again added impetus for personal development. The first report , written by Constable and the British Institute of Management, stated: 'Employers should seek to create personal development programmes for all managers' (Constable 1987: 22). The second report written by the National Economic Development Office and Handy (Handy 1987) again promoted personal development: 'One possibility is a development plan for every manager' (Handy 1987: 18).

Business and management education has also caught on to personal development. Many institutions now offer courses and in some cases masters level degrees incorporate personal development too.

Lastly new technology: computer-based training, interactive videos, distance learning and the Open University all support the processes of personal development. The success of the Open University Business School with its ever increasing annual student enrolments is but one example of the application of personal development.

Who is it for?

This question concerns us. Clearly the knowledge worker, the high-flier and the manager can all benefit from personal development techniques.

But what about the secretary who is trying to move out of being a secretary, the middle-aged clerical worker, the disillusioned administrator?

Very often personal development courses do not reach those who perhaps most need it. Over the three years we have been running workshops only three clerical workers and one secretary have attended out of 60 plus participants. Part of this is because organizations restrict entry to workshops to higher grades. Other reasons include individuals' bad experiences of unstructured training activities, individuals' unwillingness to take risks, poor publicity by the management developer, and in our case one workshop which was a wash-out (and bad news travels fast).

We would like to see personal development on offer to any person who would like to try it. Maybe this is unrealistic because organizations usually pay for these workshops. However, one recent experience with a rehabilitation centre for the mentally ill would suggest that entry to personal development should not be restricted by grade, status, intellect or any other criteria.

Why do organizations sponsor personal development workshops?

According to Burgoyne's model (Figure 6.2) management development and corporate strategy need to fuel one another. At a minimum management development workshops have probably often been level 2

	Levels of maturity of organizational management development
Level 6	Strategic development of the management of corporate strategy —the learning company
Level 5	Management development input to corporate strategy formation —MD audit input to strategy
Level 4	A management development strategy to implement corporate policy —helps implement strategy
Level 3	Integrated structural/development tactics —individual based
Level 2	Isolated tactical management development —response to crisis/local problems
Level 1	No management development —only natural processes

Figure 6.2 Burgoyne's model

activities like a lot of management training. For our workshops we would place most of them at level 2 or 3. They were advertised, publicized and sold best by previous participants.

Why did the workshops become part of the menu for management training? What were the organizations hoping to achieve?

A number of factors were involved: the training managers were aware of the Handy and Constable report recommendations. I had pushed my bosses/clients to allow us to pilot personal development courses, as I believed passionately in the approach. Also the organizations had invested in distance learning and self-managed learning resources: libraries and rooms where individuals could read texts, watch videos, use computer assisted learning and use interactive video programmes. Some of the subjects covered in the resource libraries were part of the corporate strategy—marketing, customer relations and financial awareness.

So we can infer that personal development programmes do operate at level three, i.e. there is an individually-based link between development tactics and the organization's structure.

Could personal development operate at level 6 in the learning company? A quick answer may be a tentative 'yes'; however the issues raised by this question require more thorough coverage than the intended scope of this chapter.

Organizations increasingly require flexible, highly skilled individuals who can manage a number of different functions and who are prepared to move around the organization. Personal development workshops can help to broaden specialists as well as help specialists to plan their own careers.

An opportunity cost of personal development courses is that some participants may decide to change their employer and/or speciality as a result of attending a personal development workshop. Our experiences suggest that this may happen to 5–10 per cent of participants. However, perhaps these individuals would have moved on in any case.

Lastly, personal development used to be attractive on a cost basis. The attraction lay in individual's doing their own thing in their own time. However where individuals use video, or computer programs or buy courses like those of the Open University Business School costs may not be cheap. But a substantial cost benefit should be derived by individuals planning their own management development activities instead of attending courses on a 'sheep-dip' or latest fad basis.

How to organize it

I have briefly covered the organizational aspects of why personal development workshops are offered.

Figure 6.3 depicts how we see the organization of personal development workshops. Figure 6.4 shows some of the pre- and post-programme participants' experiences.

Before the workshop we like to get some idea about what participants hope to achieve from attending the course. Similarly we make sure that participants understand their active role in shaping the workshop. We also try to assure participants that it will not be a T-group type experience nor will the tutors be attempting to run psychological games.

What participants do after the course is up to them. All of them will have completed their own personal development plan. Very often small

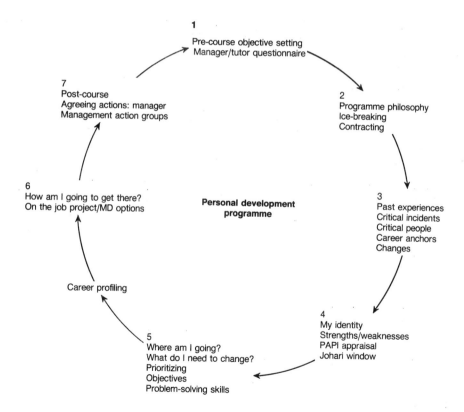

Figure 6.3 Organizing personal development workshops

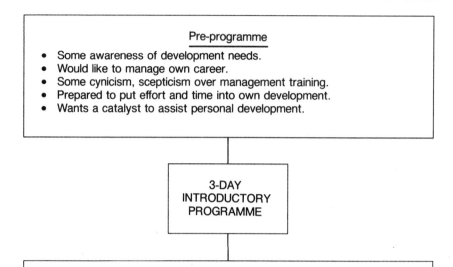

Pre-programme
- Some awareness of development needs.
- Would like to manage own career.
- Some cynicism, scepticism over management training.
- Prepared to put effort and time into own development.
- Wants a catalyst to assist personal development.

3-DAY INTRODUCTORY PROGRAMME

Post-programme
- Personal development plan.
- Builds a series of visions covering non-career aspects too.
- Realization that participants need to own the processes themselves.
- Probably starts some form of management education.
- Establishing management action groups.

Figure 6.4 Pre- and post-programme

groups are formed to share progress on individual plans and to act as a 'skunk-work' within the organization.

Tutors can be available after programmes to advise and to counsel, but the emphasis of personal development is not to instil dependence on 'expert' tutors.

What are management developers doing?

The main concern we have is that developers are good at advocating personal development for others; but poor at carrying out their own personal development.

Figure 6.5 highlights five areas where we can undertake personal development. Perhaps we can pose two questions:

1. What personal development activities are you currently engaged in?
2. What non-intellectual development activities are you currently engaged in?

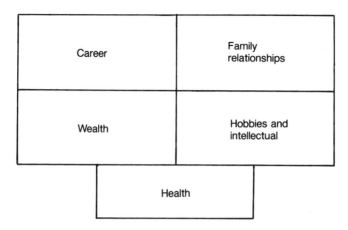

Figure 6.5 Five areas for personal development

(I have to admit to being better motivated for intellectual personal development activities than others. However currently I am training to complete a half marathon in under 90 minutes and I am causing havoc to my family by learning how to play the guitar.)

What next?

I would like to pick up one possible action point from each of the sections of this chapter:

- *Why personal development?* Let us ensure that this is not another passing fad. Perhaps we need to clarify what is and what is not personal development.
- *Who is it for?* Can we try to widen our client base? Personal development need not be restricted to managers, it is part of education for life.
- *Why do organizations sponsor personal development workshops?* In 'New Order' organizations personal development needs to be an integrated management development activity. Personal development workshops also have an important role in the managing change process.
- *How do we organize it?* There are many choices here but the key elements is participant ownership of both structure and content. We need to work hard to secure this.
- *What are management developers doing?* Not enough! Perhaps we need to try to develop local and national networks to share our own experiences and best practices.

Conclusion

This chapter has tried to cover some messy questions which surround personal development. As stated in the introduction this has not been a comprehensive treatise.

For me personal development is one of the processes that can help build the relationship between the individual and his or her organization. This relationship is often in a state of tension as the individual tries to meet their needs and at the same time satisfy the requirements that the organization makes. What we need to learn is how to generate a constructive tension in which both the organization and the individual thrive. Personal development can be part of this constructive tension.

References

Brown, Mark (1988) *The Dinosaur Strain*, Element Books, Dorset.

Burgoyne, John (1988) 'Management development for the individual *and* the organization', *Personnel Management*, June, 40–4.

Constable, John (1987) *The Making of British Managers,* Stanley Hunt, Northants.

Handy, Charles (1987) *The Making of Managers,* HMSO, London.

—— (1989) *The Age of Unreason*, Business Books Ltd, London.

Harvey-Jones, John (1987) *Making it Happen*, Guild Publishing, London.

Peters, Tom (1988) *Thriving on Chaos*, Guild Publishing, London.

7
Opening up learning in the Prudential
Naomi Stanford

Introduction

In this chapter I look at open learning in the Prudential and focus on one particular programme—the Open University's 'The Effective Manager'.

I show how the use of open learning in general and this programme in particular are beginning to help in creating the climate for self-development in the company, and in doing so are affecting the culture of the organization.

Before proceeding further I would like to explain what I mean by 'climate' and how this affects 'culture'. The prevailing attitudes, standards and environment of a particular group (in this case learners) contribute to the 'climate' of a specific aspect of the organization (in this case self-development). When these attributes of self-development—initiative, self-direction, learning autonomy, and so on—reach a point where they are valued by, and transmitted to, other groups and successive generations in the organization, a change in aspects of the culture can be discerned.

This does not imply a linear process from creating a climate to cultural change. Indeed, within Prudential the already changing culture allowed the introduction of a method of training delivery which in turn facilitated the creation of a self-development climate, which then itself contributed to cultural change.

This change is at a level of ethics and values, and would require a more detailed treatment than there is space for here. However, there is casual evidence of it. For example, the long-standing policy of Prudential 'growing its own staff' (to the extent that there are Prudential couples whose children also work for the company) is giving way in the personnel and accounts areas to the recruitment of professional staff from outside the company. Large numbers of new staff, often coming from very different types of organization, inevitably influence the culture of the Prudential.

Again casual evidence suggests a feeling among long-serving staff that the previously service-oriented culture of the Prudential is giving way to a profit-oriented culture with a concomitant shift in values.

As you read you will realize that this is not a blueprint but a selective case study. I do not, for example, discuss the complicated interplay of politics, personality and environment which accompany the use and further development of open learning in the corporation, neither do I detail the processes and procedures which support the open learning system which exists now.

What I do discuss are eight aspects of open learning which relate to the introduction and continuing use of The Effective Manager. These are:

1. the 'previous' culture of the Prudential;
2. the 'new' culture;
3. the responses of the training function to the new culture;
4. open learning in the Prudential;
5. The Effective Manager programme in particular;
6. running this programme;
7. what we have learned from this programme;
8. where we should be going with open learning.

The 'previous' culture

I came to Prudential with no previous experience of an insurance industry. Working in the environment it is easy to see how Prudential exemplifies the role culture (Handy 1987: 190) or process culture (Deal and Kennedy 1988: 119) typical of a long-established, traditional insurance company. For the major part of its history Prudential has been a bureaucratic, hierarchical, paternal organization, by definition risk averse and to the closed end (right) of the spectrum illustrated in Figure 7.1.

The new culture

In the last few years, and due to a number of factors, this culture has begun to change. The most publicly visible demonstration of this (both internally and externally) came in September 1986 with the launch of the new Prudential corporate image. Employees received information and

Factor	Open	<-------------------------->	Closed
Stability of work	much change	<-------------------------->	Little change
Prevailing management style	consultative	<-------------------------->	autocratic
Is authority recognized mainly by	ability	<-------------------------->	position
Is decision making	decentralized	<-------------------------->	centralized
Are decisions usually made at	lowest practical level	<-------------------------->	highest level
Target setting	staff set own targets and get agreement	<-------------------------->	targets are imposed
Are staff subject to	self monitoring	<-------------------------->	close supervision
Are staff expected to	achieve	<-------------------------->	conform
Control	initiative encouraged	<-------------------------->	frequent interference
Promotion is based upon	quality of achievement	<-------------------------->	length of service

Figure 7.1 Organization culture
Source: reproduced with permission from Open Learning In Industry (Crown copyright, permission of Controller of Her Majesty's Stationery Office)

in-company publicity about the new Prudential; among these were booklets on 'Prudential's New Identity', 'Prudential Corporation' and 'Prudential Guidelines for Organizational Change'. Reading through these it is obvious that the company wants to retain the associations of Prudential with qualities of prudence, wise conduct, wisdom, security and strength, peace of mind, sound investment and integrity, but has forged the new identity to apply these qualities in a chaotic world. One of the booklets explains it thus, 'in the increasingly competitive and complex world of financial services, our new identity is an outward sign of how we are changing. It projects the new dynamism found in all parts of the organization' (*Prudential's New Identity*, 1986).

Many changes are occurring within the corporation which are less dramatic than a new identity but which, nevertheless, also indicate a move away from the closed end of the spectrum (Fig. 7.1 illustrated above) towards the open end. A move which is both apparent and actively sought in many parts of the company. From my perspective (as a training analyst) I have seen how changes in the training and development sphere both reflect and develop organizational change.

Responses of the training function to the new culture

The reflection of organizational change showed in changes in the training function. In July 1985 the first management development adviser was appointed to the corporation. About this time a computer based training unit was established, the training department was reorganized to include a tier of internal training consultants, and the supervisory and management courses offered came under scrutiny. All these were among indicators of responses to the need to train staff to meet the 'new normal' where organizations

have to face significant and far reaching change, such as mergers, expansion, contraction, responses to competition, relocation and restructuring—to say nothing of changes to management style or organization culture which may be either the cause or the effect of some of those very changes (Fricker 1988: 337).

(Within Prudential I saw all these changes occurring simultaneously, albeit in various parts of the organization.)

The development of organizational change showed in work done by internal training consultants and development staff which stimulated demand for training and highlighted the need to move away from a menu of 46 conventionally delivered supervisory and management courses towards a more flexible approach to meeting training needs. As a result of this thinking, I was appointed in January 1987 with a brief to supplement and replace the conventional courses with open learning where appropriate. I also took over responsibility for the OU School of Management programme within the company, although at this point only The Effective Manager had been piloted and recommended for corporation use.

Open learning in the Prudential

We now offer fourteen internal open learning courses in supervisory and management skills as well as most of the range of OU School of Management programmes. The former are offered in a variety of modes which reflect the need for trainees to feel part of a learning group, to practise skill development in workshops and seminars, to complete their programme to schedule and to improve their job performance. Generally speaking the knowledge-based parts of the training programme are studied independently using a variety of media; while the skills-based elements are developed in group settings. The independent study also involves discussions with peer group learners as well as line manager supervision.

It has rapidly become evident that the 'new' learning techniques involved in open learning are part of the self-development process of trainees. I will explain this further. Generally, training can reflect a dissemination orientation or a development orientation. The dissemination orientation is one that sees learning as the acquisition of facts, concepts or skills; where the tutors are subject experts responsible for organizing and sequencing of material, and assessment is concerned with measuring the proficiency of the learner.

The development orientation sees learning as an enhancing of personal competence and meaning making where tutors are resource people and co-learners, and assessment is collaborative and based on mutually agreed criteria (Boot and Hodgson 1987: 7). Within Prudential open learning the elements of 'conventional' training are minimized and opportunities to give learners' choice and self-direction are optimized.

From the Prudential documents mentioned earlier, it is clear that corporation training in general should reflect a development orientation in order to help move the corporation towards a more open culture. As the following quote illustrates the corporation has declared a commitment to developing self-motivated and self-directed staff.

Significant investment is being made to increase the staff's awareness of the overall direction of the Corporation so that they can undertake their own responsibilities more effectively as a result of their understanding of the wider context. We believe this process of communication is two-way, however, and actions that result in providing employees with the opportunity to be consulted about the direction of the business, and in particular about how their own job can be done more effectively, are encouraged (*Prudential Corporation* 1986).

Training with a development orientation requires trainee involvement, participation and collaboration in the process. Within Prudential we have selected open learning material which both reflects this orientation and which supports trainees through their programme in a way that develops the personal and interpersonal skills of trainees and line managers. (The latter play a significant part in supporting the trainees.)

The Effective Manager programme

As I have said I do not describe in any detail either the administrative and managerial systems, or the marketing of open learning in the Prudential. What I will do in what follows is show you briefly how these aspects—administration, management and marketing—work in a particular open learning programme in a way which supports self-development in the trainee: The Effective Manager—Open University School of Management.

We chose The Effective Manager programme as we felt it was apt for our staff for a number of reasons:

- Using twelve workbooks as a core it covers a range of managerial topics under four main headings—You and Your Job, You and Your Team, You and Your Organization, and You and the Manager's World. Additional material includes a text *Understanding Organisations*, six audio cassette tapes, three TV programmes, and supplementary readings.
- It is well-structured material with immediate relevance to the trainee. For example, the frequent activities direct students to use the course material to analyse, examine or assess their own work contexts. A typical example is in Book 10, 'Coping with Organizations'. The topic under study is conflict. As an exercise the learner is asked to 'Think back over the previous working week and ask yourself whether you have observed or been involved in any of the following conflicts (tick as many boxes as necessary) . . .'
- It is strongly supported by the Open University system. Each student is allocated to a tutor who is available for the period of the course to help and advise students, and who marks the three assignments each student has to submit. Additionally students must attend a residential weekend, and up to four tutorial sessions at a local study centre.
- It reflects a development orientation. Students pace themselves to preset points, and to a large extent choose their route through the course. They are also able to decide how deeply to study each topic.
- It introduces staff to unfamiliar methods of learning which brings confidence to other situations when they have met this challenge. Many staff are apprehensive about studying largely independently through a variety of media, particularly if they have been away from study for a long time.
- It challenges assumptions about the managerial role as well as about methods of learning. The activities constantly ask students to rethink their role as manager. One Prudential student remarked, 'I now manage in a completely different way.'
- It is very cost-effective. The six-month programme costs in the region of £600 and represents approximately 240 hours of student study time.
- It is available to small or large numbers of people distributed through the UK. This is a major benefit to Prudential which has offices throughout the UK. Staff can be enrolled at their local Open University centre without having to come to the Prudential central training unit.

- Its structure allows staff to meet people from other organizations. Tutorials and the residential weekend are found to be particularly useful and many Prudential students say that meeting managers from other organizations is the most valuable part of the course.

Running the programme

The trainee

Prudential staff eligible to take The Effective Manager course are likely to be in grades 5 or 6. That is below middle-manager level but with sectional or departmental responsibility or they may be of equivalent grade but a technical specialist, for example a financial services consultant. Usually they have had no recent supervisory or management skills training. One staff member explained his reasons for enrolling on the programme like this, 'I was recently promoted to the post of departmental manager. My previous role had been a purely technical one. I feel I owe it to myself and my staff to study and acquire managerial skills.' Other staff put forward other reasons, some wishing to update management skills, others to develop a fresh attitude to their job, or to increase personal effectiveness and efficiency. Some staff liked the idea of the challenge the studying set as exemplified by this staff member who said that the studying would 'satisfy my need to see that I can still learn and acquire new skills and cope with change'.

Marketing the course

Staff find out in various ways that the course exists. They may be nominated by their manager who has details of courses offered, they may be referred through the appraisal system, or through being advised by a training consultant. They may hear through word of mouth or by being invited to attend a presentation of the programme through personnel officers.

Presentations are given in the two months preceding the closing date for applications. They are held for general audiences (and already received nominations) advertised through the personnel operations manager, or for specific audiences at the request of a manager or training consultant.

The purpose of these presentations is to let intending applicants know exactly what they are letting themselves in for. Each component of the course—workbooks, audio tutorials, video programme, tutorials, tutor marked assignments, the residential weekend and the exam—is discussed. There is often a member of the OU staff present and always a Prudential staff member who has taken the course and can answer questions from his or her own experience. These briefings allow people the informed choice of whether to take the programme or not and staff who have not been to a presentation are discouraged from applying to take the course. Any staff member who decides to enrol must have the support of his/her manager.

Enrolment profile

A typical Prudential OU student is male, aged 31–35 with either a degree or a professional (usually ACII) qualification. He will have worked for the company for five years and be in a section manager or technical specialist role. He is more likely to be working in a central than a divisional office. About 50 per cent of staff who take the programme are promoted in the year following the course. Figure 7.2 illustrates the enrolment pattern since the course was first offered in the Company.

To date 25 per cent of Prudential students enrolled have been women which reflects the organizational employment pattern of women concentrated in the lower grades without access to this course. However, this pattern is expected to change as more women take the various women into management courses (including the Open University one which Prudential piloted) and then proceed to develop their careers.

Company involvement in the programme

Once staff have enrolled on the course there is little company involvement. The names and locations of all students doing a particular presentation are circulated to that student group and it is suggested they arrange to meet each other periodically. About halfway through the presentation staff are formally invited to meet each other to discuss progress so far and towards the end of the course they meet again for exam revision and to provide feedback on the value of the programme. Again an OU staff member is present at this review meeting. As well as this students have a contact number for advice and support.

At each presentation's review meeting staff are asked whether they would like more company involvement (for example a specific Prudential

Nov. 1985	Nov. 1986	May 1987	Nov. 1987	May 1988	Nov. 1988
M 5	17	9	16	4	43
F –	4	1	7	8	9

Figure 7.2 Enrolment pattern of men and women on The Effective Manager programme

tutor) but so far this has not been an area of concern. As one student remarked, 'we were left largely to ourselves. I felt OK about this.' Another said, 'I personally did not find a need to use it [the support system]. I felt I was able to cope reasonably well on my own.'

Also at the review meeting students are asked in various ways that they thought of the course and what they have gained from it. These responses enable us to gauge the suitability of the material and learning method without looking too closely at how 'successful' the course has been. This latter form of evaluation is the responsibility of the nominator who assesses differences in work performance over a period of time and provides feedback through the appraisal system.

Student response to the material
Staff are favourable impressed with the content of the programme. The twelve workbooks which form the spine of it are seen as the most useful: 'course book material generally excellent', one student remarked. The residential weekend was considered a great strength of the programme. 'The weekend was excellent in helping to crystallize many of the subjects covered in the course, and while hard work, was stimulating and enjoyable.' Another student said that the weekend was 'One of the highlights. It was well run with good facilities. It enabled me to meet and exchange views with a broad spectrum of people from other organizations.'

The videos, audio tapes and set book were less well received. 'The video was rather old fashioned and difficult to take seriously', while one student criticized Handy's text for being 'too wordy and American'.

The tutorials were found to be patchy. Some students had very good experiences here while others found them a 'waste of time'. The tutor-marked assignments were 'very worthwhile and rewarding' though some students admitted finding them difficult to produce.

Student response to learning method
At the review session students are asked to respond to the following enquiry: 'The course was primarily an open learning course. Please comment on your experience of this method of study in terms of where you studied, the time you needed, family support necessary, and any other relevant aspects.' Additionally students are asked 'What were the advantages and disadvantages of studying by this method?'

Most students are unfamiliar with open learning techniques and found that although they liked the choice of 'time, pace and place' for study they found the required self-discipline, motivation and efficient time-tabling difficult to include into their existing work and domestic commitments. As this student said, 'I found it more difficult than anticipated because I was out of [studying] practice, but support was there when needed. The biggest problem was rearranging personal commitments to accommodate the course.' (Incidentally this staff member has now applied to do a further OBS course.) Another commented, 'The discipline involved in this type of study was very difficult—I used a lot of personal time, far more than expected. I did, however, work when it suited me best and this was a benefit. It could be, and sometimes was, too easy to stop.'

Students were challenged both by the method of learning and the content of the programme.

What we have learned from this programme

Over the three years we have been sponsoring this programme we have learned a number of things.

Content of programme

Although staff could see the relevance of teaching that there is a commonality of managerial skills they felt that case studies and assignments would be more gripping if they related specifically to the financial services section. The issue of relevance to the student is one of which the School of Management is aware.

Learning style

We have had very few dropouts (less than 4 per cent) but we do not feel that open learning is a method of learning suited to everyone. One student summed up her response to open learning by saying, 'Never again will I study in this way.' The company does offer a range of training options—CBT, conventional training, text-based open learning, action learning, etc., but this can be confusing for the customer. How to get a 'best fit' between trainee and course delivery is an area of discussion among training/development staff at this stage.

Company involvement

As we send relatively large numbers of staff on the programme we wonder whether an in-company course or Prudential only tutor would be appropriate. Geographical location of staff and potential administrative and support difficulties have not made this a workable proposition as yet, but is one which is continuously reviewed.

Management support
In this programme (and in all other open learning programmes we offer) we have found that it is essential that the trainee's immediate superior be *actively* involved in supporting the trainee for the duration of the programme. This is an area which now needs the greatest amount of work within the company. Running supporters' workshops is one of the schemes being looked at to involve line management staff in training. It is true to say that open learning courses in general, including Open University programmes, have had little, if any, positive endorsement from senior managers. For open learning to be seen to be a credible training option it is essential that it is supported from the top down as well as the bottom up.

Application of new learning
We have found that many trainees are unable to apply their newly acquired skills in their job, mainly because their job role is not renegotiated with their manager to take account of skill development. This naturally leads to dissatisfaction, frustration and a feeling of 'Why did I bother to do the course?' Once trained, staff need to be given the opportunity to practise what they now know. We feel that better line manager support and involvement would alleviate some of the dissatis-factions which lead to comments like 'Now I've done the course, how do I get my manager to learn what I know?'

Integration with other training
I have already mentioned that there are various training options available to staff. We have not yet solved the problem of making this fit into an understandable, cohesive, integrated training pattern. We are considering ways of making choices easier for the potential trainee. And we are also considering having training accredited, so that gradually the employee can build up a number of credits which will result in a nationally recognized certificate. Using a variety of training methods in a develop-ment orientation should ensure that these structural patterns retain learner-centredness.

Where we should be going with open learning

I cannot relate this aspect specifically to The Effective Manager programme which is just one of a range of courses offered. The areas that we are working on are as follows:

1. The integration of training so that methods are not the focus of

attention. The aim is to provide training courses that offer the delivery method most suited to both the topic and the learner's situation.

2. The development of a development orientation in training. This means training trainers out of a didactic 'tell them what I know' mode into a more facilitative role.

3. The effective marketing of the internal training unit perhaps with a specialist marketer. This has become an urgent concern as, within the Company, the Prudential central training unit now competes for custom with external training agencies.

4. The development of a clear understanding of where training can reflect and change organizational culture and where it is appropriate for it to do so.

5. The refining of topics and materials to suit specific as well as general applications/target groups. As far as open learning goes this means tailoring activities, case studies, and examples not just to the broad financial services sector but to sections of it—pensions, unit trusts, and so on.

6. The much higher degree of management involvement in staff development, even at the basic level of briefing staff before they take a course. We feel that the manager has as much to learn from supporting trainees as the trainee staff member benefits from the involvement.

7. The development of trainers so that they are confident to support open learning actively in terms of briefings, reviews, supporting line staff, etc. In practice this has involved team meetings, seminars devoted to open learning and the mooting of a plan to accredit trainers in the delivery of open learning.

8. The appropriate use of each training method. (For example, OL/CBT is not good for skills training but can be used in conjunction with direct training.)

9. The formation and adoption of a code of practice for training/ development to which all corporate trainers work.

10. The agreement to use a corporate label for training/development which does not separate the method from the intent but which will include all methods. This arose from the development of CBT, open learning and 'training' as separate entities. The new training manual includes all methods in one directory under a single logo.

11. The examination of issues of accreditation/assessment, particularly in the light of NCVQ and the Management Charter. Some moves have been made in this direction. For example, thirty staff piloted an open learning supervisory management introductory programme

accredited by the National Examinations Board for Supervisory Management.
12. The reviewing and evaluation of all aspects of the open learning system when it has been running two years.

Summary

I have outlined above the experiences of Prudential Training Services in running text based open learning courses over a two-year period, with particular emphasis on The Effective Manager programme. What we have learned from this has informed our thinking about training and its role in the changing culture of our organization.

Specifically we have learned:

1. that open learning has a significant role to play in facilitating the self-development of an individual;
2. that the methods of open learning encourage change in the training function and develop the trainers involved;
3. that both these aspects have an impact on organizational development and change.

This last aspect is the most difficult to quantify and evaluate since the organization as a whole is in a constant state of change.

However it is also the most interesting one for exploration since the creation of a climate for self-development (and the maintenance of it), requires some understanding of many factors which cause and influence organizational change and development. We still have a long way to go on this.

References

Boot, R. and V. Hodgson (1987) *Beyond Distance Teaching Towards Open Learning*, Open University Press, Milton Keynes.
Deal, T. and A. Kennedy (1988) *Corporate Cultures*, Penguin, Harmondsworth.
Fricker, J. (1988) *Open Learning in Transition*, National Extension College, London.
Handy, C. (1987) *Understanding Organizations*, Penguin, Harmondsworth.
Prudential Corporation (1986) The Prudential, London.
Prudential's New Identity (1986) The Prudential, London.

8
Learning resources centres
Julie Dorrell

Introduction

Self-development has become a rising star in the constellation of management development in recent years due to pressure on organizations to offer more learning opportunities to individual members of staff. This pressure is coming from a number of sources:

- internally from the employees themselves, and the need to have a more flexible workforce;
- externally from the government and from the fast-changing business environment, particularly the expectations of an enlarged 'home' market from 1992.

My experience in helping to create a self-development scheme for Forward Trust Group led to my offering a workshop on the practical aspects of initiating learning resource centres at the Lancaster Conference in September 1988. This is the example I shall take, later in this chapter, to show what factors need to be considered, what the practical steps are, and finally what can be achieved by using distance learning resources in this way.

When the end of my contract with Forward Trust came in sight. I decided to set up on my own, as JLD Associates.

My purpose was to advise other organizations, across a wide spectrum from financial institutions to local authorities, on how schemes like this might be introduced. I had come to believe strongly in the use of distance learning for self-development and wanted to promote it further. The purpose of the present chapter is to make available to a wider readership the substance of what was offered at Lancaster.

Assumptions behind the resource centre approach

The general assumptions underlying this approach are that:

1. people are better motivated to learn if they are offered a choice of learning resources, rather than having 'training' foisted on them;
2. those who have suffered in a classroom situation in the past can learn on their own, at their own pace, without competition, with no one looking over their shoulder and no fear of making fools of themselves;
3. a positive attitude towards continuous learning is fostered;
4. by offering individuals the chance to develop themselves to the fullest extent of their ability, and on their own initiative, a more satisfied body of people is created;
5. resource centre learning can be more easily integrated on the job than course-based learning.

Benefits of self- and continuous development

Stating the assumptions behind the learning resource centre approach leads on to the benefits of continuous development.

Benefits for learners
I believe that self-development allows the individual to discover latent talents, perhaps not apparent before. This stems from being able to continue development beyond formal school and further education through life, allowing for scope and hope, particularly for late developers. Using distance learning resources to make some learning available throughout the year, on a continuous basis, allows the learning to be applied more readily. Skills and knowledge are thereby increased in parallel on a continuous basis. This also helps to meet the greater demand for training, and it can be undertaken at the workplace, in the home or while travelling by car or train.

Benefits for the organization
These include:

- offering larger numbers of people learning opportunities;
- pre-course resources being available to produce a basic level of understanding among participants, thus saving the trainer time and money, and the learner time off the job;
- financial savings on travel and accommodation costs;
- individuals being able to learn, while fitting in with work loadings;

- some learning opportunities can be provided as soon as and wherever they are needed;
- cost-effectiveness when resources are used by large numbers of employees;
- individuals come to take more responsibility for their own training once they have control over their learning processes;
- managers also learn to take more responsibility for the learning undertaken by their staff.

Disadvantages

There are, of course, some disadvantages to using this approach. Some people find it difficult to learn on their own, particularly when they are not used to doing it: the isolation faction comes into play.

Others cannot convince themselves that it is 'legitimate' to use a learning resource centre during working hours, for instance for reading a book, however work-related it may be. They fear that if they are seen doing so by senior management they will be deemed to be 'skiving'. Small companies very often find it impossible to use the learning resource centre approach because they cannot afford the initial capital costs involved. It is also not as cost-effective for them as for larger organizations, because they do not have the numbers of staff to make it so.

Example—the Forward Trust Group 'TALENT' experience

(TALENT = Total Approach to Learning Employing New Technologies)

The scene was set in November 1985, when a training consultant, with the assistance of furniture and equipment suppliers, produced a mock-up of a learning centre at the Forward Trust Group Management Conference. This was done to introduce the concept to managers, and to test their reaction to this proposal, before embarking on the establishment of the four regional learning centres. Forward Trust's starting point was their need to introduce major changes in the financial services compliance regulations relating to the Consumer Credit Act 1984. They had a computer-based training programme tailor-made and the question then arose: 'How do we deliver this training?'

Learning centres—quiet study areas, in which staff could learn in their own time and at their own pace, away from the distractions of telephones and colleagues—seemed to fit the bill. Later the idea of learning centres was widened to include video and audio equipment, computers, books and other text-based learning programmes.

A good learning environment is essential and space in which to establish a learning centre was often at a premium. The initial pilot model learning centre in one region, furnished and equipped with three workstations, was a rather 'grand' version. The Phase II model was considerably smaller and more economical, both in relation to space and furniture requirements. This was partly in response to financial pressures as well as those of space. The first four regional learning centres were for branch and regional staff. Three more were then added catering for head office staff in London, operational staff in Birmingham and the factoring organization based in Worthing.

The realization that *all* staff, particularly those in outlying geographical areas, would still *not* be able to have access to learning resources, led Forward Trust to seek 'something else'. That 'something else' turned up at Texaco, where we went to see how their ASSET mail order system worked. (ASSET = Acquire Skills by Self Education at Texaco; see Cooper 1988.) This kind of system was adjusted to suit Forward Trust and added to the resource centres, to become part of the total TALENT scheme.

The mail-order system consisted of:

- a catalogue of learning resources, divided up into relevant sections; a short synopsis on each resource enabled potential users to decide which materials were appropriate for their purposes, symbols identified the medium of each resource;
- a library or stock of learning resources: training videos, audio-cassettes packs, computer-based training programmes, and text-based learning programmes or books;
- a manual or computerized method of logging resources in and out, keeping a record of availability and showing stock levels at a glance.

Once the scheme was complete, in the sense that decisions had been made as to what precisely would be offered, and to whom, there was an internal marketing job to be done.

First, it was necessary to get across the concept of self-development. Second, it was important to explain how Forward Trust's own scheme would work, answering questions such as:

- What is TALENT?
- What is it for?
- What's in it for me?
- What's wrong with courses?
- What resources are available?
- Where can the learning resources be used?
- What are learning centres and where are they?

The newly introduced internal newspaper was used as both an introductory and promotional tool, together with personal presentations down the line. A specially commissioned video was made to introduce the concept of self-development, demonstrating the analogy with the sportsman or woman. This video was very well received and did a lot to increase understanding of how people could help themselves by using the learning resources and learning centres.

We were seeking to gain the vital commitment from managers at all levels and generally change attitudes to training, away from: 'What has the training department got by way of courses?', or 'Can I go on a course, please?' (training as a perk), to 'Training is a continuous all-year-round process for which I personally take a large share of the responsibility' and 'How can I improve my skills and/or knowledge because I know I need to get better at, say, accounting, as our department is about to become an autonomous profit unit?', or 'I don't seem to get the results I should like from my reports. Perhaps I could express my ideas better and achieve the desired outcome.'

With hindsight, there were some things which could have been done differently. First a copy of the TALENT manual was issued uninvited to every single member of staff, regardless of their individual attitudes to the scheme. It was thought to be the right thing to do at the time, so that each person would feel included and understand that it was for everybody, not just graduates, managers, or the highly motivated.

It might have been better to announce the availability of the manual, and get individuals to request it, by use of a reply slip or some such device. This would have made the initial desire and move to acquire the manual come from the individual.

Second, the assumption was made that access to learning resource centres was essential for all users. In fact, once the mail-order system and the manual were introduced, much of the necessity for learning resource centres was weakened. Staff could, in many cases, borrow books and video and audio cassettes to use outside the office. The only real need for learning resource centres remaining was for computer-based training, because few people had personal computers at home.

Some learning resource centres were underused for several other reasons:

- bad siting, due to pressure on space;
- use by staff for meetings and actually working in, despite continued exhortations to keep them as dedicated learning areas;
- inertia on the part of some staff to use them at all;

- protestations of being too busy by others, particularly senior managers.

Three years on from the main launch of the TALENT Scheme at Forward Trust, the general demand for learning resources is still good and there is heavy use of them. Each year, following the time when appraisals are undertaken, there is an increase in demand, above the normal year-round level. Demand decreases during the summer months of July and August, when many staff take holidays.

No major evaluation has yet taken place on the scheme or the resources used, although large numbers of evaluation sheets on the resources have been filled out and returned.

The learning resource centres themselves are not in general used as much as had been hoped for, but two of the remaining six (two in the Midlands having been amalgamated after office relocation) have a 30–40 per cent usage rate. Given that the company had started up learning resource centres in the financial sector, which were relatively untried at the time, and that they are still running, I believe the scheme can be deemed successful.

The way ahead for self-development—using readily accessible learning resources

Self-development can be greatly assisted by the use of distance learning resources, either:

- in learning resource centres; or
- through a mail-order catalogue.

Individuals can make their own training plan, perhaps with guidance or assistance from their manager, where they have one. They can then use the learning resources available to achieve their own development in directions they feel are suitable.

Use of learning resources can be tied in to appraisal schemes, providing managers with a training option to meet the training needs of their staff.

There are many decisions to be made by organizations wishing to use these cost-effective methods of providing training and learning opportunities. To begin with they have to look carefully at themselves as an organization, decide where they are going and how they want to get there. They need, very often, to come to a *commitment* to offer learning opportunities for their staff and to give that commitment the financial backing needed to create those opportunities.

Having reached that stage they should, perhaps, examine what training needs they believe they have and look at how best to meet those needs. Improvements can be made on the Forward Trust scheme.

1. A 'help line' can be organized with someone always ready to offer:
   (a) suggestions,
   (b) advice,
   (c) to pass the learner on to someone who can help,
   (d) to assist any learner who might feel isolated or blocked in their learning.

2. Instead of handing out the catalogue to everyone, each staff member can be offered the catalogue and have to make a positive choice to receive it. This makes the impetus come from the individual and increases motivation.

3. The catalogues themselves can be more economically produced, using desktop publishing methods and binders into which a title sheet can be inserted.

4. Physical learning resource centres are not needed in all organizations. Some would do better with a mail-order-only system. This depends on the availability of computers for computer-based training, video equipment and so on, together with the working conditions at the various business locations under consideration.

5. Interactive video was already on the market when the TALENT scheme was introduced. It was not incorporated at the time because it was viewed as a large new capital expenditure item, which should be monitored carefully and perhaps introduced later on. Midland Bank, to whom Forward Trust belongs, had already introduced interactive video for its much larger number of staff and branches. It is an excellent learning medium, and is quite widely used by some large organizations in this country now. It can very well be incorporated as another medium among those already in use for distance learning.

Summary/conclusion

Self-development using distance learning offers considerable advantages in developing individuals, by motivating them, but is not necessarily suitable for all organizations. The size and type of business carried out may make it unviable or not particularly cost-effective. Using learning resource centres can provide organizations with a well-educated, flexible body of employees, who can help it to achieve its aims and objectives.

Reference

Cooper, S. (1988) 'Self-development in Texaco' in Pedler *et al.* (eds), *Applying Self-development in Organizations*, Prentice-Hall, London, pp. 211–19.

9
Open learning at W H Smith
Bob Johnson

'When open learning isn't open'

If you push the average trainer into a corner and ask for a definition of open learning, you'll probably get something like: 'Open learning is learning that takes place at a time, place and pace convenient to the learner.'

A definition like that is very seductive. By implication, the learner is responsible for his or her own learning. That should mean that, provided an organization makes learning opportunities available to its staff, it doesn't need to force, bribe or persuade them to undertake training. If time, place and pace aren't fixed, that makes open learning a very flexible medium. A responsible learner will adjust his or her learning round the needs of the job and the business and, who knows, may even decide to take some of it home! And of course, a learning method which goes on in the learner's own workplace, with the learner providing the motivation and commitment should mean that we can cut down on central training and support costs.

W H Smith has been using open learning as a central strand of its management training programme since 1985. Our experience during those years led us to believe that not only are these assumptions dangerously unreliable but even the definition of open learning we started with is seriously flawed.

Until 1985 all of W H Smith's management training had been in the form of traditional residential courses. They were popular and considered worth while. When the twice-yearly calls for nomination went out, most courses were fully subscribed and several were heavily over-subscribed. End-of-course questionnaires and action plans gave convincing testimony to their success. The training department enjoyed a healthy reputation among both course members and their nominating managers.

Working on the basis that 'if it works, leave it alone', there was no apparent reason to change this course-based approach to management training. Except one. In 1985 W H Smith's managing director Malcolm Field asked: 'How do I know what return I get from the investment I put into management training?'

As a result, in that year the company's training department took a critical look at itself in order to answer three fundamental questions:

- How can we ensure that the training we provide is relevant to the needs of individual managers and of the company?
- How can we quantify the results of training?
- What should we be doing to make training more cost-effective?

As we researched these questions, we were forced to face some worrying realities.

- We did not know all the key skills of our managers.
- We did not know the standards to which our managers were expected to perform.
- We were using residential training as our one and only response, regardless of the skill involved.
- Managers often attended courses for reasons totally unconnected with training needs.
- We had no mechanism for measuring the outcome of the training managers experienced.

As a result of our research and the brainstorming which followed it, we recognized the need for a training system which would 'measurably improve job performance by identifying the specific training needs of an individual manager and providing him or her with training to meet them'.

Four years after the event, both the problem and the solution seem self-evident. The jargon of 1989—competencies, performance testing, performance standards—very much address the problem we were facing. Not at the time, though. We were, therefore, involved in designing a new approach to management training which we thought revolutionary. We called it 'performance related training' and it worked like this.

1. Identify individual training needs

To achieve this stage, we first needed to identify the key skills of a manager's job. By interviewing jobholders, analysing job descriptions, asking their managers and seeking confirmation from directors, we were able to identify the key skills of a job such as retail department manager which might be relevant to as many as 1200 managers across the company.

The second step was to design exercises to test those skills. These were a combination of written tests, practical work and role-plays. We then set standards for each exercise by having it undertaken by members of the target group who were recognized as being of an acceptable standard in that skill.

These exercises were designed into a week-long residential programme—effectively, a low-cost assessment centre. These programmes, which we called 'profiling centres', were designed to be attended by all newly promoted managers within six months of appointment.

2. Provide training responses

As the result of attendance at the profiling centre, managers can identify their own personal training needs for the job to which they have just been promoted. The manager's involvement in this process cannot be stressed too highly. Members of the W H Smith training department who were responsible for development performance related training were concerned that managers undertaking it would feel threatened or resentful at what they might see as 'being weighed in the balance and found wanting'. In fact, the feeling of threat was less than we had anticipated. Junior managers came along with the typical attitude, 'I don't know anything about being a manager, so you can't show me any weaknesses I'm not already aware of'. By contrast, the profiling centre was often a boost to confidence, because managers achieved a higher standard in certain skills than they had anticipated. More senior managers, particularly those who felt that they had 'arrived' professionally, found it more difficult to adjust to the performance measurement used in the centres. Even so, this feeling was usually overcome by emphasizing that the exercises weren't a question of 'passing' or 'failing'. They were intended to identify training needs in order to meet them.

Our concern that managers might resent having their performance measured against a standard proved groundless. The most usual reaction, in spite of a sophisticated appraisal system which has been in use for many years, was: 'For the first time I really understand what the company expects of me.'

By the end of a profiling centre, most managers have recognized their training needs and are keen to know what they can do about them. At this point they attend an interview with a tutor, in order to negotiate priorities and agree relevant responses. This is very much a two-way process. The amount of training to be undertaken depends on the personality of the manager and the importance of individual skills to their situation. For example, all retail managers need to be competent in the company's financial control system. However, some junior managers only have one member of staff, which means that personnel skill like appraisal and selection interviewing are less important.

Which takes us back to the analysis of management skills which was carried out at the start of the process. As a result of that analysis, we came up with two main groups of skills. The first of these were interpersonal: team management, selection interviewing, counselling, for example. We decided that the most suitable response to needs in skills like these was a residential course, where managers could practise, learn from their experience and practise again.

Our second group consisted of subjects to do with knowledge and procedures like financial interpretation, security and legislation. It was in such areas that we decided to use open learning. Used in this way, open learning would allow managers to study the material as often as they liked to ensure they understood it and to apply the skills in a very practical way in their own work environment.

Deciding to use open learning was only the first step. It was then necessary to resolve the form that it should take. The first question we had to answer concerned the medium to be used. The majority of managers in W H Smith trading operations have frequent and intensive customer contact. Their working lives are varied and unpredictable. Open learning therefore had to be in a form which could be started and stopped with a minimum of inconvenience. In addition, open learning was on trial—the approach was new to the company and had to prove itself. Further, the training department itself was going through a major learning experience. It was important to keep that learning within manageable bounds.

For all those reasons, we went for text-based open learning. Our reasoning was that:

- booklets could be picked up and put down quickly and easily;
- if it failed there would be no hardware costs to write off;
- we could concentrate on structuring open learning, without concerning ourselves with complex issues of programming or inter-activity.

That still left us with several decisions to make. We had to come up with a style of text which would stand out from the welter of paperwork which arrives on a manager's desk each morning and which would be effective for managers who, in the main, had proved their competence in practical, rather than academic, ways. We also had to make sure that learning removed from the centre really did put right the shortfalls in performance which had been identified through the performance related training process.

The first two criteria resulted in a design for text-based material which was:

- 210 mm × 210 mm—an odd size deliberately chosen to make it distinctive;
- printed on quality paper, in two colours, with careful attention to page and cover design and the use of graphics;
- short—typical packages involve between two and four hours of study-time;
- job-based—frequent activities are designed to relate the package to practice, not theory.

Ensuring that open learning in W H Smith does indeed correct the skill needs which have been identified has meant that the company's approach has to be less 'open' than the definition with which this chapter started. If a member of staff has a training need in customer legislation for example or stock control, or health and safety, it is both dangerous and potentially costly to give them the freedom to complete it if and when they choose. Our approach, by contrast, has been to make the line manager responsible for setting targets and deadlines and making him or her aware that all open learning should be completed within twelve months of attending the profiling centre.

Nor do we leave the staff member and the manager on their own during this period. The open learning package which has been recommended is recorded on a database together with the deadlines which have been set. The relevant sections of the database are sent out for updating on a quarterly basis. Exception reports are produced if the learner has not met the agreed target. And, finally, local trainers make regular visits to all learners to monitor progress, to ensure line managers are supporting learners and to overcome any problems which may arise.

So far, though, this process, which some may see as unduly restrictive, only ensures that the package has been completed. It gives no guarantee that the manager's performance is now up to the required standard. Which brings us to the third and final stage of performance related training.

3. Confirm performance standards

We had already used exercises to identify training needs. So it was logical to use further exercises, of comparable design and content, to make sure managers had learned the skills in which they needed to be competent. These are undertaken both after open learning texts and at the end of residential courses. Exercises are assessed by line managers, local trainers or by members of the training department, depending on circumstances.

So far this chapter has been largely factual. It has dealt with the context in which W H Smith uses open learning and the form that open learning takes. From here, we need to move into the realms of philosophy and it is at this point that the author must make his own position clear.

In my opinion, a definition of open learning which defines 'openness' only in terms of what is convenient to the learner is unsuited to an organizational context. Organizations like W H Smith offer training primarily to make their staff competent. Lack of competence is nothing to be ashamed for, particularly for newly appointed staff, but it *is* something to be tackled and overcome as quickly and efficiently as possible.

Open learning offers a training method which is convenient *to the organization* because it offers flexibility of time, place and pace.

Of course, it allows staff to learn without having to attend a training centre. It means they can use odd corners of their time which would otherwise be unprofitable. There is nothing to prevent them working through a section again if it didn't make sense the first time. But, in important ways, it's not open when used in this way. The skill the learner lacks is important to the job. So it must be learned quickly—and to a set deadline. The performance standard, too, is set. There is an exercise to take at the end of this package and the learner is expected to reach the standard. Progress will be monitored throughout—by the manager, the local trainer and by the centre.

Does this mean, that the W H Smith version of open learning involves an unjustifiably directive manipulation of the method? Does it take away people's freedom of choice and, if so, is that wrong?

I don't think so—and experience bears this out. Managers in W H Smith enter an informal contract with the company by which they will receive experience, development and, if they're good enough, promotion in return for accepting the performance standards of the company. To a large extent, this approach to open learning parallels the overall culture of the company. Staff are given clear direction and a lot of support. In fact other training initiatives which have been less prescriptive have led to younger staff in particular expressing a performance for *more* guidance and direction.

So experience has shown that this system for monitoring open learning provides a series of benchmarks, targets and deadlines which managers seem to welcome. It answers the question 'What is expected of me?'

which many appear to find important. In the same way, the support structure has had positive results. Line managers are expected to meet their staff every two weeks or so, in order to review progress and discuss open learning they have been working through. Of course, not all managers do this particularly well. It has been significant that learners with difficulties have been those whose managers have been too busy, or not sufficiently committed, to spend time regularly with them. The fact that these progress reviews take place during normal working hours places a further limitation on openness.

It is important to stress, however, that performance related training does not simply create robots. Managers are given standards to meet. Accepting a management position is assumed to mean acceptance of those standards as well. Open learning represents one means of achieving them. Individual managers are free to negotiate their priority training needs and to a limited extent, their timescales for completion. They share a responsibility with their line managers to ensure that their training is satisfactorily completed.

The techniques described in this paper are designed to ensure that managers achieve the levels of competence expected of them. Most welcome the security, protection and confidence the support structure provides. Very few complain about a lack of freedom. After all, that's what they're paid for!

10
Corporate strategy and individual development in Hoechst UK

Barry Allen

Introduction

Hoechst UK Ltd, is a subsidiary of the German chemical giant, Hoechst AG. The company has four major UK sites, including its London headquarters building.

Employing some 1100 people, Hoechst UK's business base is founded in a wide-range of industries including chemicals, plastics, fibres, dyestuffs, pigments, agro-chemicals, pharmaceuticals and animal health. Major occupational groups, within the company, range from research and product-development, through manufacturing, marketing, sales and distribution to finance, accounts and information on technology. It is this very diversity in the business base and the complexity within the employee functional-groups that gave rise to the needs addressed in this chapter.

For several years Hoechst UK has had a well-developed approach to training and development. The two important gaps in this over-all approach have been:

1. a lack of an acceptable means of uniformly identifying training and development need across the company; and
2. a lack of a means of relating corporate strategy and objectives to the development of individuals.

In 1982 Hoechst UK's senior-managment team established a manpower planning and development unit within the company. The over-all purpose of this unit was to help line-managers to ensure that they always had sufficient numbers of staff, appropriately trained and experienced and highly motivated towards the achievement of their own and the company's objectives. Hoechst UK wanted to be in a position of never *having* to recruit from outside, although it would *choose* to do so when appropriate.

The two long term objectives were:

1. to further enhance staff morale and motivation, through:

   (a) each individuals' appreciation of their own contribution to the company's goals,
   (b) the recognition and reward of staff for their efforts and results,
   (c) the development of action plans geared towards personal growth,
   (d) the provision of opportunities for staff to display individual potential for growth;

2. to improve corporate effectiveness and efficiency through:

   (a) the identification of training-needs, related to the ability to achieve objectives,
   (b) the structure utilization of personal strengths, in the achievement of higher standards of personal performance,
   (c) structured opportunities for job-enlargement,
   (d) shorter learning-curves for those in new jobs,
   (e) improved internal recruitment,
   (f) external recruitment restricted to lower levels of the organization,
   (g) improved manpower planning,
   (h) reduced staff turn-over.

The overall 'model' that was first established in shown in Figure 10.1. In developing this first model we had three clear goals in mind. In this chapter is described the progress that we have made in achieving those goals; specifically to develop:

1. a uniformly applicable competences-schedule which can be used in performance appraisal, in assessment of training needs, in producing the content and objectives of corporate training events, in identifying potential for personal growth, in internal and external recruitment;
2. a performance appraisal system which provides links between individual objectives and performance and company goals, between personal performance and reward, between individual training needs and company training events, and which helps in the process of identifying potential for personal growth;

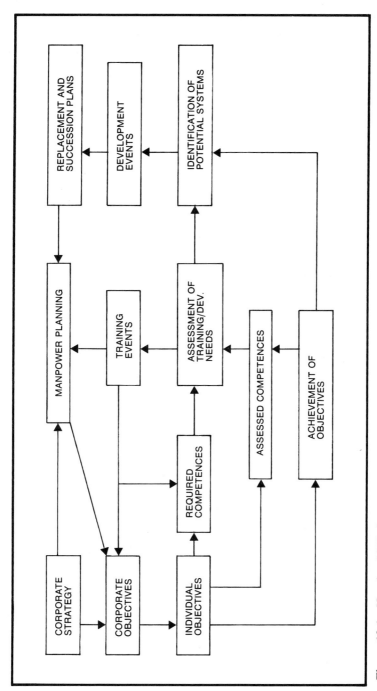

Figure 10.1   Hoechst UK's human resource strategy

3. an improved manpower planning system which links busines goals with manpower needs forecasts, which links manpower needs forecasts with replacement and succession plans and with training events, which link replacement and succession plans with identification of potential systems.

Development of job competences

Over the past few years we have used a modified form of repertory-grid to help us to establish a system of job analysis. Our concerns were to identify a range of knowledge, skills and attitudes that could be applied uniformly throughout our very complex business structure. We were seeking to establish a 'common language', that could be used across all of our functional activities in each of our fourteen major business areas. This common language would help to improve, even further, the processes of:

- internal and external recruitment;
- developing the content of in-house training courses;
- developing a system of rewarding effort;
- developing a system of identifying potential for growth;
- developing a system of identifying individual training needs;
- establishing individual development programmes.

We were seeking to become able to identify and describe work-'behaviours'. These 'behaviours' we called 'job-competences' and we saw them as being more than knowledge, skills or attitudes. In defining competences for line-managers, we asked them to describe what it was that someone had to be able to do in order to do a specific job really well. The example that we used, of a salesperson, assumed that more than product knowledge was needed in order to be able to sell. There had to be the skills of converting product features into product benefits. There had to be the skills of persuasive communication. There also had to be the appropriate attitudes towards finding, and calling effectively upon, new customers. In our use of repertory-grid we asked for information concerning what *good* performers did that differentiated them from the not-so-good.

The 'prizes' that we sought, in establishing a company wide language for describing both people and jobs, were:

- an aid to line-managers in external recruitment, making it easier for them to answer the question, 'Can this person do this job?';
- an aid to line-managers in internal recruitment, making it possible for

them to be presented with a company-wide list of people who 'can do this job';
- a means of specifying, precisely, the competences required *in* a particular job and thus defining the content of any training needed *for* that job;
- a means of 'measuring' effort, uniformly, across the company, thus adding a further measure of 'fairness' to our reward system;
- a means of assessing whether the capacity for higher-level competences was present, thus determining the existence of potential for growth;
- a method of specifying the content of development programmes and a means of measuring their effectiveness.

Our conceptual model for clustering the competences that we identified is shown in Figure 10.2.

Within Hoechst UK we have identified thirty-nine competences, each with its own hierarchy of performance-levels. Each 'level of competence' is a description of observable behaviour and we have tried to keep these descriptions 'simple'; for example, in 'verbal communication', we have restricted the behaviour to 'conveying clear messages'; the ability to 'influence or persuade others' is a different competence. As well as striving for 'simplicity' we have also sought to achieve a sufficiently wide range of competence-levels; no job within Hoechst UK requires

Company specific competences	*Functionally specific competences*
'Knowing the company tunes and how to play them on the company piano'	'Knowing how to play any companies' tunes on their instruments'
Ability to use company-related knowledge, effectively	Ability to use a range of professional craft, clerical, manual or managerial skills effectively
Company-relevant competences	Transferable competences

Personal commitment	*Self-direction*
At its lowest level, being punctual and attending regularly. At its highest levels, actively seeking out additional responsibilities, developing self, personal mobility, accepting new tasks	At its lowest level, doing urgent things quickly and allocating appropriate resources to important things; appropriateness of prioritization. At the highest levels, acting in own role appropriately for its departmental and organizational contexts
Personal competences	Job-context competences.

Figure 10.2   Competence clusters

competence-standards *below* our lowest levels, no job requires competence-standards *above* our highest levels. In using an hierarchical approach to the competence-levels we have established the convention that an analysis which shows that a job requires 'competence 10, level 4' is also showing that levels 1, 2 and 3 are required. These competences, established through agreement with the job-holders and their boss, are used to assess both job-requirements and job-holder performance-levels.

Competences in performance assessment, training and development needs

By defining every job in terms of required competences we have given ourselves the bases for:

- assessing performance in 'input' terms as well as 'outputs';
- assessing individual training needs;
- assessing individual development needs;
- assisting in the identification of potential.

Individual job-performance can be likened to a production process. In production the inputs are raw-materials, energy, and the production process; the outputs are 'finished goods'. In individual performance, the inputs are available resources and competences; the outputs are measurable achievements. In Hoechst UK we believe that all jobs have measurable achievements, outputs, and we can now measure the individuals' inputs or competences. As these competences are expressed in terms of 'observable behaviours' and are assessed, annually, by agreement between job-holder and line-manager we have added 'effort and commitment' to 'achievements against targets' in our performance appraisal procedure. We believe that this addition is valuable from three points of view:

1. We can 'recognize and reward' effort even if achievements are not as high as planned. Such 'under-achievement' may be as a result of factors outside the control of the job-holder.
2. We can focus more quickly on training-needs in performance-assessment discussions if we are not merely focusing on 'outputs'. Under-achievement against target *may* indicate the existence of a training need. Under performance against required competences will show which training need exists, if any, or inappropriate attitude or lack of role-clarity.
3. Where an above-performance against required competences exists, then it is probable that a development need exists; a member of our

staff has the ability and willingness to take on additional responsibilities, or higher-levels of responsibility, or to make greater use of personal strengths within the present role. (The existence of such development needs is not as easily identified through recognizing over-achievement in *'output'* terms.)

Within Hoechst UK, the identification of individual potential-for-growth is a continuous process.

Competences in job analyses

Through the process of line-manager discussions, it is possible to analyse present jobs, in terms of task-content, and to derive required competences from task-content. All existing jobs within Hoechst UK, up to business-unit head, have been analysed in this way and the list of required-competences for each job has been built into our jobs database, held on computer.

Not only can we express present jobs in required competences terms, we can also describe our future jobs similarly. The manpower forecasts, that we derive from our manpower-system modelling, tell us not only how many people at what levels of the organization will we need, but also what must these people be capable of doing and from where we are likely to be able to 'recruit' them.

The lists of required competences, which we produce from our job-analyses, are of considerable value in external and internal recruitment, in measuring individual performances, in defining individual training and development needs and in identifying individual potential for growth. Because we have a comprehensive jobs database it has also become possible for us to develop a very accurate 'menu' for each of our corporate training events.

Competences in training events

Hoechst UK is a complex business organization. We have business units based on some fourteen industries; we have subsidiary and associate companies with other business interests. In each of these business units similar jobs may have different titles, different jobs may have similar titles. In order to ensure that our twenty-odd corporate training events are relevant to all business areas we have developed their contents on the bases of job competences and not on 'job titles' or 'task-content'.

If we take the function of 'supervisor' as an example, we have defined this function as being 'responsible for the day-to-day activities of others, including establishing individual work-loads, assessing work standards, informal discipline, monitoring daily work-performances and on-the-job coaching and counselling'.

Regardless of title, this is the primary, supervisory role in Hoechst UK. All line-managers know that our 'first-line supervisors' course is based on the competences derived from the above definition. all 'about-to-be' supervisors, or those with the prospect of becoming supervisors, who attend this course find all of the content relevant. They may need other competences; some 'supervisors' are also involved in formal performance-appraisal or staff selection or allocating tasks. Such supervisors will need to attend more than the 'first-line supervisors' course. Our programme of training events has been designed so that all competences required, in jobs up to middle manager, are covered. By reading the courses' synopses, all line managers know the competences being addressed by each event.

Identification of potential system

There are three core elements in the identification-of-potential system that we have developed over the past five years. These core elements are as follows.

1. The annual performance appraisal system. This is an open discussion between the job-holder and the immediate boss. The four areas of discussion are: achievements against objectives, competences displayed compared with competences required, training and/or development needs and future objectives.
2. Development workshops, at which objective assessments are made of job-related strengths and weaknesses and which are described much more fully, later in this chapter.
3. Parent, grandparent and uncle/aunt discussions. These are intended to provide a 'three-dimensional' picture of members of staff. The three 'dimensions' are provided by the parent (immediate boss), grand-parent (boss's boss) and aunt/uncle (boss's peers who have some knowledge of the staff member).

Data gathered from the above three core elements are entered on our expert computer system, PARYS. This information is updated at least annually and is the basis of our people database; this latter is a very valuable tool in the process of internal recruitment.

To allow people to grow as far and as fast as they are able, we have to ensure that we can identify the potential for growth throughout their careers within the company. Our four sources of recruitment are our youth scheme; which now includes an 'industrial scholarship scheme', sandwich course students or other work-experience students, graduates, recruited directly from universities and polytechnics, other graduates, or non-graduates, from other organizations.

Youth and sandwich-course students have pre-recruitment assessments made of them and are, obviously, not recruited unless these assessments are 'good'. Recruits from other organizations bring with them some 'reputation', a record of previous achievement. Only graduates recruited directly from universities or polytechnics have no 'previous record of job-performance'. The one event which is geared solely towards the identification of 'under-utilized talent' is our development workshop. Originally designed for one level of management across the whole of the company, development workshops are now conducted as an hierarchy, for all levels of management, across all functions and within all business units. At higher levels of this hierarchy the workshops are conducted across all business areas within Hoechst UK and now include subsidiary companies within the group.

Development workshops

Development workshops have become part of Hoechst UK's 'culture', since we conducted the first in 1985 (Griffiths and Allen 1987). While containing many of the elements of assessment centres, development workshops go much beyond them. They are the most exciting and rewarding personal-development activity that I have been involved with in twenty years.

The objectives of the development workshops are:

1. to give delegates insights into themselves in terms of work interests, work preferences, managerial styles and job competences, expressed as relative strengths and relative weaknesses;
2. to give delegates opportunities to consider their jobs in the contexts of department, division, company and parent company; to encourage them to 'look further ahead than to-day; to look more widely than here; to look higher than this level';
3. to cause delegates to work with peers, in teams; to provide opportunities for developing an appreciation of other functions, to develop a deeper understanding of interfunctional relationships;
4. to produce agreed development-plan outlines that enable greater use to be made of personal strengths, that specify improvement activities for key, relative weaknesses and which provide a basis for discussion on personal development with the immediate manager.

The pre-work consists of a series of questionnaires which the delegates complete and return for scoring. Half of these questionnaires are 'bought-in'. We have developed the other half internally and have 'validated' them with our line managers.

The workshop itself consists of individual exercises, group discussions, practical 'leadership' activities formal inputs, group presentations and plenary sessions. Considerable benefit is also derived from the 'after-hours' socializing. Throughout the workshop, feedback is given to each delegate and an *agreed* profile of relative strengths, relative weaknesses, managerial style and personal preferences is built up. Although immediate managers of the delegates attend the workshop as 'coaches', they do *not* give feedback to their own staff. Feedback is given after each exercise by other managers, acting as coaches. At the end of the workshop, the final debrief of the delegates is conducted, again, by a manager other than their own. This final debrief is a review of the whole workshop and lays down the broad areas of development need, for later discussion with the immediate boss.

Immediate managers are expected to arrange discussions with those staff who have attended a workshop. These discussions should be arranged within two weeks of the workshop ending. The outcomes of these discussions are longer-term development plans.

Development plans may well contain agreements on formal courses to be attended, or open-learning packages to be worked through. In such cases, members of the training function would normally be involved in an advisory/counselling capacity.

Much more commonly, however, development plans include the use of specific 'strengths' to take on additional responsibilities (job enlargement) or to do more of the same (job enrichment) or to become involved more with other functions (job broadening). Development plans also include projects, involvement in new working groups, 'secondments' and 'appreciation visits'.

All development plans are agreed between boss and delegate, but the delegate has to have ownership of, and responsibility for, the plan. Boss and delegate arrange a review of the plan on an at-least-annual basis.

One element that may be incorporated into an individual's development plan, but that is not 'open', is that which stems from a succession plan. In Hoechst UK we do not make 'open' to members of staff our replacement and succession plans. Such plans are formulated as a result of the higher-level, parent, grandparent, uncle/aunt discussions. As a result of such discussions the responsible 'parent' will ensure that the necessary development actions are built into agreed development plans.

Replacement and succession planning is the term we use to describe 'internal recruitment'. Sometimes 'replacement planning' has to include 'people broking'.

Internal and external recruitment

Our manpower forecasting process enables us to develop meaningful succession plans. We can reasonably forecast our future people needs in terms of numbers, status level and jobs' contents. We know when specific retirements will occur. Our succession plans indicate the job to be filled, the current job-holder, the likely date that a successor will be needed and a shortlist of potential successors. Although this looks relatively simple, it should be borne in mind that the retirement of one business-unit head will lead to four potential promotions occurring. While we do not attempt to have succession plans for all four levels of managements we do need to have knowledge of the 'potential' at all four levels.

'Succession plans' cater for the orderly, expected movement of staff throughout the company. Another element in internal recruitment is 'replacement planning', an attempt to cater for the unexpected and the potentially damaging. We have identified 'key jobs' and 'key staff' for whom we need to have emergency replacements. In this definition a key job is one which, if it became vacant, and could not be *quickly and very effectively* filled, would cause us serious business difficulties. 'Key people' are those who fill a unique position, one which has been developed by and for the job-holder because of a unique combination of competences and experience in the company, or knowledge of the company. Such staff are, by definition, almost irreplaceable in an emergency.

Our intention is to have replacement plans for every key-job-holder and contingency plans (job splitting, perhaps) for every key person.

Whenever a forecast vacancy occurs we will have asked the question 'Should this job remain unchanged?' If the answer is 'yes', then ideally, a successor will have been groomed and tested for the job. If the answer is 'no' then the changed job will have had a successor groomed and, ideally tested, for the new role. If the job is to be split and allocated to more than one other person then, ideally, they too will have been groomed for what will be their new jobs.

Unexpected vacancies, too, provide an opportunity to ask the question 'Should this job remain unchanged?' Our most recent experience of non-key jobs suggest that the answer is often 'no'. In such cases we have used the opportunity provided to create new roles, containing many of the areas of responsibility of the old, but changing the total job to satisfy our present/future needs more fully. When such new positions are created we may need to 'engage in people broking'.

People broking

Whenever a job is described in 'competences terms' it is possible to use this job-analysis as a 'trawl' through the people database to find all those members of staff whose personal competences closely match those of the vacant job.

Once a 'list' of such 'possibles' has been produced, it is possible for informal soundings to be taken of possible interest in applying for the position. This approach to people broking does *not* replace the need for internal advertising and 'normal' recruitment; people broking supplements internal recruitment.

Manpower planning systems

There are five broad elements of Hoechst UK's strategic and tactical development of people:

1. Performance appraisal
   - the cascading down of company objectives to individual objectives (not as autocratic as it looks to be here!).
   - agreement on what are the required job-competences.
   - assessment of performance against these two sets of criteria.

2. Identification of training needs
   - from performance appraisal to individual needs.
   - from job analyses and individual needs to the contents of training events.

3. Identification of potential for growth
   - from performance appraisal, from development workshops, from parent/grand parent/uncle/aunt discussions to individual development needs.
   - from manpower planning to recruitment needs, to replacement and succession plans, to development plans and development events.

4. Individual development	• from development workshops, from performance appraisal, to personal growth-job-enlargement, job-enrichment and/or preparation for higher-level jobs.
5. Manpower planning	• from corporate strategy to forecasts of needs. • from age profiles, wastage to internal audit. • from internal audit to internal and external recruitment and to individual development needs.

The manpower forecasts are based on historical data (wastage rates) current-staff audits (including age profiles and known retirement dates) and the company's five-year strategy.

Hoechst UK's long-term strategy is determined by three major factors:

1. the parent company's strategy, as an internal industrial-giant;
2. the parent divisions' strategies and objectives;
3. the UK as an economic, industrial environment.

Since 1986 there has been a greater clarity in the statement of corporate strategy and objectives. A process now exists which enables the component divisions of Hoechst UK to develop corporate and team objectives. These are derived from:

1. Hoechst UK's objectives;
2. the parent-Divisions' objectives; and
3. the views of divisional managements concerning the future business and economic environments in which they will be working.

While individual objective *are* 'cascaded down' from team-objectives, this process is not entirely 'autocratic'. 'What targets/objectives are stretching but attainable?' is a question asked of job-holders very early on in the objective-setting process. The responses are listened to!

From the long-term strategy and objectives, forecasts of our future manpower-needs are made.

Summary

Individuals within an organization have the need for opportunities for personal growth. Organizations have the need to make the best use of their most valuable resource, people. Not only are these two needs compatible, the means of their satisfaction can be identical.

Fully effective individual development will only occur in those organizations whose senior management actively support and fund the total process. The first steps in ensuring that such active support and funding are available are:

1. to show that the process is aimed at helping the organization to achieve its long- and short-term objectives;
2. to demonstrate how the beneficial outcomes of individual development can be measured; and
3. to clearly state what 'benefits' will accrue to the organization when it 'buys into' individual development.

This chapter describes Hoechst UK's attempt to draw clear and quantifiable links between the statement of corporate objectives, through recruitment needs, training events and identification of potential systems, to personal growth. Individual, self-managed development and individually targeted training are key elements in this process. We believe in the mutuality of the value to be gained from personal growth, for the individual and the company. It is an important part of Hoechst UK's management philosophy that people should be encouraged to grow as far and as fast as they are able. We subscribe entirely to the belief that all development is about 'learning', rather than 'being taught'. We believe that organizations can provide development opportunities but that individuals have to seize them. In that sense, we believe that *all* development is self-, or individual, development.

Reference

Griffiths, P. and B. J. Allen (1987) 'Development workshops at Hoechst, UK', *Journal of Management Development*, **6**(1), 11–18.

11
Management learning contracts: the training triangle
George Boak and Peter Joy

Introduction

Open learning is an approach to education, learning and development which provide participants with a wider range of choices than the traditional classroom-based courses. Typically there is choice about *what* is studied, often in the form of a choice between a wide range of modules. Typical, too, are choices about when, where and for how long the study is undertaken. These choices are so often made possible by the provision of materials—interactive workbooks or video packages—that open learning is often wrongly taken to be synonymous with distant learning. Management learning contracts are a means of providing effective training and development in management skills, through bringing together the parties involved in training and providing a mechanism for making the right choices.

There are three people (at least) involved in the training and development of any employee; the individual trainee, or *participant*; the tutor or *trainer*, and the person who must release the participant from work—the *manager*. These three actors form the immediate training triangle, and their actions and motivations will determine the degree of success of the training episode.

Management learning contracts

A management learning contract is a signed or formal agreement between *participant*, *manager* and *trainer*, about what the participant will learn, how that will be assessed, and the means of undertaking the learning.

Participants are managers or supervisors and the focus of the contracts has been upon the development of management skills, but the principles would apply in other fields.

Since 1986 over five hundred contracts have been negotiated. Each contract has been scheduled to completion within a three to eight week period. The majority of management learning contracts undertaken in this period have formed part of a programme leading to a recognized qualification.

The skill areas covered have been diverse, including those of analysis, financial, statistical, job or value; information technology; dealing with people, including persuasiveness, interviewing, coaching, chairing or contributing to meetings, teambuilding, assertiveness; time management and goal achievement; and various communication skills—including those of fluency in other languages.

The response from managers to the use of management learning contracts has been very positive. On the whole they have appreciated the responsibility given to them by the method, and the opportunities this opens up.

A number of principles of learning and development acted as foundations for the development of management learning contracts (Boak and Stephenson 1987). Malcolm Knowles (1975) points to the factors affecting the motivation to learn in adults as being:

- the opportunity to participate in the experience, from decisions on what is learned, through active participation in the process, to playing a role in evaluation;
- the perceived relevance of what is learned;
- the availability of feedback on performance;
- the consequences of learning, or failing to learn.

Using management learning contracts as part of a development programme immediately increases the learner's participation. This in itself enhances the relevance of the programme.

Where real challenges are faced, by taking advantage of learning opportunities in the workplace, the consequences of action are also real and motivation is again enhanced. The co-operation of the trainer and the manager in providing opportunity, support and feedback are also of great value.

The difference between management learning contracts and the academic, research-based learning contracts discussed by Knowles lies in the greater emphasis of the former on skill development, and in the extra involvement of the employer's representative.

David Kolb (1976, 1984) and Honey and Mumford (1986) have provided the most recent formulation of the process by which skills are developed. By passing through a series of stages, summarized in Figure 11.1, the individual develops a specific skill.

There is a danger in conventional training and development programmes of concentrating for too long on the knowledge element, and mistaking knowledge for skill. Management learning contracts provide a means of structuring skill development through each of the four stages.

In particular, the value of action can be recognized in the use of management learning contracts. As trainers, we have encountered managers who have 'done' assertiveness/interviewing skills/motivation (etc.) courses and yet exhibit no signs of changed behaviour bar one: the ability to repeat the underlying theories and describe how the course was run. The management learning contract approach is heavily indebted to the action learning philosophy of Reg Revans (1980).

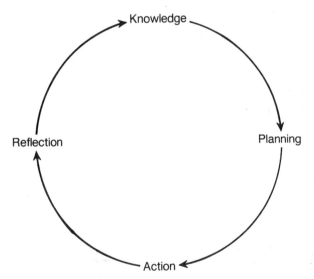

Figure 11.1 The learning cycle

Contracts and projects

Project work is a familiar component of many management development programmes of more than three or four days' duration, and management learning contracts are often mistaken for projects by participants and managers. Both are exercises running over a period of time, involving research work and individual application. Both may be chosen by the individual participant, and both may result in a written report. What's the difference?

The key difference is that a management learning contract concentrates on *learning*—that is, on the acquisition of knowledge and/or the development of individual skill.

The learning is defined in advance and the success or otherwise of the management learning contracts is judged on a measurement of that learning. A project, on the other hand, will usually involve the analysis of a situation, the preparation of recommendations for change, and sometimes the implementation of those recommendations. It is about changing a situation, not about changing the individual. It will almost certainly involve the acquisition of knowledge and perhaps the development of skills (particularly planning, information-handling and analytical skills) but it does not *concentrate* on skill development and in most circumstances is of limited value and unpredictable in developing the individual. A project, however, may be of more immediate benefit to the organization as represented by the manager, and even to the individual participant, by focusing on the accomplishment of a task or tasks.

A project can be used as a vehicle for learning, of course, but only if learning becomes the focus, rather than the quality of the project report itself, does the value in development terms approach that of a management learning contract.

Making it work

Preparing the ground
Two processes are necessary before effective management learning contracts can be negotiated: these are priming and diagnosis.

Priming means preparing the participant and the manager for the roles they will have to play. Devising and undertaking a management learning contracts requires more initiative, ingenuity and active effort than many participants and managers expect. In addition to simply explaining what a contract is, they have found it is essential for the following reasons:

- To emphasize the fact that contract objectives are *learning* objectives, to make the distinction between contracts and projects. Although the current means of assisting diagnosis of learning needs are far from perfect tools of analysis, they do provide a focus on learning and a glossary of terms for describing skills which can usefully distract participants from their more immediate, short-term project-based problems. The diagnosis also makes discussion between manager and participant more specific, less emotionally difficult, and therefore more careful.

- To explain the reasons for using management learning contracts. This is typically done by reference to the learning cycle, as above, and by the use of the learning styles questionnaire (Kolb 1976). It is important here to emphasize the fact that management learning contracts do work, and that participants can develop their skills. The fatalism with which people can regard themselves as simply 'not good at interviewing' or 'not very organized' is not at all conducive to change for the better. Depending on the participant, the priming process may involve discussions about the role of personality in determining behaviour. (The fact is that participants *can* improve their interviewing and self-organizational skills through the use of management learning contracts. As trainers we know that. It is necessary for participants to believe it too.)
- To explain the responsibilities of the three parties to the contract, emphasizing the initiatory role that lies with the participant. It is important, too, to make clear arrangements for assessment, and thus to emphasize the responsibility of the participant to take action within a particular period of time.

Diagnosis means making an assessment of learning needs, and will lead to decisions about the subject of the contract. We have used a range of methods to help participants make their diagnosis, including a computer program and a blockage questionnaire.

Discussion with the manager (line manager and/or mentor) can help, as can discussion with the trainer—where the latter acts as a counsellor. It is important, however, for the participant to accept and to act on the diagnosis, so that he or she owns the contract.

An aid to diagnosis is exposure to a model of good practice. Without this, participants may identify problem area—because of negative results or feelings of stress—but may be unable to identify the skills they wish to improve.

The trainer can help here in providing access to models of good practice. The degree to which this model can be adapted by the participant should vary depending on the contract. Two examples illustrate this.

In one case, the participant wanted to be able to use a personal computer. He had no experience whatsoever of using one. He was aware of a learning need, but incapable of expressing it any more precisely. Discussion with the trainer indicated that, of the basic types of program, a database would be more useful to him than a spreadsheet. After explaining the options to him, the trainer recommended that the management learning contracts should focus on database and they discussed the data that might be included. A specification was drawn up of the number of fields that would be included and what the participant would be able to do in order to demonstrate his ability. Access to a PC and to an introductory manual was available in this case from the manager.

In a second case, the participant wanted to improve his ability to make useful contributions to meetings. Again, he was aware of a learning need—which related to a particular, regular meeting—but unsure how to go about improving. The trainer made some readings on meetings available and suggested that the first part of the contract should be for the participant to identify the skills he felt were important to contributing to meetings, and then to assess himself against those skills to determine his priorities for development. (In this case the participant also asked his manager to assess him.) He would then aim to make progress against his areas of greatest need. (In this case the testimony of his manager formed part of the assessment.)

In the first example, of information technology, the criteria for skilful performance are fairly well established. The same is true of most skills relating to financial analysis. In addition, in the example given, the participant was starting from ignorance.

In the second example, the criteria for skilful performance are not well established. This is true of most, if not all, of the interpersonal skills. That being the case, it is important for participants to decide and define the criteria against which they wish to be judged, and the readings or advice made available must give them scope for doing this. The criteria participants produce must be justifiable, and this should be part of the contract assessment.

It will be apparent by now that the needs analysis recommended by the rationalist school of training and development is here being undertaken largely by the participant, with the trainer and in many cases the manager acting to help clarify the participant's thinking.

Having prepared the ground, through priming and diagnosis, we are ready to negotiate the contract. It is very easy to fall at the first fence.

The first fence
Without adequate priming and diagnosis, the tendency is for a participant to make much less effective progress towards drafting a contract. Where a draft is made, the tendency is for it to be:

- a project, not a contract; or
- a knowledge-acquistion contract; or
- a broad skill area contract.

In addition, there is a tendency to be over-ambitious.

Part of the priming and diagnostic processes will continue into the actual negotiation of the contract. If the participant presents a clear draft, then much of the negotiation is simply confirmation or amendment of that draft. The correct role of all three parties to the discussion at this point should be to clarify the needs and wants of the participant and to make an accurate assessment of opportunities and resources available to carry out the management learning contract. There are four things to watch for.

1. Setting the target Management learning contracts work best when they have realistic, limited targets. This may mean focusing on improvement in one or two specific areas, as in the examples above. This can be difficult for participants to grasp—particularly in the interpersonal and personal skill areas—and may lead to resistance to tacking areas of need with management learning contracts or to over-ambitious targets which are not met.

This point cannot be emphasized too strongly, because even small changes in approach to interpersonal skills can have a large effect.

It follows that an accurate and realistic assessment of the current level of skill or knowledge of the participant is necessary to determine how much stretch is in the target, and this is something to which all three parties can contribute.

2. Ownership of the contract For reasons of motivation, commitment and relevance, ownership of the management learning contract should remain with the participant. Some of the processes present in the situation, however, may conflict with this.

The manager may be the participant's senior, and a leader–follower relationship may be firmly established. Directions, suggestions or hints of the manager may be followed in the contract negotiation as they are followed elsewhere.

From the manager's point of view there may be 'obvious' learning needs which the participant should address, and the management learning contract may be seized upon as an ideal opportunity to make this happen. Less legitimate, in this training and development context, is for the manager to seek to use the management learning contract as a means of getting the participant to tackle an outstanding project. It is true to say that there can be significant personal development for individual managers in overcoming these problems. The trainer may be accorded the blind respect normally expected by tutors and trainers, and the participant may be willing to follow suggestions made from this quarter—even though they may not make much sense at the time.

From the trainer's point of view it may seem quicker and easier to make suggestions rather than ask questions. There may be 'obvious' training needs. Inexperienced management learning contract negotiators are likely to feel more comfortable when they are giving information in a traditional trainer mode rather than seeking it.

For all that a manager might see a problem the participant ignores, or the trainer be able to save valuable time by going straight to the heart of the matter, the danger in both cases is loss of commitment and loss of ownership.

If the management learning contract is successful, that success is a shared one, and the realization by the participant that he or she can learn and develop independently is blocked.

If the management learning contract runs into problems less effort is spent in tackling them than if the participant has chosen the route. Responsibility for failure, as well as success, is diluted.

3. Dependencies The classic dependency is introduced in this way. The participant wants to improve his or her skills in computing. A new desktop publishing system will be installed in his or her office next week. He or she needs to find out what it will do, how it works and then train up the other staff in the office to use it. Of course, the new desktop publishing system rarely arrives on time, and when it does it takes two visits from the software house to get it to work at all.

A basic dependency is the participant's own time. Job changes and unexpected fluctuations in the workload can hit the best laid plans. Other dependencies, built into management learning contracts by assumption, are:

- access to resources and to information;
- access to opportunities to practise, e.g. to chair the meeting, to interview the applicants.

The partners in the training triangle should be wary of accepting plans of availability at face value. The extent to which the contract will stand or fall due to a dependency should be established, and the contingency plans discussed.

4. Being explicit Good communications practice applies to the agreement of a contract. The trainer, as facilitator, should make sure that all three parties have the same understanding of the objectives, activities, deadlines and performance measures of the management learning contract. This may involve simply discussing the participant's written proposal, or it may involve amending it to make it more explicit. Typically, for example, the participant will offer 'a written report' as part of the assessment. It is useful to discuss, and often to include in writing as part of the contract, what the report will include, how long it will be and what criteria will be used to judge it.

Assessment
The purpose of assessment is to establish whether the participant has indeed learned what he or she set out to learn. The fact that the management learning contract will be assessed also acts to motivate the participant, or to add social pressure to natural self-motivation.

For each learning objective there should be a performance measure, and so before the management learning contract begins participant, trainer and manager must decide suitable ways of determining whether knowledge or skills has increased. An account of progress, and of problems encountered and overcome, can provide an appropriate frame for the evidence the participant undertakes to produce. The evidence may take a variety of forms:

- demonstration—as in the ability to use a technique or to display a skill, such as use of a computer;
- testimony—of the manager, or of some other individual who is naturally a witness to the participant's display of improved skill;
- recordings—audio- or videotaped evidence of skilled behaviour;
- written reports—particularly useful for summarizing conclusions or indicating improved knowledge or understanding;
- oral reports—particularly valuable in that they allow interaction through question and answer, and enable a thorough testing of the participant's understanding.

Some areas are very difficult to assess, particularly the interpersonal skill areas. The aim of management learning contracts is to develop skilled behaviour in a 'real life' situation and on the whole we have avoided assessment of role-play behaviour or assessment of skills in mock interviews, because of the unreal elements in those situations. How then can significant skills—like the ability to carry out a performance appraisal, or a disciplinary interview—be addressed?

The approach that has been taken to date leans on the learning circle philosophy. The aim of management learning contract may be to improve the *action* (i.e. the behaviour) but where the action is not observable, an *account* of the action taken, together with reflections on success or failure, a statement of the principles of effective performance (i.e. knowledge or theory) and an action plan for future development, serve as reasonable surrogate measures. Tutors are trained in 'behavioural event interviewing' to improve their capabilities in this area (Klemp and McClelland 1986).

Participants can benefit because:

- contracts are of their own choosing and should therefore be relevant to their needs;
- in addition to other skills, they improve their *learning* abilities with appropriate support and guidance in drawing up the contract they will see real improvements in skill, knowledge (and, usually, self-confidence).

The managers can benefit because:

- they become involved in training and development in a safely constructed role;
- they have an opportunity to influence and evaluate the activities of the trainer and the participant.

Trainers can benefit because:

- they tackle a wide variety of real problems, and see real developments in skills and attitude.

The cost of these benefits is simple; the contract process is one which provides a challenge to all three partners, particularly those who are undertaking it for the first time–whether participant, manager or trainer—after experiencing only traditional training methods.

The future

Future trends in this area are three-fold:

1. The impact and popularity of management learning contracts is likely to lead to an increase in their use. This has been observable particularly in the last three years as client organizations apply the management learning contracts method to a range of development situations.
2. The move towards defining competences needed by effective managers (Boyatzis 1982) may provide broad outlines for management learning contracts, within which participants may define their own

specific learning objectives. There may be an effect on motivation: that remains to be seen.

3. The use of action learning sets to discuss and support contracts has been successful in most cases in our experience to date. Each individual determines, in the end, their own contract, but the development of relationships in the group has led to more challenge, examination and self-assessment than the relationship with trainer and manager alone can provide.

Work still remains to be done in each of these areas—in training effective management learning contract negotiators, in using competence statements and in compiling and maintaining learning sets where they are appropriate. But a working method of reaching difficult training and development needs is already available in the form of the management learning contract.

References

Boak, G. and M. Stephenson (1987) 'Management learning contracts: from theory to practice', *Journal of European Industrial Training*, **11**(4), 6.

Boyatzis, R. (1982) *The Competent Manager*, Wiley, New York.

Dearden, G. (1989) *Learning While Earning*, Learning from Experience Trust, Oxford.

Honey, P. and Alan Mumford (1986) *The Manual of Learning Styles*, Honey, Maidenhead.

Klemp, G. O. and D. McClelland (1986) 'Behavioural Event Interviewing' in Stenberg and Wagner (eds), *Practical Intelligence*, Cambridge University Press, Cambridge.

Knowles, M. (1975) *Self Directed Learning*, Follett, Chicago.

Kolb, D. (1976) *The Learning Style Inventory*, McBer and Co., Boston.

—— (1984) *Experiential Learning*, Prentice-Hall, New York.

Revans, R. W. (1980) *Action Learning*, Bloud and Briggs, London.

12
Using personal construct psychology in self-development
Fay Fransella and John Porter

Introduction

Professor George Kelly's Psychology of Personal Constructs *(PCP) was published in 1955. It provides a framework for working with all psychological aspects of the person. PCP basically says that the sense we make of the present world, as it ebbs and flows around us, is based on how we have interpreted our experiences in the past. This process of trying to make sense of the present PCP calls construing.*

We construe by peering at the world through a set of *constructs* which we have created for ourselves over the years. We each peer at the world through our own personal pair of spectacles. Sometimes we all agree about what we see, sometimes we look at the 'same' event as others but *see* something different.

For instance, let us pretend you are one particular sort of person who is about to go through the door to a meeting. You have a fair idea of what the meeting is going to be about as you have been to other, similar meetings. As you look at the people already there you find your predictions proved correct. Each is sitting in their usual place; each doing what you expect he or she to be doing—Jim is smoking vigorously; Mary talking in a rather loud voice to anyone who will listen; David sitting quietly minding his own business.

One important feature of construing is that it is about the future. It sets up a series of predictions. You have worked out ways in which these meetings are similar to each other and from these you expect (predict) what is likely to happen in this coming one. The better able we are to construe events, the more control we have over those events—control in the sense that we are in a position to plan our own behaviours if we can predict the behaviours and feelings of others.

But you suddenly notice that there is something unusual about this setting—something you have not predicted. There is a stranger standing quietly in the corner. You may possibly feel a twinge of anxiety at this moment. If we are faced with something we are unable to construe immediately we find it difficult to know precisely how to behave toward that event.

All our feelings about things relate to how we construe them. PCP covers all aspects of our experience of the world.

So, you hastily pull out some constructs in your repertoire and try them on for size. Is the person likely to be a superior or not? Is the person standing there alone because he is shy or because he is very confident and content to watch the scene as it unfolds?

At a more personal level you may be asking yourself whether your not having been told about this new person is because you are not considered important any longer. Of course, you are not consciously saying all these things to yourself, they are just ideas that float through your mind.

Of one thing you can be fairly certain, the view through the spectacles of that stranger standing quietly against the wall will not be identical to your own.

In the examples which follow we will show how:

1. PCP analysis of a person's construing of their working environment can indicate areas in which anxiety may occur;
2. these anxieties can be reduced through a better knowledge of self;
3. how processes of personal change (learning) can be initiated and assisted by assisting people to see alternative perspectives.

There are always alternative ways of looking at things

Whatever you decide will determine how you will behave. For one unique feature of PCP is that all behaviour is the experiment we carry out to check up on our construing (predictions) about the event facing us.

This means that, to understand how others experience events, we have to *ask* them. There is no room in personal construct psychology for third-party interpretations. Standing quietly in the corner may be interpreted by some as indicating a shy person, but PCP understanding necessitates asking the person standing in the corner what he is doing from his standpoint. Asking does not have to be direct in order to elicit information. It can be embedded within group interactions or through the processes involved in repertory grid construction.

Misunderstanding frequently arises when managers try to anticipate or understand what their staff are thinking. Instead of trying to enter into the world of that other person they apply a 'managerial' interpretation. Their view must be the right one; after all, they are senior!

Why should self-awareness be important? Only by knowing about themselves can people (in this chapter we are concerned with managers) test alternative constructions about the reality which confronts them. Only then can people be invited to become their own 'personal scientists', try on different perceptual goggles and experiment with alternatives for themselves, their staff, company and even customers. This is the process of learning which we believe is essential in the learning organization. It starts with the individual.

We are going to introduce one individual and a group of individuals who have taken the bold step of being personal scientists. They have solved personal and organizational problems through allowing themselves to consider alternatives by taking personal charge of and responsibility for their own psychological processes and behaviours. The examples are drawn from industry and commerce and involve real problems which inhibited personal or management group 'output', performance and reduced morale.

The individual example concerns a middle manager who wanted to change aspects of his personal style in order to be able to be a better manager. Our group example is drawn from a senior management team who found themselves faced with the need to improve their levels of communication and co-operation.

Qualitative assessment of construing

One very useful procedure for data collection and glimpsing a person's processes is a technique Kelly used to deal with his statement that 'if you want to know something about someone, ask them, they may tell you' he called it *self characterization.*

We have used this technique extensively in widely differing work and management contexts from overseas sales performance to heavy engineering production. The following example sticks out as being particularly interesting because nobody knew the nature of the problem!

Let us call the manager in question Alan. He was introduced to us by his own senior managers as a most promising person who for some reason was not living up to his own and others' expectations. The problem was that nobody knew why. He was certainly a valued member of his team, liked by both seniors and subordinates, competent at his job, but yet . . .?

The first stage in the process was to gain his agreement to enter into a joint exploration with us of his 'world of work'. An important aspect of the relationship was the guarantee of confidentiality of the content of our explorations. As with all personal construct interventions our first meeting involved mutual personal introductions and an outline of the techniques and theory which we would be using.

At the end of the first meeting Alan was asked to spend some time before our next meeting in preparing a character sketch. The instructions for writing this type of sketch were very carefully drafted by Kelly as follows:

I want you to write a character sketch of Alan, just as if he were the principal character in a play. Write it as it might be written by a friend who knew him intimately and very sympathetically, perhaps better than anyone ever really could know him. Be sure to write it in the third person. For example, start out by saying 'Harry Brown is . . .' (adapted from Fransella and Bannister 1977).

At our next meeting Alan arrived with his character sketch. It contained few surprises. Indeed it confirmed much of what we all knew—that Alan was a friendly, helpful, conscientious sort of chap. Like most people he had his ups and downs. When on the down side he did his best to explain his position and make himself liked; doesn't everyone?

Our next approach was to look at the sort of constructs he used. According to Kelly's fundamental postulate, our processes are psychologically channelized by the ways in which we anticipate events. So we looked to see if there was anything unusual about Alan's constucts which would lead him to make predictions (and hence behaviours) of a type which other people might find unusual. We used processes of eliciting by triads involving people at work, the data from the self-characterization and laddering to find out the more superordinate, or more personally important constructs. No blinding flashes of inspiration came to either of us.

Something was wrong. Quite simply the investigator was imposing his own construct system on to the investigation of the problem. By putting so much effort into looking *for* something we were missing the obvious. Maybe we should have been looking for the lack of some construing process?

At our next meeting I conducted an experiment. I intentionally made a rather silly comment about something which I knew was within Alan's sphere of specialism. His response was swift and most definite. He very quickly and firmly told me how I had got it wrong, then proceeded to help me with a new and more helpful perspective. Maybe this was it. Alan *could not* sit back, listen, and let others make mistakes or sort out their own problems. He *had* to help by telling people the way forward. We reviewed his self-characterizations (by now he had written a number covering various contexts); not one of them contained any constructs around the area of listening. Of course he listened—but only in so far as it provided him with the lead in to *telling*.

During these various processes Alan had developed his self-confidence. He was now totally aware of himself. His response to this new information was to try some limited behavioural experiments. On occasions he would not comment at all in a conversation. On others he would wait a while, them make his comments and suggestions but with reference to, and including others around him. He became more popular, proficient and efficient. In PCP terms we see this as the individual trying on new constructs and having them validated. Validation is important for enabling the person to incorporate them into his construct system, continue to use them and further elaborate their meaning.

Some important points emerge from this intervention. Firstly, a PCP intervention process does not necessarily require anyone to *give up* aspects of themselves. On the contrary the process is most often one of building. Secondly, personal change becomes easier the more the person knows about him- or herself. Finally, a PCP intervention process keeps the *client* not *the consultant* in control of where he or she is going.

This same process of intervention can be used in any situation where aspects of the person are affecting performance.

The case of Alan describes the use of the 'self-characterization' analysis for just one person. It need not be restricted to such applications. It often forms a valuable addition to team integration process. By getting each member of a team to write their own self-characterizations plus an additional characterization of the team itself, they become more deeply aware of the environment within which they find themselves working.

With a small amount of additional facilitation they may swop their accounts of the team and so learn more about each other's perspective. This is one of the procedures available to managers to monitor change after formal workshops or other interventions.

Quantification of construing with repertory grids

Our second example involves a small management group and their processes of 'learning' how to become a management team. We are not concerned here with mechanical skills of interpersonal interaction, such as would be needed to solve simple puzzles, but with enabling senior managers to operate at a more strategic level by increasing the level of understanding and sharing between them (Critchley and Casey 1984). In order to achieve this objective we have to concern ourselves with the underlying attributes (constructs) of and about the persons involved and how these affect the various role messages—or role episodes, sent and received between them (Katz and Kahn 1978).

Neither are we concerned with any pre-ordained categories of personality, trait or behaviour style. We start instead with a blank sheet upon which to determine the individual role structure(s) and team culture as revealed by the individual's construing systems and the sociality and commonality between them. Only when this is done can we help a person determine where he or she is in relation to his or her ideal about themselves, each other as members of a management team, and the team as a whole. The approach used is both qualitative—what are the values used, and quantitative—how relevant is each construct, how important is it, and to what extent does each member and the team as a whole measure up?

PCP investigations do not end without attempts to understand others by interviewing or listening to them in other ways. Professor Kelly was also a physicist and mathematician. He devised a technique for enabling numbers to be attached to the relationships between the units of his theory—*constructs*—the repertory grid.

Very briefly, a construct is a sort of psychological dimension which defines what something is as well as *what it is not*. It is essentially a *process* of differentiation which goes far beyond the words in which it is described. For example, suppose we present a manager with three *elements* or aspects of his work context as follows:

my job   my ideal job   my boss

If we now ask him to nominate some similarity between any two of these *elements* that makes them different from the third he may say, 'Two of these would *get information and feedback* about what is happening.' Next we ask for the opposite of *get information and feedback*. To which he may reply, '*kept in the dark*'. Thus we have elicited one construct using the 'triadic' method. An important feature of every construct is that one end (pole) will be preferred to the other. People differ from one another and may not always agree about which is the preferred end.

According to the theory, constructs are organized into a system whereby some are more abstract and important (superordinate), others are more concrete and of lesser importance (subordinate). Techniques of interviewing, laddering, pyramiding and elaborating, enable the PCP investigator to uncover much of the structure of a person's 'construing system'.

Repertory grid technique enables us to quantify aspects of a construct system. The procedure is quite simple. Figure 12.1 is a repertory grid sheet designed using some constructs elicited from a manager. The top of the grid contains the *elements*, by name or role title. The column is '*My job now*'. The *constructs* are written at the side.

If the person thought that his job involved 'Getting information and feedback about what was happening' to a maximum extent, he would place a '1' in the appropriate cell for element 1, construct 1. Alternatively if he saw his job as very definitely having 'no idea of what is going on' he would place a '7' in the cell. If there was really nothing to choose between them he might place a '4'. Intermediate ratings of '2' and '3' are degrees of favourability and '5' and '6' degrees of unfavourability. '*My job now*' is rated against each of the constructs in turn.

In the second column is a second heading, '*My job as I would like it to be*'. Each person repeated the procedure exactly as he did for '*My job now*'. There might be up to about twelve different headings (elements) like this, including other members of the management team, and other departments of the company.

But very often you want to know more than just how people see their job and so forth. You want to know just how important each construct is for those individuals. Importance of constructs is measured by placing them in pairs and asking on which the person would be most willing to change from the preferred to the non-preferred side. For instance, would they be more willing to be treated as a child rather than as a responsible adult or to be concerned with 'rules' and 'timekeeping' rather than concerned with quality and output of work. As all constructs are paired with all others in a 'resistance-to-change grid', it is simple to derive a score of the number of times any given construct 'resists change'.

So what happens if you feel strongly about being treated like a child rather than as a responsible, trusted adult? One common response is to behave like a child. 'If that is what they think of me, I'll give them something to complain about.'

It is important to note that interpretation of the relationships between the constructs and their relative importance takes place within the framework of PCP.

A special application of the grid in self-development

If self-development is, in part at least, to take place within a group setting, then the *exchange grid* is extremely useful. This involves each participant completing a grid in which the elements include at least one

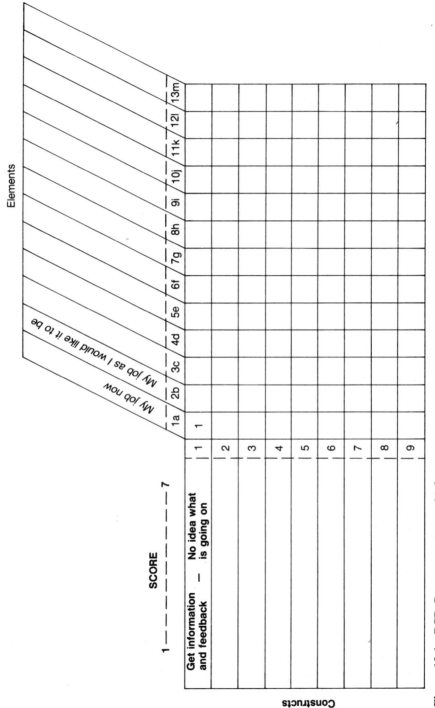

Figure 12.1 PCP Centre repertory grid form

other member than himself—it could be a grid made up of all the other members. In this instance, members are going to work in pairs.

First, up to six constructs may be elicited and laddered as described earlier. Each person then rates his own constructs on the elements using a 5- or 7-point scale.

Next each prepares a blank grid on which their own constructs and elements are written.

Now they go into pairs and fill out their partner's grid *as they think their partner has done*. After this they look at these grids and discuss any discrepancies—or similarities for that matter.

The procedure we used with a management team was a combination of the conventional repertory grid method and the exchange grid described above. Members of the management team were interviewed individually. Constructs about themselves, their jobs, colleagues and the overall context of their management team were elicited using triadic and dyadic methods, and by self-characterization, as described previously. Their construing systems were further investigated by the processes of laddering, and pyramiding in order to obtain constructs across a wide range of superordinacy. These constructs were incorporated into an individual repertory grid which each person completed.

Analysis

We started by looking at the raw data (see Table 12.1). The main issues for consideration in this case were the manager's current perception of his role, his ideal position and his perception of a 'group' role when meeting and working with his colleagues (management team).

How we feel about something, somebody, or even our own situation depends on how closely that person or situation is similar to, or easily described by the preferred pole(s) of our constructs. So to gain a feel for how this manager *felt* about her situation we calculated the mean scores for the elements 'Self in ideal job', 'Self now' and 'Group' (management team) across all constructs.

Element—(person or situation)	Mean score
Self in ideal job	2.00
Self now	3.15
Management team	4.85

Since a score of 1.0 implies that an element is regarded totally favourably, these figures indicate some discrepancy of role perception between self and ideal and an even greater gap between ideal and the

Table 12.1   Repertory grid: raw data for one manager

Pole	/Contrast		*	1	2	3	4	5	6	7	8	9	10	11	12	13	14
deliver service	/fail to deliver	1	*	4	3	6	2	6	4	4	4	5	3	4	2	4	3
selfish	/help others	2	*	6	5	5	6	6	4	6	4	6	4	4	5	5	4
strategic	/seat of pants	3	*	2	2	5	2	3	3	3	5	2	3	4	3	3	3
considerate	/offhand	4	*	5	6	3	6	3	3	4	5	4	5	4	4	4	5
led by market	/business mind	5	*	5	5	4	6	3	3	4	3	6	5	3	6	4	3
controlled	/disorganized	6	*	3	3	6	2	4	5	4	3	5	3	4	2	4	4
honest	/out for self	7	*	3	2	5	2	3	4	3	4	3	3	3	3	3	3
help others achieve	/suppress others	8	*	3	3	5	2	4	5	4	3	4	4	1	3	3	4
worker	/slacker	9	*	2	2	4	2	5	5	2	4	2	4	3	2	4	3
responsible	/irresponsible	10	*	3	2	5	2	4	4	4	3	3	3	4	3	3	4
know own role	/confused	11	*	5	2	6	2	4	5	4	4	2	4	2	5	4	5
confident	/lack confidence	12	*	5	2	5	2	3	3	3	4	2	3	3	5	3	3
good with people	/cuts people out	13	*	3	2	4	2	5	5	3	4	2	3	3	3	3	4

```
                    * * * * * * * * * *   *   *   *  Department Z
                    * * * * * * * * * *   *   *  Colleague G
                    * * * * * * * * * *   *  Colleague F
                    * * * * * * * * * *  Department Y
                    * * * * * * * * *  Colleague E
                    * * * * * * * *  Colleague D
                    * * * * * * *  Colleague C
                    * * * * * *  Colleague B
                    * * * * *  Department X
                    * * * *  Colleague A
                    * * *  Ideal Job
                    * *  Group
                    *  Admired manager
                    Self now
```

Source: Tschudi (1988).

management team. This calculation gives us a feel for how, on average, the person feels about these elements.

However the 'average' may disguise some important underlying frustration. To find out more we need to know the importance of the constructs. Rank order of importance was calculated using a 'resistance to change' grid (see Fransella and Bannister 1977). When the four most personally important constructs only were used and the mean scores recalculated for these constructs only, the results were as follows:

Element—(person or situation)	*Mean score*
Self in ideal job	2.00
Self now	3.25
Management team	5.25

The score for the management team has considerably worsened indicating that the role dislodgement will be even greater due to the relatively greater importance of these constructs.

These mean scores alone do not tell us about the implications of the role dislodgement.

In order to estimate the implications of the role dislodgement on the behaviour and feelings of this manager a principal components analysis (Tschudi 1988) was performed on her individual repertory grid to reveal the construct and element relationships.

Such analyses provide easily interpreted *meaning* to the complexity of personal grid data. It combines all construct relationships with the elements in such a way that self, ideal and 'group' are seen in the context of the whole (see Figure 12.2).

In this diagram the *ideal, self* and management team (*group*) can be seen in a more or less straight line with perceptions of ideal and management team lying at the opposing extremes. The perception of *self now* is somewhat in the middle, slightly on the preferred side of most constructs.

We can see clearly from this plot that the manager wishes personally to develop or be more like her ideal and the *admired manager*, but when she has to work with her colleagues she has to accommodate an environment which *she perceives* as being more like the *opposite* of her preferred self.

When the results of the analysis were fed back to this person she found some comfort in the *knowledge* of why she found working with her colleagues so uncomfortable.

The process was repeated with all other members of the team. Not surprisingly the results were similar. Not only in terms of the unfavourable nature of the perception of the management team, but also in terms of the actual constructs which emerged. This similarity of construing might have been predicted through Kelly's commonality and sociality corollaries and by a view of the 'team' as a cultural entity as defined by Schein (1985). Indeed Schein describes the existence of value hierarchies within cultures in a similar way to the personal construct hierarchies described by Kelly.

With so much similarity between members of the management team it was a simple procedure to combine the common aspects of their repertory grids and produce a common team perspective.

At this stage we had derived a picture of the management team's culture in terms of its underlying values, the view each person held of him- or herself and their anticipations of what it meant to work with each other. The curious fact is that each person thought him- or herself to be

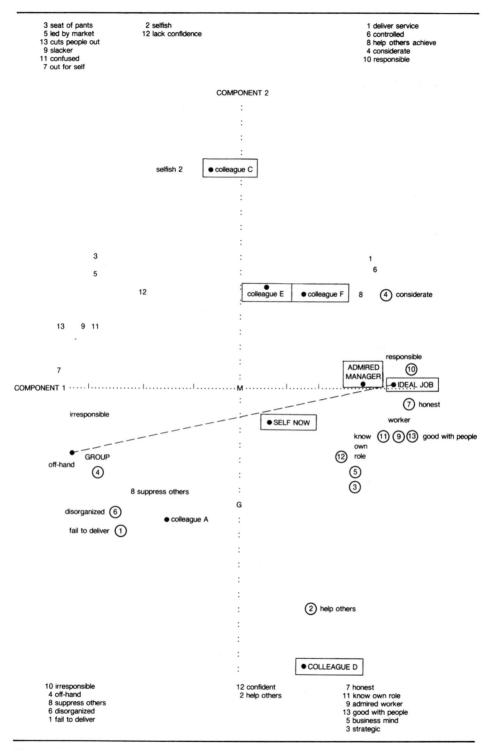

Figure 12.2 Principal components analysis plot (simplified)

more or less alright. They even thought of each other *individually* in reasonably positive terms. It was the dynamics of the *group* that was unacceptable to them.

Our problem was that no one person could be identified as being the cause or origin of this non-preferred culture. Nevertheless we can predict from personal construct theory that individuals who find themselves forced by outside pressures to be the opposite of how they wish to be will suffer anxiety. They will also try to reduce risks to themselves by stopping involvement in the management team context. And this is exactly what was happening.

In just the same way as personal change involves individuals knowing more about themselves, so it is vital for any team to be aware of its culture—each other individual's 'construing system' and the interactions between each other and the team itself. To achieve this a workshop was held in which the whole team participated. They were introduced to personal construct theory's philosophy of constructive alternativism, in terms of the problem that faced them. That is nobody among them was a prisoner of that situation; each was free to rethink his or her own and the team situation; each could adapt and change *if he or she wished*. All that was needed was the data and a framework within which to plan the changes.

The event was heavily task-based with occasional emphasis on construing processes—we were after all solving a team problem and not teaching psychology!

Together we worked through the interpretation of the repertory grid computer analysis of the construing of the whole group. At the same time each manager looked at his or her own results and reflected on any similarities and dissimilarities. Finally, they were led to look on themselves as a 'cultural group' and take personal and group responsibility for the origins of the emergent culture. More importantly each person started to see how others in the group could hold alternative perspectives of the same event(s). These alternatives were of course judged against each person's own set of perceptive 'goggles'.

The remainder of the workshop involved each person getting to know his or her colleagues. Initially there were protestations that 'of course we know each other, we've worked together for years'. But the data from the grids said not. People often need an excuse or reason to get to know each other. To help the individuals to break the ice the personal repertory grids were intially used as a source of data.

Table 12.2 shows the extent to which the people or elements fit into the personal construct model which the individual has of the group or team environment. In this case principal components have accounted for only

Table 12.2 An individual repertory grid: factor scores

		Vbl	1	2	Dist-n	:	Dist	Var-r	Acc
A	Self now	1	−0.443	0.301	0.536	:	0.340	0.689	16.770
B	Admired manager	2	−1.502	0.046	1.503	:	1.085	1.322	89.103
C	Group	3	2.008	0.666	2.116	:	1.473	2.527	85.812
D	Ideal job	4	−1.922	−0.002	1.922	:	1.389	2.002	96.354
E	Colleague A	5	0.959	1.053	1.424	:	0.799	1.145	55.737
F	Department X	6	1.346	−0.088	1.349	:	0.973	1.304	72.619
G	Colleague B	7	0.012	0.967	0.967	:	0.365	0.297	44.971
H	Colleague C	8	0.544	−1.814	1.894	:	0.790	0.835	74.689
I	Colleague D	9	−0.609	2.273	2.353	:	0.965	1.093	85.092
J	Colleague E	10	−0.230	−0.794	0.826	:	0.343	0.343	34.281
K	Department Y	11	0.009	−0.962	0.962	:	0.363	0.924	14.289
L	Colleague F	12	−0.514	−0.826	0.973	:	0.485	0.944	24.944
M	Colleague G	13	0.022	0.026	0.033	:	0.018	0.111	0.303
N	Department Z	14	0.321	−0.846	0.904	:	0.394	0.465	33.490

0.303 per cent of the variance in the scores attributed to colleague G. So why is colleague G different? Like the stranger in the room referred to earlier on, can he be anticipated? What better opportunity to go and ask. Thus each team member was given the right to introduce themselves to somebody they previously thought they knew.

Initially, heavy use was made of the personal and grouped repertory grid results, but soon everyone graduated to observed behaviours at work. Previously taboo areas were opened up. At the end of the day the whole group went away with a group action plan *and* a series of *personal* plans for small personal changes and better understanding of each other. In addition they took with them techniques for asking questions in a non-threatening manner and for really listening to the answers and seeing the possibility that their colleague has a different *but equally valid* alternative view of the same reality.

Epiloque

This team continues to monitor its own progress. It has initiated mechanisms for exchanging ideas and sharing feelings, a new process which has allowed them to be more creative. In addition to these informal interpersonal processes, a formal monitoring process has been set up.

The team reports an easing of interpersonal relationships, fewer but more efficient and effective meetings, and more rapid decision-making processes. There is less departmental thinking and a more co-operative holistic approach. Their new 'goggles' have revealed new realities.

Conclusion

We believe that PCP provides the conceptual framework and techniques for helping people find out about themselves, to design processes for personal change and learning, and for actually putting those strategies into effect.

References

Critchley, W. and D. Casey (1984) 'Second thoughts on team building, *Management Education and Development*, **15**(2), 163–175.

Fransella, F. and D. Bannister (1977) *A Manual for Repertory Grid Technique*, Academic Press, London.

Katz, D. and R. L. Kahn (1978) *The Social Psychology of Organizations*, John Wiley & Sons, Chichester.

Kelly, G. A. (1955) *The Psychology of Personal Constructs*, W. W. Norton, New York.

Schein E. H. (1985) *Organizational Culture and Leadership*, Jossey-Bass, San Francisco, Washington, London.

Tschudi, F. (1988) *FLEXIGRID v. 4.4*, University of Oslo, Norway.

Part III   The future: challenges and questions

Introduction

If the tendency in Part II of this book was to suggest that individual self-development can be usefully harnessed with collective organizational goals, Part III tends to bring out the essential tension between the two and illustrates that the problem posed by Argyris thirty yeas ago and quoted in the Preface is still strongly with us. Here we move from the firm ground of ideas that work to the messy world of unresolved issues.

The first four contributions focus upon differences. Chapter 13 illustrates dramatically the possible organizational consequences of undertaking self-development without prior thoughts about 're-entry',while Jacky Underwood works with inner variety and how you can make this work for you. Pauline Kidd and Sally Watson handle the 'hot potato' of women's development in the male world of management, as do Maggie Smith and Janice Leary who widen the perspective to wonder if opportunities will ever be equal in work organizations.

The final three chapters in the book address the themes of learning community and learning company. The first is exampled as a design for short development programmes while the ambition of the last two extends to creating the whole of a learning organization. If these are a fair sample of work on this theme then the public sector, and perhaps particularly the health service, is at the forefront of the developments. John Edmonstone's points that the public services tend to be both bureaucratic in form and yet full of autonomous professionals, thus creating massive managerial problems of ambiguity over goals, task obsession and low risk taking, are well made. There are no simple solutions to these problems. Does the learning organization offer a way forward?

13
Organizational effectiveness and self-development: the essential tension
Robert Adlam and Michael Plumridge

Introduction

One of the basic predicaments for an individual is: 'Am I to live for myself or am I to live for others?' And, similarly, one of the basic predicaments for an organization is: 'How far can we, as a collective, demand the effort and energy of our constituent individuals without creating a disabling alienation from their personal and social needs?'

In his analysis of personal distress, John Heron exposes the heart of this problem with characteristic power and simplicity:

Persons can only be persons in relation. They can only realise their authentic personal needs in corporate systems of interdependence, in coherent and stable social structures which, by virtue of their nature, tend to be conservative. I postulate that, even in the most enlightened organisational development, tension and conflict will arise on the interface between individual need and corporate purpose. What makes an organisation enlightened is that it has built-in procedures for acknowledging such conflict and working constructively with it (Heron 1977: 7)

While Heron grasps the nature of the problem, we believe that his analysis falls short of addressing two additional points. Thus, it is our contention that the procedures an organization develops for enabling effective individual and organizational progress are massively dependent on the skills and techniques—in practice—of enablement *and* the fundamental value stances of the individual and the organization.

Further, in the light of the recent persuasive analyses by Garratt (1987) and Pedler, Burgoyne and Boydell (1988) concerning the relationship between 'learning' and organizational survival, we believe that contemporary organizations must learn to learn from the experiences of their constituent members and must learn to unlock the powers and energies of their members through enabling rather than disabling structures.

These issues concerning the tension between individual and organizational development constituted the fundamental 'ground' against which we set out to study the problem of organizational effectiveness and self-development. In the first instance, in our exploration of this problem, we drafted out some simple preliminary ideas. We began by reflecting upon the existential situation confronting an individual within any organization. Our thinking took the following course: the constant problem for individuals is how to get their needs met. The vast majority (and, in a sense, *all*) can only be met in collaboration with others; the individual is necessarily enmeshed in a world of others. The eternal dilemma for individuals is that, once they embark upon social relationships, this very act demands the surrender of their individuality—to some degree.

This 'surrender' involves the modification not only of behaviour but also of their most deeply held values and beliefs. In consequence, organizations inevitably produce an identity crisis for the individual. Fundamental existential questions such as 'Who am I to be?', 'What can I become?', 'What am I becoming?' are always—at some level—on the individual's agenda.

The corollary of this problem from the standpoint of the organization is how to achieve organizational effectiveness by utilising the maximum potential effectiveness of its individual constituent members. Organizational effectiveness implies a strong sense of a shared common purpose or, at the very least, the removal of constraints which may stand in the way of achieving individual effectiveness. In order to achieve this, the organization must develop a climate in which the needs of its members carry at least equal weight as its market position; it must have sophisticated mechanisms and, perhaps more importantly, sophisticated behaviours, for seeking, listening to, interpreting and taking account of the needs and aspirations of its individual members; it must be able to enable, energize, empower and empathize with each of them.

Developing an appropriate workshop design

When we were asked to mount a workshop at the Lancaster conferenceon self-development, we were faced by the problem of how to address these issues which none the less we both approached from different perspectives, but which constituted the central problem for each of us. One of us embraced the perspective of a humanistic psychologist and personal growth facilitator; the other, that of a management and organizational developer. Both of us had arrived at the conclusion outlined above by our own logical and experiential means, although they have been extensively documented elsewhere (e.g. Argyris 1957, 1964; Schein 1985; Heron 1977 and forthcoming; Pedler 1989).

Everyone seems to be aware of them and their implications for the transfer of learning and for the effectiveness of organizations. Why is it then, *if the issues are so well understood*, that the associated problems are so persistent, and apparently so intractable? Why is it that people who quite evidently 'know' about the problem find it difficult to adjust their behaviour in ways to help overcome it?

Such, then, were our considerations as we reflected upon the problem of producing an experiential design which would explore the relationship between self-development on the one hand and organizational effectiveness of the other. From the outset we had the notion of splitting the group of participants into two halves, one which would be a group of 'self-developers' (who would undergo a challenging self-developing experience), the other an 'organization group' about to receive the group of self-developers back into the organizational compass. *The crux of the experience would lie in the interfacing of the two groups and the subsequent reflection and review.*

There were several constraints to be taken into account. The first of these was, 'time'; the conference organizers could give us no more than two hours. The second was that we would be competing 'in the marketplace', i.e. the open forum of the entire conference, with four other workshops to be run in parallel; we needed, therefore, a marketing and sales strategy. The third was a lack of control over accommodation; we would not predict the kind of environment in which we would have to work. In addition, there was the different problem of having no control over the number of people who would opt into our workshop; if we had less than 6 it would hardly be viable for designing a rich learning experience; if, on the other hand it were to be more than 20 it would be extremely difficult for two facilitators to manage. Even if we were to obtain an ideal number which we estimated to be between 12 and 20, we would have to cater for the fact that we would be dealing with experienced and well-informed participants who would be very keen to learn, and who would be looking for a very demanding learning environment.

What we were seeking then, in our design, were three crucial ingredients. First, it must be a significant experience from which people could learn. Second, it must in some way mirror the ways in which people in organzations interact in dealing with certain kinds of problems. Finally, it should provide an authentic personal experience wherein personal insights would be raised and enhanced personal development would be sought. This latter requirement was formidable.

In terms of both structuring a learning event and building in a real learning design the following model was created:

Stage 1 Introduction and climate setting (whole conference open forum)—15 minutes.

Stage 2 The group to be sub-divided into Organization Group (henceforward O) and Self-Development Group (henceforward SD); attractive alternatives for membership in each group were to be offered—10 minutes.

Stage 3 The two groups O and SD to work in parallel, O considering what an organization needs to do in order to support self-development and to prepare to handle the re-entry of SD, and SD to undergo a significant self-development experience—60 minutes.

Stage 4 Interface between the two groups, i.e. the re-entry with O group holding the initiative—20 minutes.

Stage 5 Self-development group reflects and responds.

Stage 6 Whole group, i.e. O and SD group together, debrief, reflect, and review personal learning—20 minutes.

This design was created, not only to manage the constraints and challenges presented by the conference structure and participants, but also to remain true to a number of our fundamental educational principles including trust in the ability of persons to learn from experience and confidence in a group of adult learners to invent, and implement their own designs and structures.

Running the workshop

This process will now be elaborated upon in order that the reader may get a feel for what happened and how participants responded.

The two groups O and SD were duly constituted. The facilitator in the SD group, with a number of reassurances and ground rules, set a relaxed and supportive climate and brought the group into a highly aware 'here and now' state of mind by means of a short *gestalt* (noticing) exercise. They were reassured that it was 'okay' to forget constraints and anxieties.

He then led them through a guided fantasy commencing with an invitation to recapture their experiences as 'a six year old' focusing on three elements:

1. establishing a picture of the kind of child they were, e.g. to imagine general descriptions that they might apply to themselves;
2. imagining their situation and feelings at family events—such as, for example, Sunday lunch;
3. remembering thoughts and feelings of their position in school.

He then said that he was going to ask them, in a few minutes time, to draw pictures of those impressions in whatever symbolic way they chose. They were then brought gently back from the fantasy into the 'here and now' by means of some breathing exercises, and some preparation for becoming fully present in the 'here and now', in readiness for drawing their 'pictures'. At this point the facilitator offered two examples, which he himself had drawn symbolizing his own childhood. Each individual then set about the task with great intensity and commitment. Upon completion the facilitator asked them to analyse their pictures in four dimensions; what did they 'mean' in terms of:

- inclusion v. exclusion
- control v. being controlled
- affection v. indifference or hostility
- engulfment v. isolation

Once this analysis had been completed, they were asked to look for insights in terms of 'what aspects of your relating at six years old do you bring to your present ways of relating in groups?' They were then asked to reflect upon their personal effectiveness by asking themselves: which of these would enable one to be more effective in groups, and which patterns might need to be transformed in order to be more effective in groups?

Meanwhile, the organization group had split into two separate O groups. Once they had acquired flipchart paper and pens they happily set about discussing and listing very comprehensive support mechanisms which the organization would need to provide. This exercise, which was well and thoroughly carried out, sprang largely from the 'head' rather than from the heart. Occasionally, one member would remember the forthcoming interface and ask, 'But what are we actually going to *do* when we meet them?' Such interventions drew responses such as 'Well, listen of course! But we'll just have to play it off the cuff.' As they began to realize the probable difficulties of the re-entry meeting there was a tendency to criticize the design of the workshop by saying such things as,

'But in real life we would have held a briefing with them before they went away on the self-development programme.' There was even support for one member who said, 'We paid good money for this programme and we must make sure we get our pound of flesh in return!'

By the time the interface came around the O groups had constructed a substantial list of support mechanisms (see Figure 13.1) but were largely unprepared for the face-to-face meeting itself. (Because the 'O' group had split into two, the SD group was asked by the facilitator to divide itself into two groups.)

And so we reached stage 4 and the meetings duly arrived. Both developed in quite different ways but the outcomes were largely similar; that is, suspicion, hostility, frustration and conflict were generated. The two 'sides' missed each other by a wide margin.

Proceedings in one group were certainly not helped by the fact that the meeting had to take place in the room where the SD group had carried out their artwork, and there it was—arranged over the floor. As the O group entered one of them was heard loudly and lightheartedly to say, 'Oh look, a Picasso!' This remark, naturally produced instantaneous resentment and hostility and the 'meeting' never really took off; the SD group was thereafter in no mood to be 'interviewed'. In the other group the O group were much more earnest and really

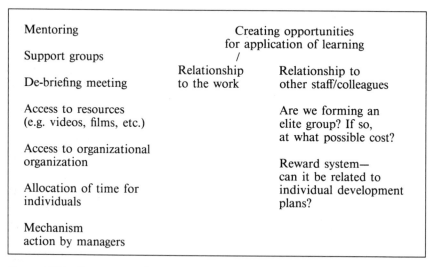

Figure 13.1 Support mechanisms

Note: This was the model of support systems created by one of the 'O' groups and their notions are—at least in part—congruent with contemporary ideas for enabling personal and organizational development.

wanted to understand the experience which the SD group had undergone. Unfortunately the latter were still needing space to reflect upon their personal learning and the more insistent the O group became in 'wanting to help' the more the self-developers grew increasingly irritated until one of them exploded: 'For God's sake, get off my back!' The O group showed great patience and persistence, however, and eventually a woman member of the SD group tried to help them by showing her picture and interpreting it in terms of her needs. She had grown up in a Nigerian village with a great deal of space around her and when she came to share her insights and said with some passion, 'I feel so frustrated and claustrophobic when shut up in an office in this 'organization', the O group were left speechless and the meeting petered out.

This 'speechlessness' appeared to be induced by a number of factors. In the first place, both frustration and fatigue were taking a hold as the O group had tried very hard to approach the problem from many angles. Secondly, there was considerable evidence of mounting truculence and an attitude of 'you wouldn't understand anyway!' from the SD group. Furthermore the final statement of the last speaker seemed to defy any possible organizational reply. It seemed that several of the O group had turned in on themselves in bewilderment at their own apparent impotence and were reflecting upon this quite awesome experience; it is possible that they were so overwhelmed by their empathy with the last speaker that they no longer felt capable of fulfilling their organizational roles.

By the time that the whole group came together in order to debrief and review the whole exercise little of the allotted two hours remained and we now had nearly twice as many subgroup experiences (because of the various subdivisions) to debrief than we had catered for in the design.

There was still a good deal of tension about but there was also a great deal of personal reflection going on. Many were amazed at what had happened, i.e. the tremendous difficulties encountered in the interface groups, and it was quite evident that many participants had derived insights into the focal issue of the workshop, i.e. the tensions underlying the relationship between self-development and organization needs.

In addition, participants had begun to identify the kinds of attitudes and behaviours necessary for enabling personal growth within organizations. One woman put this particularly well by suggesting to a number of participants that the word 'delicacy' described the manner in which organizations should interface with individuals.

Learnings

In the light of the experience of this workshop, and two subsequent applications of the design, a number of lessons emerge:

1. Unless those responsible for supporting the growth and development of others in the organization are themselves actively engaged in their own self-development they cannot actually tune in to the quality of the experiences of self-developing others. Nor can they begin to understand or implement the support and helping skills which are needed. In the absence of such help and support the self-developer is liable to lose both the heart and the will to persist with and to implement any action plans which they had in mind.

2. Even if those responsible for developing others and themselves are active self-developers the interface with those returning from a self-development programme requires skills of very high order. These include listening, empathizing, reflecting, confronting skilfully, and the use of sensitive and appropriate questions. These skills are not easily or quickly acquired and if an organization is to place itself in a situation to support self-developing employees it will initially have to invest heavily in a cadre of highly skilled developers who can give the necessary support to those others embarking on the self-development route. To emphasize this point it will be recalled that these who participated in this workshop at the conference on self-development were, for the most part, sophisticated and experienced trainers and consultants to whom these are foundation skills. Even they experienced great difficulty, and failed to connect effectively and harmoniously with re-entrant self-developers. How much more difficult, then, is it going to be for managers who may well be less skilled and less experienced, especially if the situation is complicated by hierachical differences?

3. The responsibility for self-development also lies in large part with the self-developer, including responsibility for re-entry into the organization. This is easy to forget, in a supportive and permissive 'course' environment. It is also easy to forget the realities and constraints of organizational life. We would contend that trainers and developers must pay close attention to this problem where they explore the 'transfer of learning'. In our experience this element of training remains undeveloped although the work of Egan (1985) is an exception.

    Nevertheless only the individual self-developer can really know the 'back-home' situation and it is incumbent upon them to empathize with others in that situation and to make realistic adjustments to their behaviour and expectations. Sensitivity, empathy and awareness of the needs and difficulties of others are crucial skills and attributes to be forged in the self-developer.

Interestingly, Lyons (1988) in her work, *Constructive Criticism*, offers some useful suggestions in this respect for self-development generally. Lyons argues that 'individualism' as a value is ultimately unhealthy and that interactions between persons should be predicated upon the need to 'protect and educate'. We would argue that a fundamental principle underpinning the activities of self-development is that of citizenship. We mean by this a commitment to 'giving and receiving', a recognition that 'the whole is greater than the sum of its parts', and a willingness to understand the tragedies of the human condition.

As we have said earlier, development is a two-way process; the self-developer must constantly be aware of the 'greater good', i.e. the needs of the organization as a whole. Those responsible for the integration of the entire organizational system are frequently faced by unpredicted, and indeed often unpredictable, market or socio/political/economic forces which call for a sharp organizational focus. In such circumstances, the developmental needs of the individual are apt to receive short shrift; perhaps, quite legitimately so. It is, however, incumbent upon higher management, in these circumstances, to make it known to all organizational personnel that they are aware of the sacrifices being asked of them. It is also incumbent upon individuals to perceive and to accept, that there is such a thing as the 'greater good'. It follows that part of the process of self-development within an organization is to acknowledge an organizational perspective on problems.

4. Both parties in the re-entry situation, i.e. the self-developer and the organization representative, need time and space to prepare for re-engagement. Anyone returning from any course is likely to need time to integrate what has been learned into their own frame of reference and there may be a whole residue of issues raised on the course which have not been fully absorbed, understood or interpreted. If the course has been a useful self-development experience, considerable space and time may be necessary for such reflection, interpretation and integration. Frequently, quite fundamental values, ideas, and the implications of behaviour patterns may have been brought into question: hence, much work will be needed for quite radical personal reassessments and life/work planning. This process can be greatly assisted by a skilled organizational counsellor who concentrates on helping self-developers come to terms with all of

this, and does not hurry them into quick decisions, nor attempt at this vulnerable stage, to produce or impose convenient organizational solutions. One possible consequence of this turbulence for the learner may be that, in the short term at any rate, performance will not change (it may even decline!) before eventually rising to a new and higher level.

5. The ultimate cost of any organization as a learning system is the extent to which it can reconcile individual and organizational needs in such a way as to release and support the inherent energy and creativity of its individual members. This is unlikely to happen unless the organization holds and demonstrates such a value by providing an infrastructure capable of supporting it and the will, the wit and the skill to implement it.

Thoughts for further development of the design

The briefing of the organization group needs to be tight and to stress that participants should not adopt organizational roles but should take on the problem as faced by a typical organization. We also feel that, with hindsight, we might have offered this group the opportunity to have one of its member briefed by the facilitator on the aims and methods of the self-development workshop prior to event. More seriously, we would not again attempt such a workshop within the span of two hours and would regard three hours as the bare minimum; the main reason for this is that far too little time was spent on the debrief and review. The experience had evidently been so powerful that the atmosphere was laden with uncertainty, doubt, and the desire to talk; unfortunately we did not have time to work with all this data. Furthermore, we had scarcely begun to extract learning outcomes. To this extent we were disappointed with our efforts. There was, in fact, the need for a much more thorough exploration of participants' learning.

Discussion

The results obtained from this workshop design raise a number of issues for the processes of management and organization development. In this final part of our work we intend to focus on some of these. From our perspective, development is not something which an organization can do *to* its members nor can organizational leaders (with or without the help of consultants) do it *to* their organization. It is, rather, a process which has to be carried out *with* people and, unless we have some investment in maintaining individuals in states of psychological dependency, we believe that the developmental process is most likely to succeed if opportunities are provided for individuals to 'work things out for themselves'. For us, there appears to be no real alternative to helping individuals define, own and solve *their* problems. Not surprisingly, when such a process is followed, individuals often perceive and define problems differently from their managers; choose very individual (and often idiosyncratic) ways of approaching their solutions and come up with solutions which do not conform with those of their managers and of their organization. The reconciling of such different perspectives and the ensuing potential conflict requires from those entrusted with the management of others, social and 'people' skills of the highest order. And, furthermore, at the heart of such skills, lies the capacity to project oneself into the world, or the frame of reference, of the other. This is a prerequisite for any authentic helping process. To this extent, we commend the perspectives outlined by the late Carl Rogers (Rogers, 1961; 1980).

Similarly, we would want to say that Gerard Egan's work *The Skilled Helper* (1986) offers a powerful working model of enablement and demonstrates clearly the importance of gaining access to the psychological terrain of another person's world. How, then, can organizations be helped to embark upon such processes?

While we are aware of spectrum of possible strategies ranging from interventions into the operational and task systems of organizations to the more therapeutic emphases of individual sensitivity training, we would want to highlight, in the first instance, two broad strategies for enhancing individual development. The first approach is essentially skill-based. Through an interpersonal skills programme, participants have the opportunity to discover the ways in which they interact with others and the types of effect they have upon persons. Although the focus of such approaches is upon skill-acquisition and skill-building, there are the inevitable confrontations with oneself-as-the-interactor. In consequence, deeper shifts in values, attitudes and beliefs are made possible.

Alternatively, individuals can pursue self-development through personal growth experiences, groups and courses. In this case, deeper personal transformations provide the background against which developing skill performance may be enacted.

We believe that the pressures and problems of organizational life alienate us from the inner world. Rather than addressing our inner life, we focus on the outer world. But, in our opinion, the process of achieving a balance between the inner and the outer world actually *promotes* a valuing of others, a desire to help and an appreciation of community.

Hence an organizational culture valuing the process of inner reflection or an organizational culture permitting a process of 'inner-dwelling' is to be encouraged.

We also believe that 'turning inwards' is not sufficient of itself. It is in the very act of trying to help others that we are likely to be allowed a sense of their inner selves—of their thoughts, values and feelings; and, that process unlocks for us many insights into our own selves. It is as if, in the process of other characterization, that we achieve some purchase on self-characterization. This opening of others to self and self to others is a prerequisite for reciprocal behaviour and therefore the foundation stone of our own growth and development. Opportunities for such behaviour are constantly with us if we choose to take them.

From the organization's point of view, the crucial issue becomes its capacity to develop, support and underpin the learning and development of its individual members. Clearly, the role of organizational leaders and managers is fundamental in this respect. As Bradford and Cohen (1984: 8) have said: 'There must be the commitment to help people reach their potential and to support their efforts to improve ... The situation does not require a totally skilled leader but a leader who is willing to learn to become more skilled.' It should be noted that this stance goes beyond the acquisition of skills and depends upon a value position which states: 'I can always learn to do things better and I can learn from anyone.'

We would simply wish to note here that, for us, the value stance of leaders, managers and indeed of persons generally, is the primary concern. The current debate (Charter Group Initiative 1987) in management circles around so-called competencies and their development is apt either to make assumptions about the values underpinning such competencies or to overlook them altogether. This causes us very real anxiety. For us the development of applied ethics represents a very real departure for the promotion of each organization's health and effectiveness.

In our experience, we need, at the organizational level, to create a caring, supportive culture which will enable and empower people to become all that they are capable of becoming if we are to free them from the sickness of alienation and the plague of inertia. In this respect, we find Schein's work (Schein 1984; 1985) on organizational cultures a seminal framework for any fundamental development of an organization's purposes and values. Clearly though, Schein leaves us with no illusions as to the magnitude of the task. Similarly, we strongly support the approaches of Bradford and Cohen (1984) and Harrison (1983) with regard to their prescriptions concerning organizational 'spirit' and climate.

We believe that only by creating a caring, supportive culture will organizations be able to transform themselves into learning systems capable of innovation and constant self-renewal. The acid test of their capacity for such self-renewal will lie in the ways they approach the issues raised by the learning design used in this workshop. That is to say, do they really have the values necessary for them to be truly committed to learning, development and support *and* do they have the skills to provide the environment to help constituent members derive learning from their work and life experience?

To end on a poignant yet provocative note: A writer on police organizations once described her attempts to introduce a change process as 'bending granite'. Interestingly however, we know that if we penetrate the structure of matter we discover a fantastic world of fluidity, flexibility and power. We take this as an optimistic metaphor.

References

Argyris, C. (1957) *Personality and Organizations*, John Wiley & Sons, New York.
— (1964) *Integrating the Individual and the Organization*, John Wiley & Sons, New York.
Bradford, D. L. and A. E. Cohen (1984) *Managing for Excellence: The Guide to Developing High Performance in Contemporary Organizations*, John Wiley & Sons, New York.
Charter Group Initiative (1987) FME/CBI/BIM, London.
Egan, G. (1985) *The Skilled Helper*, Brooks/Cole Boston.
Garratt, R. (1987) *The Learning Organization*, Fontana/Collins, London.
Harrison, R. (1983) 'Strategies for a new Era' in *Human Resource Management*-Fall 22(3), 209–35c 1985, John Wiley & Sons, New York.
Heron, J. (1977) *Catharsis in Human Development* Human Potential Research Group, University of Surrey, England.
— (forthcoming) *Dimensions of Facilitator Style*, Human Potential Research Group, University of Surrey, England.
Lyons, G. (1988) *Constructive Criticism*, Wingbow Press, California.
Pedler, M. (1987) *Applying Self-Development in Organizations*, Manpower Services Commission, Sheffield.
— (1989) Personal communication.
— T. Boydell and J. Burgoyne (1988) *Learning Company Project Report'* Manpower Services Commission, Sheffield.
Rogers, C. (1961) *On Becoming a Person*, Constable, London.
— (1980) *A Way of Being*, Houghton Mifflin Co, New York.
Schein, E. H. (1984) Coming to a new awareness of organizational culture, *Sloan Management Review* 25, 3–16.
— (1985) *Organizational Culture and Leadership*, Jossey-Bass, San Francisco.

14
Your inner team: dealing with internal differences
Jacky Underwood

Introduction

My aim in this chapter is to assist those who wish to clear the internal blockages which are hindering their effectiveness in dealing with others. The method is through getting to know and negotiate with your 'inner team' of sub-personalities—the different aspects of yourself which manifest themselves as discrete patterns of behaviour. The text is interspersed with exercises which are crucial to the learning. The different stages are: recognizing your ability to switch role and behaviour, identifying your helping and hindering behaviour patterns, finding out the positive intent of 'negative' patterns in order to release the energy for productive purposes, and negotiating with your inner team over internal conflicts and differences. Each section is illustrated with examples drawn from my own experience and from the reports of those who have used the concepts and exercises with me in training events.

We all play many different roles in our lives. Most of us will be aware to an extent of how our behaviour varies as we move from one role to another. For example, some people will experience themselves as confident and assertive at work, shy and retiring in social situations; others have the reverse experience. A man may be conscious that, as a son, he acts differently than as a husband or as a father. A woman, burdened by the double load of responsibilities at home and at work, may be able to access the playful, light-hearted side of herself only when deep in a creative hobby or personal interest. These various 'selves' are our 'sub-personalities', so termed since each has its own distinctive behavioural traits, posture, gestures, tone of voice. We normally shift from one to another without thinking, as if guided by some inner knowing which assesses which sub-personality is appropriate to the circumstances. These different patterns of behaviour, and the motivational drives underlying them, give us our potential for responding flexibly and creatively.

The potential is there—and yet, many of us can experience difficulties both with becoming aware of how we are behaving at any given moment and, also, in controlling and choosing a behaviour appropriate to the situation and context. So, at times, it can seem as if I am actively hindering myself, preventing myself from working effectively or communicating clearly and directly with other people. At other times, the self-sabotage pattern may take the form of an internal 'stuckness', an unaccountable inability to act on a project dear to one's heart, or a sense of being undermined by one's own negativity.

My purpose in this chapter is to introduce you to the concept of sub-personalities so that you can begin to work with the positive energy of your various behaviour patterns. You will be familiar with the idea of team-building: a group that needs to work closely together commits itself to an honest self-appraisal so that the full resources of the team may be harnessed to its purpose. When you get to know your sub-personalities, you are accessing the power of your 'inner team', ensuring that the different aspects of yourself pull together rather than pull you apart.

The method which I described for identifying and communicating with your sub-personalities is one you can use for yourself and in working with other people. *It is important that you go through the processes and exercises.* Reading alone is not sufficient. As you read, you may well find your imagination responding, conjuring up ideas, images, different sensations. These are useful, yet they only touch the surface of the riches which your sub-personalities will present to you once you devote quality time to the exercises. Some aspects of our sub-personalities derive from the way we are socialized into our everyday roles in life, others derive from our unconscious minds. By going through the processes I describe, you allow these hidden parts of yourself to speak—and these are the parts which hold the key to releasing your full potential.

Sub-personalities

The term sub-personality is derived from a school of psychotherapy called psychosynthesis (Assagioli 1986). The concept is adapted here for use in personal and management development settings. Those who are familiar with transactional analysis (Stewart and Vann Joinnes 1987) will readily grasp the basic idea, which is that we all use different aspects of our selves ('ego states' in TA) in our daily interactions with others, moving from one to another without thinking. The TA model links these different states of our selves to stages in the development cycle, referring to 'parent', 'adult', and 'child'. We can, for example, faced with an authority figure, find ourselves responding in a 'childish' way—either rebellious or compliant. The ideas as used in psychosynthesis work with a wider cast of characters, assuming that our character traits are derived from social, organizational, and cultural influences as well as from the family. Our sub-personalities, then, are behaviour patterns organized around the different roles or functions we play in our lives.

Exercise 1 Listing roles

Stop reading now, take a sheet of paper, and list on it the various roles you play in your life at present. Think of yourself at work, at home, in relation to friends and relatives, in the local community, in relation to your leisure pursuits, and you as you are when alone and away from the demands and expectations of others.

Look down the list again and conjure up some sense of yourself in each role. Can you hear yourself speaking? Can you get a picture of yourself sitting, moving about? How does it feel to be you in that role? Make brief notes of what you discover and, in particular, notice what happens as you transfer from one role to another.

A frequent reaction to this exercise is to realize how unaware we are of our different selves, and also how we usually manage to keep them very separate, assuming a particular 'persona' (Greek for mask) according to the context. Sometimes we 'forget' to switch masks as we move from one situation to another. A common example is when, at the end of a tense and busy day at work, we whisk through the front door at home issuing terse demands to our nearest and dearest. This happens, paradoxically, just at that time when we most need to call forth love and support, and to give it, rather than to run the risk of setting up yet another situation full of tension and resistance.

An element of habit, of routine, in our day-to-day interactions can be functional. Certainly, it helps ourselves and others to find security and stability in knowing the 'rules of the game', 'how things are done around here'. Yet, as Rosemary Stewart (Stewart 1982) points out, managers' low awareness of how they do their jobs tends to limit their choices and the range of strategies available to them. With only a small amount of practice we can raise our level of awareness and watch our different 'selves' in action. Having ready access to this 'observing self', as it is termed, increases our ability to make conscious choices about what we might do in any given interaction.

This is particularly useful when we wish to deal with those sub-personalities which seem to pop up unbidden, as if from nowhere, often at the most inconvenient of times. An example of this might be when, under pressure and only semi-conscious of my own state of unease, I start blaming others for my predicament, either by whingeing and moaning, or through angry outbursts. At such times, it can seem as if, through inappropriate and uncharacteristic behaviour, one sub-personality has decided to sabotage the good work being done by another. There are a number of ways of accounting for such incidents. The first, and perhaps easiest to understand, is simply that under pressure we tend to revert to primitive defence mechanisms. Human physiology is still programmed as if we lived in prehistoric times; a modern-day tiger or mammoth triggers us into a state where we are primed for fight or flight (see, for example, Arroba and James 1987). Neither of these responses is deemed appropriate in the normal repertoire of a rational and balanced adult but we have available a range of emotions and behaviours from earlier in our lives before we were so well adapted to social conventions. It is often these overwhelming and seemingly childish patterns which pop up in times of stress and uncertainty (Smith 1975: Ch.1). They, equally, can be considered as sub-personalities, ones which belong to former roles and relationships.

The other way of explaining this sense of being 'taken over' by a behaviour pattern which comes apparently from nowhere is through the concept for 'archetypes'. The term was introduced by C. G. Jung and refers to universal patterns or motifs which come from the collective unconscious. Archetypes form the basic content of myth and legend and appear in our dreams and visions. They also emerge at times as instinctual behaviours or as repeating patterns in our lives. The Guzies, for example (Guzie and Guzie 1986) link eight of Jung's great archetypes to the Myers Briggs Type Indicator for identifying personality dispositions and preferences, and suggest that we can use these 'great stories' positively to help us shape our lives. Bolen (1985), writing on the psychology of women, selects seven of the goddesses of ancient Greece to characterize the forces which shape women's inner lives, as opposed to the culturally derived stereotypes which the external world attempts to impose on them. Archetypal patterns can also operate at an organizational level. Handy (1985) draws on the characteristics of four of the Greek gods to describe differing managerial styles and organizational cultures.

Releasing 'negative' energies

So far, in my examples, I have tended to emphasize 'negative' patterns. We all have, too, behavioural patterns or sub-personalities which are recognizably positive forces in our lives. The structures described in this chapter can also be used to strengthen and enrich these aspects of yourself. However, one ignores or attempts to wipe out 'negative' behaviours at a cost: their motivating drives have reservoirs of energy which, if suppressed, are likely to surface unexpectedly and with unfortunate consequences. By failing to acknowledge the anger I am feeling about some situation in my life, I can find myself for some quite trivial reason biting off the head of a valued colleague, then wishing instead I had bitten my own tongue. The anger did not 'belong' to that person or that situation, yet it needed expression. Since I failed to acknowledge it and deal with it appropriately, it found its own outlet, using an unsuspecting victim. In other circumstances I might well manage to exercise control over my rage, preventing myself from unleashing it on others, indeed, pretending it did not exist. Should I then be surprised at the arrival of a migraine or a backache? No, this is simply the energy of my anger finding an alternative means of expression for itself.

Most of us are having to deal with an unprecedented degree of change and uncertainty in our working lives, perhaps accompanied by stresses or confusion in our personal lives. Such challenges can bring out the best in us, yet apprehension, anxiety, fear, do trigger some of our most primitive behavioural responses. Just at the time when we most need to support each other, we can find ourselves driven apart. The danger is that inadvertent behaviour can be misinterpreted and responded to in kind, with the possibility of escalation into major conflict. In times of pressure, it is crucial that we develop much more awareness and understanding of our own disfunctional behaviour patterns so that we can avoid any tendency to sabotage either ourselves or others. The joy of working with sub-personalities is that such energies can be harnessed for the good. The basis of the approach I describe is to work lovingly with your 'negative' sub-personalities and to face up to the conflict and differences within your 'inner team'. You will then be better equipped to deal with conflict, change, and uncertainty in the external world. You will feel less threatened by differences between yourself and others.

The first step is to realize that you have a 'self' that is in charge of all your 'sub-personalities'. The easiest way is to make a friend of what I have termed the 'observing self'—that part of you which can be aware of and notice your different feelings and behaviours as they manifest themselves. You can then move on to characterize the different aspects of yourself. Unlike transactional analysis which has a set hierarchy of scripts (variants of the internal 'parent', 'adult', and 'child'), the notion of sub-personalities gives you a cast list as long as you wish to make it, the 'characters' offering themselves for the improvised drama of your life.

I find this idea of a play and a cast of players a useful metaphor to aid in the essential step of understanding that you, the 'core' you, are not your behaviours. You may conceive of yourself, instead, more as director or stage manager with the task of ensuring that your cast of sub-personalities are a team which works together in, rather than against, your best interests. Continuing the metaphor, you may well find you have one or two 'prima donnas' to contend with, sub-personalities a little unruly or wilful. Nevertheless, they are there to play a part in your drama and are amenable to direction once you befriend them and look after their interests.

Exercise 2   Identifying behaviour patterns

This exercise may be done alone but is usefully carried out in pairs.

Step 1:   Take a sheet of paper and, working alone, make brief notes on three of the behaviour patterns which you experience as ineffective for you: when they appear you tend afterwards to regret what you have said or done, or to feel you have in some way let yourself down. Bring to mind now the sort of situation and/or person which brings out this behaviour in you. Notice your characteristic tone of voice, gesture, body posture, breathing pattern. Follow this by going through the same process, this time re-experiencing and making notes on three behaviour patterns which you feel pleased about, ones which bring out the best in you.

Step 2:   Working now with a partner, take equal time to talk through what you have noted down. If time is short, you can select one 'negative' and one 'positive' pattern. Tell your partner about the last time this pattern manifested itself in your life. Use the present tense as you describe exactly the scene, what was going on, what you were doing, saying, feeling. Bring it to life now.

Your partner's role is simply to give good listening attention, without intervention. At the end of the allotted time, you partner will give you feedback on what she or he noticed about your posture, gestures, expression, voice, breathing, etc. This will help you to become even more clear about the 'symptoms' by which you can begin to identify this particular 'sub-personality' as it emerges.

Reverse roles so that you become the listener as your partner recounts their own chosen patterns. Listen and watch closely so that you can give good, detailed, and specific feedback.

I will give an example of my own. I know that my anger can, in spite of best intentions, blast out in an uncontrolled fashion. This used to happen particularly in meetings with male colleagues where, as a woman, I experienced myself as ignored, unheard, apparently invisible. The warning signs were a churning in my belly, a flushed neck, clenched right shoulder and fist. Then, the sub-personality which I call the Dragon would fly out fast and furious to operate a scorched-earth policy which was beginning to leave me even more ignored and isolated. I use the past tense since, these days, I am able to acknowledge the Dragon as one of the best energies I have working for me—but more of this later.

The first step, then, is to become closely aware of the physical symptoms that go with any behaviour pattern you wish to get to know better or to change. This in itself can start a change process. Returning to my own example, I found that I was able to recognize the Dragon as its energy began to rise and, in effect, to negotiate with it about who was to act in the situation. Mostly we would agree it would be my cool rational self. Just occasionally, if I thought the situation or people 'had it coming to them', I would allow the Dragon to do its worst. And my experience of just this small amount of negotiation was that my anger would come out more in control, expressing itself as a justifiable outrage that was more acceptable to others than my previous hurt raging.

Getting to know your sub-personalities

A simple 'guided fantasy' is the core structure I use to begin the process of dialogue with a sub-personality. One chooses a specific behaviour pattern which is causing concern (or a 'positive' pattern which one wishes to enrich), then one takes it on a walk up a mountain, talking with it and waiting to find out what shape and form it wishes to adopt. A key item on the agenda is to ask the sub-personality what is its *positive intent*. However unwelcome the manifestation of the behaviour pattern, it is necessary to affirm a belief that there is some underlying purpose which is functional for you, given the right context. In some cases you will find that the sub-personality seems eager and ready to reveal its name, shape and purpose in one's life. In other cases there can be an initial recalcitrance, particularly when working with a part of oneself which for years has been distrusted, neglected, even hated.

It is important to establish the right setting and atmosphere before beginning the guided fantasy. Choose a room without distractions, with the possibility of subdued lighting, where you can be free from interruptions for up to an hour. If working as a group, have the chairs in a circle or semi-circle with everyone in view of the facilitator. If you are working alone, familiarize yourself with the instructions before you start—and preferably put them on tape, leaving time in between each phase for your response. Arrange with a friend time to debrief afterwards, or record the experience in a journal as soon as possible. The telling of the story is a grounding experience which brings you fully back into 'present time'.

Exercise 3   The guided fantasy

Step 1: Sit well-supported in your chair, spine straight, head balanced lightly on top of the spine, thighs supported by the chair, legs uncrossed, and feet on the ground. Allow your arms to rest on your lap so that your shoulders are relaxed. Take you attention 'inside' with eyes closed and focus on your breathing just above the navel. Simply watch and follow your breathing and with each out-breath, allow any tension in your body to drain away, down through the chair and into the floor. With each out-breath, feel yourself getting heavier and more relaxed. As you enjoy the support of the chair, allow any remaining tensions to drain away so that you can feel more at ease, more at peace.

Step 2: Now turn your attention to that part of yourself which you need to talk to just now. Allow this aspect of your behaviour to identify itself; allow the possibility that it may not be the one you had expected to be talking to.

Step 3: Find yourself at the foot of a mountain with this part of yourself, knowing that you are going to climb the mountain together in order to converse. Start now to climb the mountain, choosing your path as you go. Your task at present is to be attentive to your companion. It may stay by your side, it may go ahead, it may follow. It may choose a completely different path up the mountain. Notice whether this aspect of yourself has a shape or form, notice whether it wants to tell you anything. At this stage you are simply to listen to anything it wishes to let you know.

As you continue to choose your path up the mountain, remain attentive to your companion. Notice any changes in it as you go along. Thank it for coming with you on your journey and ask it these questions: 'What is your positive intent for me?'; 'How are you trying to help me in my life?'; 'What would *you* like from *me*?'. Listen to its replies and notice any changes in its shape or form. Do not be surprised if it is reluctant to talk to you. Reassure it that you do now wish to learn to love it and work with it for your benefit, that you are now ready to understand its purpose in your life.

Continue together on your journey up the mountain, now nearing the top. At the top of the mountain, bring this part of yourself into the sunlight and, again, ask if there is anything it wishes to say or do. Notice any changes in it and find out if there is anything you would like to say in response. Listen to it again.

It is almost time to begin your descent down the mountain. Find some way of saying farewell for now to your companion. Notice whether it wishes to come with you or whether it wishes to stay on the mountain at present.

Now begin your descent back down the mountain. Choose your path as you go. Soon you will be at the bottom of the mountain and in a short while it will be time for you to return to this room. Take one last look around you and then begin to imagine how it will be when you open your eyes and re-enter this room. Attune your hearing to the sounds in and around this room. Take a few deeper breaths. Begin to move your hands and feet. Finally, open your eyes, look around, and, in you own time stretch , yawn, and do anything you need to make sure you are fully back in present time.

Step 4:   Choose a partner (preferably the same person with whom you worked in exercise 2) and take equal time to share with them anything you wish to say about your experience on the mountain.

Make sure there is plenty of time for the debriefing period, and for some sharing in the whole group. If you are the facilitator or guide for the process, be prepared to give additional support and attention to anyone who has had a particularly strong experience. This can usually be left to that person and their chosen partner while you maintain a sense of calmness and security in the background, giving reassurance that in a guided fantasy, strange and surprising incidents are normal. If the structure can be used on a residential programme, so much the better. It is often the case that the sub-personalities unfold more of themselves overnight. I have found that individuals have gained deeply moving insights into what had been patterns of behaviour of longstanding concern and intrusion in their lives. A number of people have found themselves accessing two sub-personalities which had been working against each other, causing pain internally, and ineffectiveness and blockage in progressing plans in the 'real' world. This may seem strange as you read it now, yet it makes good sense to those who have started to explore the ideas involved. I can report ardent and involved conversations during residential programmes where no-one was batting an eyelid at such remarks as:

'My Blob has legs this morning!'

'My pillar has split into a white dove and a black raven.'

'It woke me up in the middle of the night and told me its name.'

It is perhaps worth issuing a gentle warning, though I doubt whether anything untoward will arise. The structure is a type commonly used in self-development programmes. Individuals participating are excellent at pacing themselves in the depth of the inner journey that they take, going only into the inner conflicts and blockages which they are ready to face up to and integrate into their lives. However, it is just a possibility that a person who has been under severe stress may touch something too disturbing to handle easily. The facilitator needs to be alert to any signs of this, and to know their own limitations and boundaries. If the participant needs additional counselling or expert help, make sure you can put them in touch with an appropriate helper.

Most people will have a straightforward experience which, though surprising, makes a lot of sense to them. I will illustrate, once again using my own sub-personalities. I have already introduced you to the Dragon. In my early conversations with it, I discovered that its positive intention was simply to protect me—it got angry when it felt I was being abused by others. This certainly helped me to gain new insights into my own behaviour, and strengthened the ability of my 'observing self' to negotiate on-the-spot about which of us, myself or the Dragon, would deal with the situation. In subsequent conversations (and it is well worth continuing the dialogue with your major sub-personalities since they tend to transform over time, and in relation to each other), I discovered that the Dragon was closely linked in its purpose to another sub-personality, the Little Girl. She, it turned out, was in utmost need of care and protection since I would insist on taking her into situations which she found too challenging. Once I started to look after her needs myself, the Dragon's behaviour changed dramatically. Freed of its duties to the Little Girl, it revealed itself as my visionary in the form of the Little Dragon, which flies high, fast and free, aware of possibilities without constraint or hindrance—it is in search of treasure! Energy that was previously locked up in some old internal drama and only released as anger, is now available to me in a much more positive form.

Negotiating with your inner team

When you discover or guess that two sub-personalities are in some way linked, you may facilitate a dialogue between them. This will be particularly helpful if one appears to be sabotaging the best intentions of the other, or if the two are in some way interrupting each other with the effect of, for example, putting you into stalemate. The aim is to get each to understand the positive intention of the other in your life and to negotiate an agreement about how both might be satisfied without disrupting each other or you. There are a number of methods for facilitating this dialogue between different sub-personalities or aspects of yourself. If you are familiar with *gestalt* therapy, you might choose to 'be' each part in turn, moving from one seat to another as you change roles. You may, indeed, wish to bring in a third seat for yourself as 'director' in order to remain very clear about whose interests are at stake and that you are in charge of your inner team. Another method is to allocate one sub-personality to your right hand, the other to your left hand. This is the method adopted in the next exercise which is a 'reframing' structure used in Neuro-Linguistic Programming (NLP), a set of skills and operating principles for effecting improved communication and personal change (Bandler and Grinder 1982).

Exercise 4   Negotiating between sub-personalities

1. Assume a comfortable sitting position where you can be undisturbed for up to an hour. Allocate sub-personality X to one hand and describe it: 'You are the part of me that . . .'. Allocate sub-personality Y to your other hand and describe it: 'You are the part of me that . . .'.
2. Tell X that you value what it's trying to do for you and ask its positive function in your life. Wait for a response, then do the same in relation to Y. As you speak, look at the relevant hand, as if you were really talking to this aspect of yourself 'sitting' there.
3. Ask X whether Y ever interrupts its purpose, and whether there is anything it wishes to say to Y. Hold up hand X, turn it to face hand Y, and listen to what it has to say. You may listen to your inner dialogue, or speak aloud if the words come easily to you.
4. Ask Y whether X ever interrupts its purpose and whether there is anything it wishes to say to X. Hold up hand Y, turn it to face hand

X, and listen and/or speak as before.

5. Allow the dialogue between X and Y to continue, moving the relevant hand up as each 'speaks' in turn, and turning it to 'look at' the hand which is being spoken to. Make sure that each acknowledges the other's positive intention for you. Ask each to state what it would like from the other in order to minimize interruption, or to give assistance. If necessary, remind both that they are there to help you fulfil your life's purpose.

6. Ask each whether they are now ready to make an agreement to harmonize their behaviours in your best interests.

7. Ask whether any other sub-personalities, or aspects of yourself are involved in this disfunctional pattern. If so, renegotiate, bringing in the other 'player'.

8. When agreement is reached, bring your hands slowly together and in to your heart, to symbolize the sealing of the pact between you. Thank your sub-personalities.

Once you have become familiar with the idea of using all your different behaviour patterns for your benefit, rather than attempting to deny or suppress some of them, you will find yourself with considerably more energy and creative potential available. More energy than perhaps you realize is consumed in holding back or holding down 'negativity' that you would rather not have come to the surface. The exercises and structures I have described will allow you to face in to such blockages. You need only a firm belief that all your behaviours are functional to you, given the right context. The structures enable you to negotiate with your sub-personalities the situations in which it will be useful for them to appear; or to devise, perhaps with the assistance of yet another sub-personality, some alternative behavioural strategies for the situation which will satisfy the needs of the first. Do not be surprised if, in the period following an internal negotiation, one or more of your sub-personalities either disappears or changes its form. This was my experience with a behaviour pattern which I called the Demons. I will not go into detail about how I untangled these terrible twins. It is enough to say that they transmuted and amalgamated themselves into a much more helpful energy which I call Leigh, a sort of steward who marshalls my business affairs and maintains for me critical boundaries when I am under threat.

Putting your inner team to work

Your own imagination has probably already begun to work on the uses you could find for bringing your own sub-personalities into play. I need to say little more. I doubt you will any longer be content to fill out a questionnaire and find yourself labelled 'team worker', 'completer-finisher', or even 'shaper' (the terms are taken from Belbin's typology, Belbin 1981). Instead, you might conceive of yourself more as a shape-shifter, transforming the different aspects of yourself creatively to your purpose. You may also find yourself intrigued about the sub-personalities of your colleagues. Of course, it is best to honour their own characterizations of themselves, yet you may begin, gently, to call out the side of them you would rather deal with.

'Ah ha! I see the Black Knight is with us this morning! I was rather hoping instead to meet with your Mr Bubbles.'

'Usha, am I right? It seems that your Volcano is very close to erupting. What happened to that Cool Steel Sphere that got us through the business so smoothly last month?'

You might even enlist the support of a friend to assist you in keeping your own sub-personalities in order:

'Anil, I seem to be a bit too full of Gloria today, and I'm not sure that the Management Committee, for all its fine talk about equal opportunities, is yet ready to deal with a Woman-Who-Is-To-Be-Reckoned-With! Listen, will you just give me a wink from time to time and I'll see if I can pull out Bat Lady. It may be that a touch of Flighty-Fly-By-Night-Female who is just ever such a teeny bit confused might go down better this morning.'

I have drawn, in this chapter, not only on my own sub-personalities, but also on those of the individuals who have used the structures with me. I would like to thank them for sharing their experiences, and for the ideas they have given me for my own further explorations in working with the concepts.

References

Arroba, Tanya and Kim James (1987) *Pressure at Work: A Survival Guide,* McGraw-Hill, Maidenhead.

Assagioli, Roberto (1986) *Psychosynthesis,* Turnstone Press, Wellingborough, Northants.

Bandler, Richard and John Grinder (1982) *Reframing,* Real People Press, Utah.

Belbin, R. Meredith (1981) *Management Teams: Why They Succeed or Fail,* Heinemann, London.

Bolen, Jean Shinoda (1985) *Goddesses in Everywoman: A New Psychology of Women,* Harper & Row, London.

Guzie, Tad and Noreen Monroe Guzie (1986) *About Men and Women: How Your 'Great Story' Shapes Your Destiny*, Paulist Press, New York.
Handy, Charles (1985) *Gods of Management*, Pan, London.
Smith, Manuel J. (1975) *When I Say No, I Feel Guilty*, Bantam Books, London.
Stewart, Ian and Vann Joinnes (1987) *Transactional Analysis Today*, Lifespace, Nottingham.
Stewart, Rosemary (1982) *Choices for the Manager*, McGraw-Hill, Maidenhead.

15
The hot potato: a view of women's development
Pauline Kidd and Sally Watson

Introduction

Have you ever tried something new, taken a risk and discovered that what you ended up with is exciting, different but quite unfathomable? Well, this is what we are calling our 'hot potato'.

Single-sex training for women has grown both visibly and audibly over the past few years. A plethora of courses, seminars and workshops have sprung up in response to perhaps a growing market of women in management, the ideals of women tutors and/or clever marketing strategies. We too took this path into single-sex training, by designing and implementing women into management programmes. We would like to share with you our present 'hot potato' and take you through our experiences in running these programmes in an engineering industry.

We will explain why we see the results as a 'hot potato' and show you what we intend to do about it in the future.

We believe that the 'hot potato' of women's development has a part to play in the long term for self-development. The 'hot potato' is not really about women's development, but about these issues between men and women which frequently get side-stepped.

Which begs the question—are we truly in the business of self-development or do we, as trainers, collect models and theories and then skilfully rationalize human behaviour to fit them?

The story so far

February 1987

Sally Watson joined Water Training, a company offering management training and development. Pauline Kidd was the training officer at Essex

Water Company. A private company abstracting, treating and distributing water in the Essex area.

During a visit to Essex in May, the two met and shared concerns about the lack of managerial training for women within the industry. As a result they developed a commitment to initiating a programme designed specially for women. A pilot scheme of 2.5 days was set up at Essex Water. From this pilot programme came some powerful conclusions. The delegates displayed a massive lack of self-confidence and admitted to feelings of powerlessness. In addition, there was some mistrust and suspicion of the image of the women tutors. As tutors we felt both pain and elation: pain in the sense of covert aggression and some resentment from the delegates. Working in an all-female environment presented a shock. With no previous experience of single-sex training, the only platform of ideas we had to work from were the more traditional approaches centred around men.

The elation came from taking a risk, initiating novel ideas in a traditional industry and a sense of achievement on the final day.

March 1988

With the benefit of the Essex experience we set up a 5.5 day Women in Management programme for the industry.

As part of the programme all delegates were sponsored by a senior member of their organization. The programme started on a Sunday afternoon and was residential, enabling us to build a positive learning climate at an early stage.

On the first evening we noticed again a great lack of self-confidence within the group and some reluctance to confront the main issues. Within 24 hours the climate of the programme had changed dramatically. Stereotypes and myths about all female communities were being challenged. Team spirit and energy ran high. The relationship between tutors and delegates grew strong. Any unease and fear on the first evening was quickly dispelled. During this programme the pain came from some reactions outside the training group. We found there were strong reactions from those around us.

July 1988

A second programme was run within a smaller number of delegates. The atmosphere was more informal and we were able to attempt more in terms of experiential learning. The March experience enabled us to be more specific about individual's learning needs, to offer greater flexibility and so develop the concept of self-managed learning.

September 1988—CSML Conference Lancaster

We came to the conclusion that our efforts in the field of self-development were being treated in two very polarized ways. We were either regarded as a great success and supported, or critized harshly and given a fairly rough ride (one clear conclusion—there was no connection between the first reaction and gender). Indeed, the reactions were often so emotional that we nicknamed the problem 'the hot potato'.

Our attendance at Lancaster was a conscious effort to test out some of our ideas and share experience. We believed that until some of the misconception/myths of the hot potato could be understood, our progress with WIM programmes would be continuously frustrated.

February 1989

As a result of our learning at CSML we decided to take a definite step toward explaining the hot potato by registering with University of Salford to do some research on the outcomes of the programmes.

The pathway of management development

From our experience in management development, we believe that two pathways are emerging (see Figure 15.1).

Phase 1 is the traditional management training. This is what we would regard as the taught model. Where the responsibility for learning rests firmly on the trainer's shoulders, the trainer generating the specific objectives and following a timetable to deliver these. Thus the risk element is limited on both sides. From this approach managers develop an accepted range of knowledge, skills and language.

As more women have moved into senior positions, more have become eligible for management training (phase 2). The response had been that women have been grafted on to well-established programmes. Women have found themselves in an environment in which they had previously been excluded. The language approach and style of these programmes do not always successfully match the needs of women. Many have felt anxious, devalued and alienated within such programmes. In general women seriously lack self-confidence and therefore require an environment which encourages their confidence to grow from within themselves. In addition, some management development programmes can create simple logistical problems, for example, the lack of child-care facilities.

From the realism that women's development needs are not matched in this way, came a growth of single-sex training initiatives.

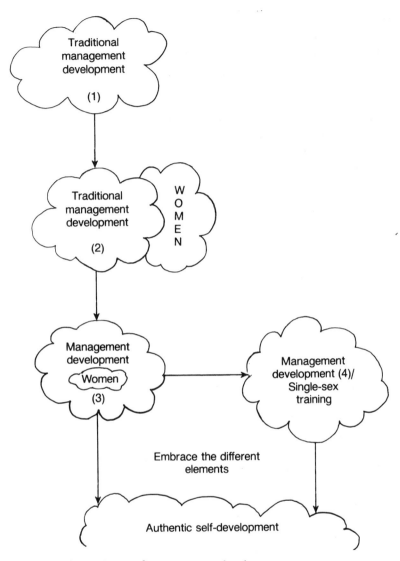

Figure 15.1   The pathway of management development

The benefits of this indicate that women learn faster in situations where they feel comfortable. The supportive environment which grows from such programmes helps the process along, leasing a freedom of thought and creative approach to problem-solving. However, we feel this approach is not the panacea, or a final stage to answering the needs of different gender groups. This is because too many negative issues surround the single-sex training approach, thus inhibiting its evolution.

We have categorized these negative issues as *internal*, i.e. within the content/process of the programme, and *external*, i.e. from the world outside the training group.

Internal

- Some women were anxious about being stereotyped.
- There was anxiety about an all-female community.
- There was a limitation on the breadth of input.
- The training group became quite insular and difficult for outsiders to 'break in'.

External

- Feelings of exclusion came from colleagues.
- Fear and insecurity came from some sponsors.
- There was a lack of clarity on the objectives of the programme.

Figure 15.1 shows two distinct paths which encapsulate our personal experiences. As trainers we had travelled extensively down the more traditional pathway. In 1987 we branched into women's development because we wanted to experience and learn about an all-female environment. At that stage we believed the way to go forward was to redress the imbalance. We needed to work and share in an all-female training environment in order to explore some of the issues surrounding the future of women's development. We found that the responses to us, the programme and its short-term outcomes were quite painful. The issue of single-sex training runs deep and for some time we were taken aback by the forcefulness of the responses. The very act of designing and running women's programmes had apparently widened and deepened this polarization.

Both the pathways are legitimate and have a relevant place within management development. We need to take the strengths of these approaches and build for the future. It seems that the two pathways are now at a crossroads and we are in danger of losing the impact and benefit by the divergence of the two pathways.

We see the hot potato as a whole set of data about attitudes, values, beliefs, etc., which have been previously ignored and dismissed. Thus, rather than ignore it, we seek to research it actively, because within the experience of all those involved in both pathways there is rich learning and growth. An understanding of such richness could be used positively to take self-development into a new era.

On reflection, we feel that single-sex training has provided a challenge that the field of self-development needs in order to grow. The hot potato is real; there is a cloud around single-sex training and it does generate anxiety for both men and women.

It is from the personal experience of the hot potato that for us, as the traditional definition of self-development is changing, we see *authentic* self-development as embracing all the different elements and experiences of those involved in self-development.

An earlier definition stated: 'personal development, with the manager taking primary responsibility for his or her own learning and for choosing the means to achieve this'.

We value and support this definition and indeed have actively worked within this philosophy. The experience of the past two years has caused us to wish to build on this definition.

By authentic self-development, we see a sharper focus with a higher level of trust and value both between individuals and between individuals and organization.

Women's training development has been and still is dismissed and undervalued. The severity of the response in itself signals a challenge for self-development.

Authentic self-development must include and encourage all contributions that may exist and grow within the total framework. Thus we believe that personal development cannot exist alone and personal growth needs a supportive network. The responsibilities are twofold and operate for both individuals and organizations.

Our present thinking has lead us to compose some criteria for authentic self-development.

Individual

1. Actively seeks new opportunities and options for learning.
2. Maintains sense of individual responsibility for personal growth and learning.
3. Have confidence to communicate learning needs and goals.
4. Values total experience and draws learning from it.

Organization

1. Actively seeks new approaches in self-development.
2. Encourages experimentation and risk-taking. Is not constrained by current models and theories.

3. Values and supports all contributions from people both internal and external to organization.
4. Encourages high level of trust between employees.

Action research

As a result of our thinking we believe the cloud around single-sex training needs to be lifted to allow for authentic self-development on a practical level.

We are planning to explore the validity of our women's programmes from two themes:

- subjective enquiry
- evalution of training

The study will involve, with their permission, all the delegates, sponsors and managers that have been involved over the past two years. As two individuals we have different perceptions and will be researching common ground from different viewpoints.

Subjective enquiry
Subjective enquiry looks at the everyday 'taken for granted' actions and behaviour of human beings. We believe that people engage in elaborate accounting practices to explain their behaviours. Locked beneath the surface of these accounts are the triggers to the stereotypical responses.

Using subjective enquiry we shall seek to understand the cloud around single-sex training—since this methodology enables us to read into worlds of all those involved with the women's programmes.

Evaluation of training
This is a structural attempt to reflect on the overall cost-benefit and worth of such programmes. It may seem almost impossible at this stage to define the factors and relationships which should be measured and assessed. The alternative to evaluating training is to rely on intuition, faith and a vague comprehension of the value. This is not the way forward for successfully rousing awareness of women's needs in training.

Conclusions

We believe that the utilization of all human resources with an organization will become more important in an increasingly competitive business environment.

The continuation of the approaches we have outlined will help to utilize some of those resources, but the danger lies in not fully developing the total resource.

There are differences between men and men, men and women, women and women. Many of us do not fit easily into the established categories. Our experience has given us some insights about single-sex training and its impact. The impact of single-sex training has provided a challenge. The continuing growth of the field of self-development needs just such a challenge.

Our hot potato is changing. At the onset it seemed to be a cloud of negative and dismissive responses. As our understanding of the issues of the hot potato grows we are starting to recognize that the responses are the key to *authentic* self-development. Such responses must be discussed, debated and researched.

16
Can opportunities ever be equal?
Maggie Smith and Janice Leary

Preparation

From the original list of conference themes we chose 'differences', agreeing there might be real value in linking 'differences' with the apparent failure to implement equal opportunities policies. From this perspective we look briefly at the current position and work which has already been done:

- The problem is discovered and defined; facts and statistics published about the implications of inequality in terms of race, gender, sexuality, disability, etc. Endless pieces of paper are generated.
- Legislation is passed; new procedures implemented; the law requires new policies of non-discrimination. In some areas genuine attempts to introduce new organizational systems are made—but how real or how permanent are the changes?
- Legislation and information take us some way, but the old infrastructures remain, guarded by old power bases and built on to institutionalized inequalities. Lip service may be paid to the needs of people whose lives are affected by the unequal treatment they receive, but little energy expanded on long-term change. Legislation may enforce some changes, but it seems that in many organizations discrimination, often unconscious, is rife and the status quo remains.

In asking why no lasting transformation has taken place, we wanted to attempt to understand what kind of developmental process might help to influence genuine and permanent change.

Attention has been paid to thinking and action, but few attempts made to confront the emotions behind discriminatory practices. Behaviour and attitudes are influenced by experiences and feelings. If we examine the basis of our beliefs and values, we access the fears which are the roots of prejudice. Insights into the source of our attitudes offer choices about changing them. Some people will opt for entrenchment and here legislation helps; maybe opportunities will never be *truly* equal, but we might reach a more balanced situation.

Many trainers avoid the discomfort of work of this kind, which may uncover very deep and painful feelings—for them as well as for their participants. It seems vital to find the courage to confront ourselves, so we begin to understand how easily we stereotype and hurt people, and we took this as the basis of our design. As trainers we know each other, have shared values and commitment and had worked together before, in slightly different contexts.

This design was new and we divided our planning meetings between:

- sharing our experiences of working on this kind of conference;
- clarifying our objectives;
- brainstorming and discarding ideas
- finally, designing the content and process.

The ground rules arose from discussion of our own minor differences—of approach, of values, of skills:

- Clear boundaries: $1\frac{1}{2}$ hours is a very short time to 'dig deep' on such an emotive subject and we were perhaps nervous of leaving more unfinished business than necessary
- The workshop would be almost entirely interactive—neither of us is comfortable with any other way of working, and we see no other way to encourage and enable self-development
- We would offer several 'taster' exercises, enabling participants to experience different ways of exploring the assumptions which underly our attitutes and behaviour and create stereotypes.
- We would use both creative and the more familiar verbal styles, to encourage the use of both right and left brain (and our own special talents).
- We would experiment with new ideas and also use some 'tried and tested' favourites.
- We would share equally in facilitating, taking responsbility for presenting different aspects (and if essential, making up a pair).
- We would look at 'equality' in the broadest sense, explore the impossibility of being totally non-judgemental and examine the roots of some of our assumptions.
- We would leave time to consider the implications of this kind of learning for use in a work context. (We failed here!)

Presentation

There were twelve participants. We began by explaining the basis of our design and the title of the workshop; before we can implement equality, if this is indeed possible, it is essential to develop our awareness of the way we regularly and automatically make assumptions about people. One of us is left-handed and used as an example her instant warming to anyone else in a group who is also left-handed, although her view may change and is based only on identifying with her own 'minority'. The workshop would focus on these unconscious and inbuilt prejudices, and exploring ways to use the learning in 'equal opportunities' work.

Exercise 1

Objectives   To explore 'mental set' and raise awareness of our response to assumptions—ours and others'.

People formed pairs to discuss the conference and their reasons for choosing this session. They were then asked to sit back and write answers to questions about their partner:

Examples

- What car do they drive?
- What is the joint family income?
- What newspaper do they read?
- How many staff do they have?
- Where did they study for their degree?
- How old are they?

They shared their results with each other, then the group explored their accuracy (or otherwise!); the source of any guesses; the embarrassment or indignation with which answers were recorded or reported.

'Income and age were difficult, especially when I got it wrong!'
'Why should I care what kind of car she drives?'

It appeared that women were less interested in car ownership, and that men were surprisingly flattered by being judged younger than their years. There was general agreement that this enlightened group would all be *Guardian* or *Independent* readers—it would be insulting to assume they read the *Sun*! Although this was pretty accurate, we did wonder how a closet *Sun* reader could then admit it?

The group questioned the assumptions *we* had made—that people drove cars, had degrees, managed staff, read a newspaper—and we assured them that this had been deliberate! We were able to explore how much we all take for granted about our peers' lives.

Exercise 2

Objectives To explore reaction to belonging to a group through an arbitrary physical criterion.

The criteria used were:

- people with beards;
- people whose hair was its natural colour;
- people whose hair was coloured artificially.

Maggie has used this exercise several times before; it is a powerful way to explore the feelings aroused by being placed in this kind of grouping. It is important for the trainer to observe the group during the first exercise and choose easily defined, fairly homogenous but possibly ambiguous criteria which leave two—or at most three—people in a minority group.

Examples of other criteria which have been used include:

- skirts, jeans and other trousers;
- under twenty-five, under forty, over forty.

We as facilitators observed the non-verbal behaviour and selection process, and later fed this back for the groups to consider. Two men with beards quickly formed the most obvious and smallest group, but there was confusion over the other two. One woman said that she was due to have the last residue of colour cut from her hair next day, so didn't really feel she belonged to either group. Her uncertainty had been very real!

People were asked to discuss their reaction to their own group and to the other two, including how were they similar and different; what they liked, disliked or envied about the others; would they like to belong to a different group?

The two bearded men displayed solidarity but were feeling isolated and vulnerable: they were aware that it was highly unlikely they would ever be joined by a female, and were sad about this. (There seemed at some level to be a suspicion that there was something amiss. Whenever this exercise has been used the reactions of the smallest group always include: feeling judged, feeling singled out, feeling cross about being picked out for no logical reason. There are *major* implications here for real life situations.)

We had noticed that the medium group seemed the most comfortable: the conversation was energized and they were oblivious of any discomfort in the other groups; they agreed that they were happy to be in this group. It may be that there is an optimum size outside which a group stops feeling cohesive, since this too is a common pattern in the exercise. Uneasy comments and challenges emerged:

'You used white criteria—black people don't colour their hair.'
'Well, I do; I'd have been in that group next week!'
'Why didn't you ask the two black people to form a group?'

We were puzzled by this question: they presumably already *know* how it feels to belong to a minority group through purely physical criteria. This exercise tested some of our ground rules, as we could have explored these reactions and any implicit racism in the group; one member did express a wish to look more deeply at the issues arising. We stayed with our decision to keep the exercises as brief tasters, explaining our reasons and the group appeared to agree. With hindsight, one of us would have liked to be more flexible; this is discussed in the Evaluation.

Exercise 3

Objectives

- To develop and use a new and innovative exercise using the more intuitive and creative right brain.
- To use a drawing to discuss differences—how we create differently, how we define and choose what is different, how we find out more about the differences and respect, understand and value them.

Janice has used colour for many years and has found it an exciting way to lead quickly into feeling and to work with the feelings 'out there' and visible on paper. It is important that the trainer is aware of the speed with which people can react and can deal with any issues which may arise spontaneously.

Participants were given five minutes to make, non-verbally, a free drawing, then put the drawing on the floor. At this stage people often feel inhibited, shy, recall past experiences of 'not being able to draw', 'not creative'. It is important to encourage people to let go of their self-judgement and allow the mind to be still.

They were asked to walk quietly round, observing the drawings, taking time to note their feelings towards them. They were to choose one which was different from their own—it might be strange, wonderful, weird, frightening, anything, just as long as it was different from their own drawing.

Still quietly, they were asked to ponder on the picture, really look and get to know the picture. The group then discussed their choices:

- What made this picture different?
- What feelings did they have in relation to the picture?

The exercise stimulated an interesting discussion; some people expressed again their fears about actually doing the exercise. We moved on to look at why they chose a particular picture. Comments included:

- better than mine, more creative, more artistic;
- more delicate;
- weird;
- dark/don't understand it;
- didn't like it.

One woman seemed to be upset by hearing her picture judged and the interpreter was unable to continue, offering later a further thought:

- I realised that saying how I felt was seen as an attack; it just hadn't occurred to me that the drawing might be precious to someone. It wasn't intended to hurt ...

One person was embarrassed by being told that his drawing was chosen because of its artistic quality. His comment was 'I can't draw, I've never been creative.' It was interesting to look at assumptions we make about our own abilities, how even these attitudes need to change! Some of the learning seems to have been unexpected, and demonstrated how people are in charge of their own learning.

Exercise 4

Objectives To explore how our view of someone is influenced by new information.

Another new design; a role-play combining imagination and reality. There has been a huge expansion in training for selection interviewing, with emphasis on the need to avoid overt discrimination, but we wanted yet again to explore how subtly attitudes might be influenced. People returned to their original pairs and were informed:

- that next week their partner was to become their colleague;
- that they would be given information about their partner and could decide whether or not to reveal what they knew;
- they could discuss their experiences in the workshop, while being aware of their thoughts, feelings and body language after they were given the cards.

Examples of information on the cards:

- This person was sacked from her/his last two jobs.
- This person is having a relationship with your partner.
- This person is having a relationship with the head of department.
- This person is anti-feminist.
- This person is HIV positive.

We asked pairs to share their reactions first with each other, then with the group, and attempted to analyse which cards had the most power. It became obvious that 'relationship with my partner' could never be tolerated. (One woman's husband was also her head of department, and this roused even more anger which precluded the possibility of a rational working relationship). This may be an unusual situation, but sexuality has an important role in relationships at work.

One person was preoccupied with wondering how someone who had been sacked from two jobs had managed to get through the interview for this one; in response to a question he said that he would have been less concerned if the phrase had been 'was made redundant', but the group seemed unclear about this. (Ask the redundant how often they are treated as 'sacked' and therefore less likely to be offered equality of opportunity at an interview!)

We were surprised that people reported being unaffected by the HIV positive card, and wondered whether this was a denial, or if our own knowledge in this field prejudiced *us*. There was one hilarious, if uncomfortably familiar, reaction:

'I didn't believe it; how could such a nice woman possibly get Aids . . . ?'

There was unfortunately no time to focus on the application of the learning to people's work settings. We asked for feedback on the workshop and several comments reinforced our own 'time' frustration. We had not expected vast insights, and while some people made useful discoveries, most seemed to be reminded of the importance of constant self-monitoring. One or two were perhaps slightly disappointed by the 'surface' nature of the session.

Evaluation

We have spent some time thinking through the design and the process, to evaluate the session and any changes we might make. These points summarize the kinds of questions trainers might ask themselves:

- *What could people take away?*
  Our main objective had been to raise awareness that we continuously make assumptions, and that, as humans, this will always be so. Vigilantly checking that they *are* assumptions, not facts ... and waiting, may help. We think that, within these limits, most participants left with thoughts of the need for this vigilance.

  One sentence seemed to extract the essence of the workshop: 'I must stop jumping to conclusions—and wait.'
- *Is there any real long-term learning in mini-tasters?*
  How many of the participants went away with *new* thoughts?

  We had intended to offer time to explore:

  What can I do now/over the next five years?
  Who can I tell/will they listen?

  There was no time for this, and we felt unfinished and frustrated. We had not expected to 'finish' by offering total knowledge of the subject, but had wanted people to take away some kind of basic 'action plan'. This leads to the next question.
- *Whose needs were we serving?*
  We had enjoyed designing the session and were eager to try out all our ideas. We had also planned a tight structure, but realize with hindsight that this was influenced more by our own anxieties than by the wishes and needs of the participants. We felt 'unfinished' because we left out the action-planning, but this may have been irrelevant to the group.
- *What were the roles?*
  We analysed which roles were thrust on us when we accepted the original invitation, and added other roles we had chosen; there were probably more. We then analysed the roles of the group members.

Janice and Maggie	Facilitators—boundary managers—learners—experts—powerholders—presenters—leaders—controllers—designers—stagemanagers
Group members	Learners—contributors—expectation-holders—experts—rebels—leaders—problem-holders—participants—thinking/feeling beings—adults

- *What might we have done differently?*
  It is impossible in self-development work and any kind of human-

relationship training to predict how a different presentation might have developed, but we could certainly have continued with the issues which were surfacing in the 'minority groups' exercise.

Our views remain comfortably, but definitely, divided! With more experience of working together we would consult the group about the way we should continue, at the same time pointing out the dilemmas. While Janice is convinced that we made the right decision in that situation, Maggie would have preferred to be more flexible.

- *What reasons influenced our decisions?*

When the atmosphere became uncomfortable and challenging, when it looked as though real issues were surfacing (as opposed to playful exercises), we noticed that we invoked the ground rules, thereby avoiding conflict. We are both experienced facilitators and would probably insist that we trust people to take responsibility for themselves and each other. Why, then, did we stick to our structure?

1. We had agreed to keep the session reasonably light, offering self-development at a possibly superificial level in order to demonstrate a wide variety of activities, which people would be free to adapt for their own work.

2. We knew there was a very limited time and were reluctant to move to an emotional level which people might not be able to handle. This seems now to be perhaps a slightly arrogant attitude; we were working with adults who were presumably experienced in this field.

3. Our working partnership was reasonably new, the design completely new, so we were perhaps slightly nervous on both counts and chose to control the boundaries as a way of controlling our own anxieties.

4. If we dealt with the 'here and now' we would have sacrificed some of the design, and may have felt we had 'cheated' the group.

5. We had made our own assumption—that this group was 'converted' to the principles of equality and non-judgementalism, so there was no need to create unnecessary conflict. (This now seems an amazing rationalization!)

Summarizing our learning: the need for constant evaluation of process

As we completed the evaluation we became aware of some familiarity, and made a connection between the process of the workshop and the way the problems of equal opportunities are often handled. The group provides a microcosm of many work settings:

- We can't get all emotional, they couldn't handle it.
- There isn't time to deal with all these questions.
- We don't have a problem here.
- No one here is racist/sexist/discrimatory/prejudiced, etc.
- It isn't part of the agenda—we'll tell you how others do it.
- Let's be practical—let's not argue.

We intend to run this workshop—preferably for much longer—as often as possible, and to monitor developments.

Until we *all* can face the totality of our fears and resistance there will be no real change in approach *either* to the needs and rights of minorities *or* to the importance of surfacing and confronting our most uncomfortable and painful feelings.

Developers must trust both themselves and others, reaching out for Carl Rogers' 'unconditional positive regard'. Self-development encourages respect for the *humanness* of human beings.

17
The learning community
Roy Canning and Judith Martin

Introduction

The origins of the learning community as an approach to management education and training are well described by Pedler (1981) and Burgoyne *et al.* (1978). The concept has been applied within organizations and has been well documented (Ambrose 1979; Barrett and Taylor 1987). Pedler sees it as a learning event with fixed time limits, existing for a more or less specific purpose. Some of the key characteristics of a learning community are:

- The approach demands that people meet each other on the same level irrespective of outside rank, status or privilege, and all share the norms of the learning community.
- Each person has unique learning needs which cannot be aggregated or equated with the needs of any other person.
- There is mutal interdependence in providing and partaking the available learning resources.
- Each person offers themselves as a resource to others in order to help them learn.

Given the above, the learning community then rests on two major principles:

1. that each individual takes prime responsibility for identifying and meeting their own learning needs; and
2. that each person is responsible for helping others identify their needs and for offering themselves as a flexible resource in the community (Pedler 1981: 69).

Our aim is to add to some of the thinking underlying the learning community model. Particularly we argue that the concept of a community is something that you cannot, like a trailer, just hitch up to some other approach. Rather if we are to think of learning in the sense of community then it does have some theoretical and practical applications which come from a wider base, particularly in the arts and political sciences. We will argue here that if we take a broader perspective of community then this leads us paradoxically to a much tighter definition and approach within the area of management education. We do this firstly by looking at how a community approach is being used in other fields and secondly by providing a paradigm for understanding how learners would work with a sense of community.

We hope that this will stimulate further debate around the issue of learner-centredness, particularly given the enormous resources being directed towards new technology and distance and open learning systems.

Community

Interestingly there has not been a lot of space given in the literature to defining what community actually means. In 1955 Hillery indicated 94 different definitions of what was meant by community.

Looking back to work done in the mid and late 1970s in management education the idea of community has mainly come from experiential learning and therapeutic institutions, particularly from T-group and sensitivity-group approaches and work with patients and staff within the mentally ill field. We think these approaches are useful but limited and it could be argued that in fact they represent closed communities which are heavily dependent on outside agents to provide the stimulus and resources for them to work.

Ideas on community learning have come from the fields of politics, art, design, education and architecture. Each in their own way has provided a more open model for community learning than some approaches from management learning and education. They offer an enriched understanding both of the concept of community and how community learning can take place.

So what do we mean by community? In community education Clarke (1987) describes five main points of entry to understanding the term:

1. community as a human collective;
2. community as territory;
3. community as shared activities;
4. community as close knit relationships;
5. community as sentiment.

Each particular approach has its advantages and disadvantages but a useful distinction is to recognize the difference between 'fact and value' when looking at community. In other words we have to ascertain the *existence* of community and the *strength* of that community in order to understand how it works. This distinction is also made within the field of community art where Kelly (1984) defines community as a set of shared social meanings which are created and mutated through the actions and interactions of its members and through their interactions with a wider society. This definition does not depend upon the location of a community but rather on a shared sense of value and purpose by its members.

Clarke again stresses the importance not only of whether a community exists but the strength of that community—'The strength of a community within any environment is demonstrated by the degree to which its members *relate* and *act* in an independent and interdependent manner.' Having shared values, therefore, is not sufficient in itself for a community to be productive, it also has to operate with a sense of interdependence and enterprise from its individual members.

We would therefore define community as a set of shared values and meanings which are constantly created and recreated through its members relating and acting in both an independent and interdependent way. The other dimension which has to be addressed when using the concept of community is the political context in which we operate. Generally communities have a strong ideological base, for example:

1. encouraging more open and democratic access to learning;
2. people to have more power and control over their learning;
3. the idea of partnership and collaboration;
4. dealing with specific problems with specific contexts with specific solutions.

A community approach opposes any form of centralization, of dependency on autocracy or any idea of a professionally expert led system. We are in other words concerned with how members of the community take charge of their own learning based on participation and partnership with others. So if we are to link community with learning then clearly we have to work within an *ideological* frame of reference, deal with the issues of power and control and re-examine the relationship between user and provider.

Learning

For us the best way into looking at learning is to use the epistemology of Bateson (1972). This framework has been taken by J. Bartunek and M.

1. *First-order learning*
   First-order learning includes the tacit reinforcement of present understanding and behaviour.
2. *Second-order learning*
   Second-order learning includes the conscious modification of understanding and behaviour in a particular direction.
3. *Third-order learning*
   Third-order learning includes learning to be aware of your own patterns of understanding and behaviour and thereby more able to change these patterns as you see fit.

Figure 17.1   Levels of learning

Moch (1987), and used to look at first-order, second-order and third-order change within the organization development field (see Figure 17.1).

Learning at the first level includes change consistent with already agreed frameworks, e.g. attending an induction course or learning how to conduct an appraisal interview. Second-level learning comes where the participant learns to change their understanding or behaviour in a particular direction, e.g. learning to be more participative and less autocratic or more sensitive and responsive to customer needs. Third-order learning helps participants to develop the capacity to identify and change their own frameworks for learning. So for instance, in third-order learning the learner would have an opportunity to explore the values and philosophies underpinning different approaches to learning; would be involved in the design, management and delivery of their own learning and would, in the process, learn how to use external agents. Within the third-order level of learning the responsibility and initiative lies with the learner and in this sense it is closer to the 'spirit' and practice of being a member of a learning community.

Another way of looking at levels of learning is to use a continuum between closed and open learning systems. The characteristics which determine whether something is closed or open would reflect the *level of learning* which in turn would be determined by the level of access participants have to the diagnosis, design, management and assessment of their own learning systems. A truly open learning system would involve the participants in the creation and management of the learning process. In other words, they are learning how to learn through participation and involvement in the process of learning. A closed learning system would treat the learner as a competent consumer (Habermas 1983) of a product designed and delivered by an external agency. There would be choice, but only within pre-defined limits.

The learning community, a paradigm shift

How we can link up the concepts of community and learning to provide a sounder theoretical base for learning community events? In order to do this we need a different paradigm—a way of thinking about the world and how we relate to it—which provides a basis for our actions (Perimutter and Trist 1986).

As individuals, we are both unique and interdependent on others and this connectedness provides the basis for our growth and learning. This new paradigm is represented in Figure 17.2 and shows independence and interdependence as inseparable as a way of being in the world. It also represents an *ideology*. In order to work within a community of learners there has to be a shared ideology which values both independence and interdependence with a sense of a 'public' self. There also has to be a sense of participation—power and control being exercised by those who are directly involved in the learning process. It is only when learners have access to the design and delivery of their own learning can we justifiably claim that the learning process is based on the spirit of community. The distinctions in this approach to the more traditional management teaching are shown in Figure 17.3.

The role of the professional

It is quite clear from the above that in order to work within a learning community expert professionals are called upon to rethink their role completely. Although offered in a different context, Rod Hackney's opinion that we have had a whole generation of professionals producing the wrong product and that learners are waiting to be released from the professional who knows what is best for them, is most apposite.

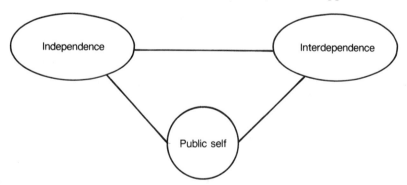

Figure 17.2 The learning community paradigm

Traditional management teaching	Learning community
Status of user Users are passive recipients of a learning process conceived, executed, managed and evaluated by others.	Users are the clients. They take control of the commissioning, designing, managing and evaluating of the learning.
User/expert relationship Remote arms length, experts commissioned by organizations. Occasionally making superficial attempts to define, consult end-users but attitudes are mostly paternalistic.	Creative alliance and working partnership. Experts are commissioned by and are accountable to the users. Experts role as enabler, facilitator and educator.
Scale of project Generally large-scale projects based on mass production.	Generally small, responsive and determined by the nature of the learners and the participants.
Location of learning projects Institutional, residential and housed by the experts. Approaches emphasize technique, style and development in technology.	Anywhere depending on the needs of the clients. Approaches determined by the client rather than by fashionable styles; could be traditional teaching methods and/or learner centred.
Motivation Return on investment and professionalism.	Aiming at self-determination and learning how to learn.
Method of delivery delivery Top-down. Emphasis on product rather than process. Centralized and specialized, compartmentalized	Multi-levelled. Emphasis on process rather than produce, flexible, specific, open, innovative.
Ideology Technocratic, competitive and undemocratic.	Pragmatic, humanitarian, responsive and flexible, collaborative, mutual support.

Figure 17.3 Comparison between traditional management teaching and the learning community

From theory to practice

When working with a temporary community there will probably be both a set theme for learning and limited resources available; for example time, learning aids or support staff. The event itself would also have to deal with 'live' issues or problems facing the individuals so that the transfer of learning would be more immediate and apparent to those taking part. In our programmes at Roffey Park we have identified some common management development themes which can be used as a basis for participants' learning about themselves and helping others learn.

Designing the learning event

In order to design a learning event which embodies the principles and philosophy of the learning community we have to keep in mind some of the key principles underlying the theory. In particular participants need an opportunity to be involved in identifying, designing, implementing and evaluating their own learning and to operate in a way where they are satisfying their own individual needs and helping others develop. In order to do this some time has to be spent on sharing values as a way of people understanding how they are going to work with each other. At this stage the trainer is much more active, encouraging participants to share some of the values around learning and some of the ways in which they could collaborate in others' learning.

The emphasis throughout is to encouraging ownership, giving participants a sense of freedom and choice and for looking at ways in which they could 'learn how to learn' and therefore use the process of learning within a different context.

Given these principles we have designed workshop-based activites that give individuals an opportunity to work as a community of learners. An example of this type of workshop for trainers is given in Figure 17.4. We have given participants the opportunity to identify from their own experience the type of issues that are important to them. This is an individual process supported by others. The first stage is for individuals and small groups to identify key areas of knowledge and skills they would like to develop, then moving on to making decisions about *how* they would like to do so. The figure gives a map of some of the ways in which people could learn. Like any other map this is an approximation to the territory and individuals would be encouraged to identify ways of learning which are outside this map but would suit their individual needs. Our experience is that managers and trainers do need to know something about the area in which they are operating in order to make decisions about what they want. This helps them to answer the next simple question.

What is a workshop?   A semi-structured training group that provides you with an opportunity to experiment with a wider range of intervention styles in managing an individual and/or a group.

What areas can I develop?   These should be based on your own work and/or areas you want to experiment with for the first time.

How is the workshop organized?   As a group we will compile a list of learning events and an initial running order for the workshop.

Who will be there and can I choose who I want?   The training can take place in a large group, small groups or on a one-to-one basis. Each individual will be encouaged to choose who they want to work with.

How do I go about developing the areas I have identified?   Here are *some of the choices* available:

1. *Discussion/problem solving*   Small group problem-solving sessions to deal with specific issues.
2. *Theory*   You may wish some additional theory inputs from the staff and/ or fellow course members.
3. *Role plays*   'Live' or using CCTV you can simulate or rehearse a situation from your own training programmes, e.g. handling a feedback session using CCTV.
4. *Structured skills exercise*   Here you may want to practise specific trainer skills using the *group* as a resource, e.g. process interventions; group management; giving/receiving feedback.
5. *Personal awareness*   You may wish to help others explore personal blocks to learning through a small/large group personal awareness session.
6. *One-to-one*   You may want to spend time with a member of staff and/or colleague on a one-to-one basis.

Can I change what I want to do?   Yes, at any stage in the workshop. It may also be that your training need(s) are met outside workshop time in other parts of the programme.

Whose responsibility is it for the workshops being successful?   As elsewhere in the programme it is a joint responsibility between the trainer(s) and course members.

Figure 17.4   An example of a self-managed training workshop (used on a trainer skills programme)

'How do I know what I need to know?'

Very often participants will have an expectation that the tutors will answer this question for them, and may be very resistant initially to identifying their own needs. Different ways in which we have helped participants overcome this difficulty include:

1. allowing the individuals to express their anxiety and fears and responding appropriately;
2. pre-course briefing, which works particularly well with in-company programmes where we would encourage discussion between participants and line managers, colleagues, subordinates and course tutors, as a means of collecting data and clarifying learning goals;
3. activities such as keeping a diary, noting events, interactions, time spent, etc. or role mapping responsibilities and relationships and identifying things that are going well and areas for improvement. Self-assessment inventories, where participants identify development needs from a list of skills, qualities, situations, etc.

If it is not possible for these activities to take place prior to attending the programmes then they can be done during the initial stages of the event.

Once individuals in small groups identify *what* they want and *how* they want to do it they come together as a group in order to set an agenda for the workshops with the aid of tutorial staff.

At this stage it should be recognized that the process can feel very messy, and a particularly difficult transition for participants who are used to lots of structure and being led by tutors. It is important to encourage individuals to acknowledge and work through this stage. It is very much a process of collaboration where individuals are making demands and at the same time offering others support in their learning. Once an agenda is put together then the workshops are learner-centred in the sense that individuals will be taking responsibility for ensuring that they meet their individual needs and will be making demands on others for assistance and resources. As the workshop proceeds then the agenda may shift as individuals' needs change and priorities become different. Thus flexibility is required. It is not a matter of working through items in sequence but ensuring that time is taken throughout the workshop to review what has actually taken place, to reschedule and to go about things differently.

We have used this type of workshop activity in a number of learning events and found it very productive. It gives the individuals an opportunity to work on individual needs and at the same time make decisions about how they learn. To date we have not encountered any problems about individuals being dissatisfied in not having enough resources or opportunities to do what they want.

It should be recognized that the workshop is used as one method among others for learning during these particular training programmes and in order for it to work successfully does need preparation from those taking part. Normally in any such event we give participants an outline of the workshop before they arrive on the programme; we also get them to think about some of the themes, some of the issues they would like to explore and we normally use some structured learning events before moving into the workshop as a way of managing the transition. We do not offer this format as a prescription for all learning events and for all individuals, our experience being that it has to be used selectively within a certain context and has to be well supported both before and after the learning event itself. However we would encourage other trainers to experiment with this type of workshop as a way of giving participants an opportunity to make more decisions about what and how they learn and to give them some degree of freedom and choice about the learning process.

Important issues to deal with in working with the learning community

The role of the trainer

Working in the way outlined above may require the trainer to have greater flexibility on how they respond to learners and in some senses to be more skilled in acting as a resource base as more demands will be made on them. The role is not a non-directive, purely resource function whereby the trainer responds passively to what is demanded of them. Our experience is that trainers need to work both directively and non-directively, to offer theory and to work at a practical level, to work in large groups, small groups and on a one-to-one basis. Learner-centredness does not mean being non-directive, as this can lead to tremendous frustration in the group. *The important point is who is making the decisions about what and how people learn.* If the individual learner requires and needs theory input and direction from the trainer then it is appropriate for the trainer to provide that. Similarly if the participant requires a less directive approach then again the trainer can respond in like. In many ways the trainer has to be more skilful. Above all they have to understand the context they are operating within, recognize and work with the express needs of the individual learner and do so by exercising a wide range of skills that the more traditional tutor would find difficulty in offering. In certain circumstances they might have to operate directively, by encouraging people to be non-directive or they might have to be non-directive in an attempt to encourage learners to take direct responsibility for their own learning. Like managing there is no one style which is appropriate in all circumstances and situations with all learners.

Managers' experience of the learning community
Participants often find it difficult to work in this non-traditional way with trainers. Their expectations are normally that of a passive recipient of knowledge-based programmes or at best practising skills within a set framework given by the trainer. Rarely would they find themselves in a position of deciding not only what they would like to do but how they would like to go about it. This training approach is, therefore, not an easy option for many learners. One recurrent issue which many participants deal with is the issue of *valuing* their own experience, knowledge and skills. We have often found individual managers discounting their own experience as unimportant while looking for something from the trainer that provides the answers. You will often find them saying things like, 'We have not learned much or there was nothing new here', or 'We had to do this by ourselves.' Although there is significant learning taking place it is not acknowledged or valued by the participant as it has not come from an 'expert' source. It is important to recognize that when working in this way the individuals need to value both their own contributions and that of their peers to the same level as that offered by tutors. Significant learning can be missed if the participants undervalue their own experience and abilities as learners.

Another issue which managers grapple with is how much to go after their own needs, and how much to offer support for others. They are faced with the issue of self-interest versus co-operation and collaboration with others and they are forced within this framework to find the right balance for themselves. Often you will find them expressing a concern about being too self-interested or not being self-interested enough. While working with others they will be concerned about getting things out of other people's learning events given that they have not initiated, designed or run it themselves. They are going to be dealing with this dependent and interdependent dynamic and each will be forced to make choices about how much time and energy they will devote to others. It is important that the trainer be aware of this and raise the issue explicitly if required.

The reviewing process
This is an important part of the learning process and may need encouragement and structure from the tutors, depending on how natural and easy the participants find it to reflect on what's been going on. Some participants may need help in thinking things through and tutors can be helpful in providing frameworks to structure the process, particularly at appropriate stages in the programme where consolidation is necessary and outstanding needs are identified. It may be helpful to encourage

participants to reflect on not only what they are learning at a content level but also at a process level. So typical questions we may ask participants to help them reflect could be: 'What am I learning about the way I support and challenge others?'; 'How have I been getting my needs met this week?'; 'Are there any patterns of behaviour I am recognizing in myself?'; and 'What are the implications of these for me at work?'

Resourcing
Another major issue which surfaces regularly in this type of learning event is the resourcing of the programme. If we are to give freedom and choice and encourage individuals to make decisions about how they learn then we will have to, as professionals, provide a back-up service that will allow this to happen. There is no point in offering people a variety of ways to learn when all there is available is one trainer, twelve participants, one training room and a series of case studies. It is important to recognize that there will be many demands made on you which will cover everything from one-to-one counselling, taking time out to do some reading, closed-circuit television work, skills exercises, case studies, theory input, to name but a few. It is therefore important when you are organizing this type of event to set up some form of resource centre for those taking part. Again this highlights that going this route is not an easy option and does require detailed planning and preparation beforehand. Normally you need a higher tutor-to-participant ratio than with conventional programmes. You need a number of different rooms available and a range of equipment which would allow you to run training sessions in parallel. It is also important to recognize throughout that individuals have the option of taking part in particular sessions and if they decide to take time out to reflect then they may need a quiet room or a learning resource library to do that.

Conclusions

We believe that to operate with any sense of community then there are a number of key yet simple principles. There needs to be shared values among those taking part and participants need to operate both in an interdependent and independent way. We also recognize that there is an political dimension in that we are looking for a less autocratic and centralized decision-making process about how people learn.

With this in mind we have described how the learning community can be used in practice on short programmes. We have described a workshop activity which can be used as part of a learning event and in doing so we have raised issues which both the trainers and participants would have to think about and deal with during the programme itself.

References

Ambrose, K. (1979) 'The development of a learning community: a case study', *Management Education and Development*, **10**(2), Summer, 141–9.

Barrett, P. and B. Taylor (1987) 'Using the learning community for management development', *Training & Management Development Methods*, IMCB Publications, Bradford.

Bartunek, J. and M. Moch (1987) 'First-order, second-order and third-order change and organization development interventions', *Journal of Applied Behavioural Science*, **23**(4).

Bateson, G. (1972) *Steps to an Ecology of Mind*, Chandler, New York.

Burgoyne, J. G. *et al.* (1978) *Self-Development*, Association of Teachers of Management, London.

Clarke, D. (1987) *The Concept of Community Education in Community Education: An Agenda for Educational Reform*, Open University Press, Milton Keynes.

Habermas, Jurgen (1983) *Modernity: An Incomplete Project on Post Modern Culture*, ed. Hal Foster, Pluto Press, London.

Kelly, O. (1984) *Community Art and the State*, Connection, New York.

Pedler, M. J. (1981) 'Developing the learning community' in T. Boydell and M. Pedler (eds) *Management Self-Development*, Gower, Aldershot.

Perimutter, H. and E. Trist (1986) 'Paradigms for societal transition', *Human Relations*, **39**(1).

Wales, Nick and Charles Knevitt (1987) *Community Architecture*, Penguin, Harmondsworth.

18
Using consultants to integrate management and organizational development
Ita O'Donovan

Introduction

This chapter examines the contribution consultants can make to the management development process in organizations. A case example of work in a local authority illustrates the role of the consultant in integrating individuals and organizational development.

Consultancy and management development

For me consultancy has three essential requirements:

1. specialist knowledge of subject area;
2. broad experience gained from the world of practice;
3. the interpersonal skills to be sensitive to organizational politics, while adopting a facilitative role in the development process.

Consultancy is seen very much as an interactive exercise between client and consultant. The consultant may be cast in the role of 'expert' in the initial stages but it is a poor consultant who fails to tap into the client's knowledge and expertise. By definition the consultant ought to be able to generate material upon which solutions to particular issues may be formulated. These too come from expert knowledge and the world of practice. The role of the consultant as a facilitator is vital; here the consultant seeks to enable individuals and the organization to reflect on their current practices in a constructive manner leading to an increased capacity to function effectively.

The term management development means many things to different people, ranging from developing systems of management control which concentrate heavily on discrete functions and reporting procedures, to an emphasis on organizational development which includes an evaluation of structures, systems and strategy: to a perspective that concentrates entirely on individual managers and a process of self-development. The latter embraces the areas of interpersonal skills and self-awareness.

These approaches to management development can be linked closely to developments within the field of organizational theory. Thus for example, scientific management is closely aligned to the concept of control; the human relations school is associated with the concept of the individual manager as an agent for development; and organizational development is closely associated with the area of organizational design.

Management development has two core elements—personal and organizational development. For me development as an idea embraces both the outer reality of environment and 'organizational goals' and the inner reality of the 'self'. The dictionary defines the word development as 'the act or process of growing, progressing, or developing'. The definition implies change; it seems only logical that the aim of management development would be to create an environment in which individuals would have the opportunity to consider and agree ways of achieving personal and organizational goals. Organizational development implies a process of examination of structures and systems to evaluate their appropriateness to cope with the existing internal and external environment. If change is present in either of the environments this may call into question the current structures and systems. The task for individuals who participate in an organizational development exercise may be to question current management strategies and styles.

It may sound incongruous to talk of 'updating' people, but they are a vital aspect of organizational life. If we take a broad range of organizations we can note that the cost of people as a proportion of overall expenditure is in the range of 60–70 per cent. It is interesting to note how much of that expenditure is related to investment in training of personnel. Very often this is as low as 1 per cent. Successful management needs to involve individuals directly in seeking to achieve organizational goals, together with an organizational design that is responsive and flexible to its environments. It follows that management development must integrate personal and organizational development. In the 1970s and '80s successful organizations were responsive not only to their employees but also to their markets. They actually consulted and listened to their customers and produced a good or service that customers said they wanted. Examples include: Rolls-Royce, Mercedes Benz, Porsche,

IBM and Hewlett Packard who have fostered an ethos of innovation and entrepreneurial spirit together with a shared sense of purpose.

Consultancy designed management development programmes

What can consultancy designed management development programmes contribute to personal and organizational development? Consultancy offers a broad-based perspective from a knowledgeable source not inhibited by internal perceptions. Specifically consultancy designed management development programmes can make the following contributions:

1. a broad-based external perspective from the world of practice;
2. a set of analytic skills to see the gaps between what an organization says about itself and the reality of what it does;
3. the ability to create a non-threatening environment to enhance learning;
4. the ability to challenge current management philosophy and practice;
5. the investigative time to create the organizational space to ask questions;
6. the knowledge to inform about changes in the external environment;
7. the ability to act as a reflector for the organization;
8. the ability to act as a facilitator so that people and the organization can develop together.

What is involved in planning and delivering

1. Initial contact involves negotiations as to the scope of the consultancy, e.g. length of time, level and number of participants, depth of investigation, etc.
2. Familiarization and investigation of client organization. This can include quantitative and qualitative methods of investigation in relation to individual structures and systems.
3. Consultants' identification and assessment of personal and organizational issues.
4. Consultants' first thoughts as to the content and process of the management development programme based on results of (2) and (3), together with an external focus.
5. Negotiations with the client as to the actual content and process of the management development programme. This will include an agreement to implement solutions generated by the management development programme.

6. Consultants design and run the programmes.
7. Consultants write a final report which incorporates the solutions generated on the programmes with their recommendations.

To illustrate this process here is a case example from a recent consultancy that I and a colleague undertook with the planning and transportation department of a local authority which we shall call 'Blue Arrow City Council'.

Planning and delivery process—step 1: initial contact

The request to undertake the consultancy made it clear that the director of the department was seeking a management development programme which would enable his officers to consider the relationship between the development of the department and their own personal development. It was agreed that the focus of the consultancy would tend towards an investigation of the performance of present systems within the department. The participants on the programme would be senior personnel. Participants would be interviewed as to their assessment of needs—personal and organizational. The director was made aware of the framework adopted by the consultants in designing management development programmes. Blue Arrow City Council strongly subscribes to the Conservative party philosophy of privatization with a vision of lean administrative centres awarding and monitoring contracts, which is favoured by the politicians. This view of the purpose of local government has strong implications for the organizational design of departments and for individual management practices.

Planning and delivery process—step 2: familiarization and investigation of the planning and transportation department

The planning and transportation department was formed in 1985 from an amalgam of two departments, planning and engineers. Since 1985 the new department experienced two restructurings, which implies a high degree of change in a short period of time. The department consists of five divisions: policy development and transportation; highways and environmental design; parking operations; development; building control. Each division is headed by a divisional director, all of whom have a direct line of accountability to the director of the department. The assistant director of the department is head of corporate management, working closely with the director. The divisions in turn are divided into subsections on the basis of functional specialism or geographical area. Most divisions may be described as tall line structures with many levels of hierarchy.

The chairman of the planning and engineers department is a member of the controlling group. He firmly believes in a private-sector business approach and constantly conveys this to his senior officers. Officers have to be responsive to members' policies and consistently seek to implement policies in the preferred style of members.

The director and the management team have introduced many central initiatives in response to policy direction. The most important being:

- a strategic plan;
- a business plan;
- performance-related pay for senior officers (that is director to assistant director divisional level);
- A bonus scheme linked to objective setting for less senior officers;
- project management for specific tasks;
- cost centre management.

All the above have been implemented or initiated within the last two years.

Stresses and strains

Blue Arrow is experiencing a period of growth with an enormous increase in property developments, both in the private and public sectors. This has resulted in an increase in planning applications, problems with car-parking facilities, both on street and in car parks. Residents on the whole pay high prices for their homes and demand quality services from their authority. This extends to general environmental issues as well as street lighting and road maintenance.

Members value the idea of 'serving the public' and are also very committed to market ideas of consumerism and consultation. They like to operate at a high profile level but this can lead to frequent changes in policies and strategies. At the same time they believe in the idea of a very cost effective department. Efficiency of output is also a priority area for departmental units seeking to enhance service delivery to clients. There is additional interest in the possibility of certain units, for example car parks becoming free standing in the competitive climate of privatization.

The departmental management team, despite changes to structures and systems, is concerned that some service delivery areas are not performing at the level required by the elected members. This has led to a degree of tension in officer/member relations. Investigation revealed the following causes for concern.

Planning applications

A policy of negotiation is in operation for planning applications, this applies across the range of applications from shop front to office block. This policy is in accordance with members' preference for consultation with clients/consumers. A survey revealed that Blue Arrow does not compare favourably with comparable authorities in reaching planning application decisions (see Table 18.1).

Blue Arrow receives 3600 applications a year which places it in the high range nationally. Applicants when interviewed made the following comments about the service they received:

- They were unhappy about the length of time applications took to be processed.
- They requested good reliable pre-application advice but this could not be relied upon.
- Applicants felt that the division did not convey their aims and objectives to them on either design or land-use issues.
- Applicants thought that officers were too demanding on design issues and often not in touch with economic reality.
- Applicants liked the policy of negotiation and the opportunity to re-submit applications.

Project teams

A project management strategy is in operation in the department in response to the need to handle novel tasks. These are usually in connection with members' priorities and deal with high-profile matters such as major developments or environmental issues. The imposition of this strategy on existing line structure has caused a classic matrix structure. This creates particular strains and questions:

- Where is the motivation for project members when their primary loyalty and reward remains within the division to which they belong?
- Who is ultimately responsible for the work undertaken by project teams?

Table 18.1 Planning application decisions: Blue Arrow v. comparable authorities

	Blue Arrow (%)	Comparable authorities (%)
Decisions issued in 8 weeks	19	41
Decisions reached between 8 and 13 weeks	26	36
Decisions reached after 13 weeks	55	23

- What are the consequences for a section when they loan or share a colleague over a long duration?

Cost centre management
The introduction to the department of a decentralized system of financial management has affected relationships with the central treasury department and also relationships within the planning and engineers department. In the first instance the department perceives the treasury as conveying financial information in a format not conducive to management decisions. Secondly within the department tensions have arisen between sections which are not of equal financial strength. This raises the issue of financial allocation/reallocation of expenditure and revenue within the department and between the department and the centre. These concerns have to be viewed in the light of elected members welcoming the opportunity afforded by competition, for operational sections to become free-standing.

Personnel
The department in some divisions experiences problems of recruitment and retention. While this must be seen within the national context of short supply in some technical and professional fields this is not the complete answer; for example:

- The ratification process for appointments is particularly lengthy (8 weeks).
- Central personnel seem unresponsive to service departments' requirements with regard to scale when recruiting.
- Generally there is not a pro-active approach to training individuals on the job to compensate for lack of technical experience.
- Members have a tight policy on human resources, but are concerned with the failure in recruitment and retention.
- Individuals experience quite high degrees of stress in the execution of their work, due to volume, politics and high levels of uncertainty as to the future position of particular units within the department.

Planning and delivery process—step 3: identification

The issues described above are a pen picture of the initial investigation, which combined the collection of quantitative data with extensive interviews of key officers in the planning and transportation department taking account of vertical and lateral positions in the hierarchy. This familiarization process provided a relevant basis upon which to design the content and process of a management development programme.

Planning and delivery process—step 4: first thoughts and concerns on programme design

Key concerns in the design of the programme were:

- the choice of media to facilitate development and discussion of the issues;
- ensuring that participants would be key actors in any proposed solutions, with the relevant scope of responsibility to act;
- the consultants to reflect the image of the department at the present time;
- the participants and consultants to work together in an examination of what future responses might be necessary so as to ensure outcomes which recognize two factors: policy direction and the implementation process;
- that the programme addresses the personal issues that develop in a climate of uncertainty and change;
- the need to link the outcomes of the programme to the management implementation process.

Planning and delivery process—step 5: negotiations with client as to design solutions

Extensive discussions between the consultants, the director and assistant director of the department, as to the content and process of the programme, ensured that the director was willing to support solutions derived from the total process. It was agreed that the consultants would submit a report at the conclusion of the management development programmes. This report would contain a clear picture of the way forward for the department. It would incorporate the deliberations of the management development programmes in the proposed solutions, together with the consultants' requirements to evaluate and make recommendations.

Planning and delivery process—step 6: design and run the programmes

Two management development programmes, each of the same design and duration, were run for the planning and transportation department.

The programmes were residential and involved the two consultants and twelve key officers. The director was not a participant, but attended the final day of the programme to listen to a presentation of the deliberations.

In designing the programme the consultants were able to draw on the research and consultancy experience of their institution, as well as receiving direct input from colleagues on particular topics, e.g. legislation, decentralized resource management, compulsory competitive tendering and stress management.

Summary of programme content and process
The programme had three foci: organizational focus: external focus; individual focus.

Organizational focus Prior to the commencement of the programme the participants had filled in job analysis questionnaires. In multi-divisional small groups individuals identified personal and organizational issues from these questionnaires with the consultants. These organizational issues were then discussed within the present evidence of the department's performance and the consultants image of the department at the present time. This discussion covered all the issues described under 'Stresses and strains': planning applications; project teams; cost centre management: personnel. It was further faciliated by the interplay of the external focus.

External focus Here the central government concern with making local authorities more accountable was examined by looking at the recent local government legislation under the broad headings of finance, housing and education. The issue of privatization and compulsory competitive tendering was looked at in detail with its structural implications for an authority seeking to adopt this message. Throughout these debates the implications for individuals were being considered.

Individual focus Change by its very nature induces many reactions; one of these is stress. Stress in itself is a normal but sometimes uncomfortable experience. Participants were given the opportunity to learn about their own causes of stress and methods for coping with them. Another reaction to a high degree of change is a climate of uncertainty in the work environment. This can have implications for individual management roles with regard to practice and leadership style. Participants considered what new skills would be required by them to manage in a climate of change.

Process of the programmes

The programmes were organized around three main inputs: sessions on major changes taking place and the forces behind those changes; discussion on financial management, management of people and group work on the real issues generated from the investigation of the department and the participants' live experience of their work environment. In the vital area of group work the consultants adopted a facilitator role, seeking to support the groups in generating viable solutions to the issues. This work was characterized by the participants reflecting on their experiences and the consultants reflecting an image they had formed of the department. The impetus for the participants to lead this process came from two factors: the material that was being addressed was relevant and real: and individuals were working towards making a presentation of their deliberations to the director on the final night of the programme. These factors combined with the other inputs to create an atmosphere that sought to find solutions to change.

Planning and delivery process—step 7: final report

When the two programmes were completed the consultants prepared a report for the director, which incorporated the deliberations and the solutions generated on the programme. The report provided the opportunity for the consultants to propose in detail a way forward for the department. The report dealt with the organizational issues of structures, systems and the personal development needs of managers implementing high degrees of change. Because of the length and detail of the final report it is not possible to include it in this chapter. What follows is a short summary of the approach we adopted as consultants. This enabled us to step back and take an analytic view of the department, while also taking account of the outcomes of the programmes.

In our view the main issue for the department was how to match its structure with the departmental strategy which was manifested in a number of key initiatives such as: a business plan, performance related pay, objective setting, decentralized financial management and project teams. The department was also going to be buffeted by changes, of which one of the most important is the internal trading requirement that is incorporated in future government legislation. There are few hard and fast rules for just what kind of organizational structure to employ for each type of strategy. Every organization is partly idiosyncratic, the result of many organizational decisions and historical circumstances; the planning and transportation department was no exception. However, there are key elements one may look at in seeking to match strategy and structure.

1. Pinpoint the key functions and tasks requisite for successful strategy execution.
2. Reflect on how a balance might be achieved between strategy critical functions, routine functions and staff support.
3. Make the strategy-critical units and functions the main departmental building blocks.
4. Determine the degrees of authority needed to manage each departmental unit, bearing in mind both the benefits and costs of decentralized decision-making.
5. Provide for co-ordination among the departmental units.

The planning and transportation department had firmly addressed itself to the first element above; we focused more on elements 2, 3, 4, and 5. The introduction of new strategies inevitably brings adminstrative problems which in turn call for a refashioning of structure to facilitate successful implementation. We concentrated on:

1. the smaller unit structure and its relationships within the division, department and with the centre;
2. the divisional structure and its relationship with the other divisions, the department and with the centre;
3. the department and its relationships;
4. the implications of the above for individual management practices.

This consultancy report and others generated in this manner have a good implementation record.

Conclusion

Here I would like to emphasize the strengths of the approach outlined above.

1. It engages the people in the organization in the management development process.
2. Proposals are more likely to be 'owned' by individuals who have helped to generate them.
3. It brings together in a challenging way the world of the practitioner and the consultant.
4. The total process is underpinned by the consultants' own institution's knowledge, based on research and consultancy.

5. The approach is suitable for management development at different levels in the hierarchy.
6. It produces proposals that integrate and take account of personal and organization development goals.

Peters and Waterman (1982) and Pascale and Athos (1986) derived their model of the importance of the Seven S's from extensive research and consultancy with successful companies in America and Japan. We can see that their Structure, Strategy and Systems fall into the category of organizational development, while their Shared Values, Style, Staff and Skills fit into the personal development category. In the view of these writers the key to management success is the integration of these elements. I am suggesting that consultancy designed management development programmes as outlined in this chapter can successfully support integrated organizational and personal development.

The independent nature of the consultant role is an important ingredient in the process of harnessing the capacity of an organization to take a developmental step forward. During the various steps we can observe that the consultant offers different contributions. During the initial contact with the client, the consultant is very much in a clarifying role, supporting the client in defining their perceived needs. The process of familiarization and investigation leads the consultant into the client's world. Here it is necessary to be sensitive to organizational politics, while maintaining independence of thought in the investigative process. It is a delicate stage where trust and integrity between the partners needs to develop. In the identification and assessment of personal and organizational issues, the consultant is very much the analyser, seeking to assess the present situation in the light of accrued knowledge and experience. There is a strong comparative performance review element in this process, balanced by an understanding of the individuality of each organization. This develops into the creative stage of deciding what elements of content and process will facilitate the achievement of a successful programme.

Step 5 sees the client and consultant exchange their professional concerns as to the requirements. This may often involve tough bargaining even with clients who view themselves as allies. Here the consultant may need to draw on the trust and credibility developed in the earlier interactions. During the running of the programme the consultant is very much the facilitator and reflector, encouraging participants to recognize the issues for themselves and generate solutions. In the final step the consultant takes on the role of adviser to the organization as a whole and by definition submits a report with recommendations and a plan of the way forward. The key to this approach lies in creating an environment where the external perspective interacts with the internal organizational view, in a positive climate, to evaluate the current situation and to decide on a developmental step.

References

Peters, T. J. and R. H. Waterman Jr. (1982) *In Search of Excellence*, Harper & Row, New York.

Pascale, R. T. and A. G. Athos (1986) *The Art of Japanese Management*, Penguin, Harmondsworth.

19
Towards a working definition of a learning organization
Margaret Attwood and Noel Beer

Introduction

This is the story of a journey which is now some three years old. It began when one of us took on a new job as manager of organizational development for Mid Essex Health Authority, a position which combines responsibility at board level for personnel, planning and other allied advisory functions with an internal consultancy brief. In the very early days of appointment the district general manager articulated his aim to change the organization's culture. This led to a dialogue (Attwood and Johnson 1987) which resulted in the recognition of the centrality of organization and management development to the drive for increased organizational effectiveness. The conceptual framework within which we are now working is that of the 'learning organization'.

This chapter describes the 'journey' thus far, explores the definition of a learning organization which has emerged as a result, together with our views about future activites which will be necessary if Mid Essex is to achieve and maintain improved effectiveness in this way.

Mid Essex Health Authority serves 290 000 people, has an annual budget of nearly £60 000 000 and employs about 5000 staff.

The work described in this paper has taken place against the background of the Griffiths Report (1983) which concluded that the NHS required a clearly defined general management function, 'the responsibility drawn together in one person at different levels of the organisation for planning, implementation and control of performance'. This process stimulating initiative, vitality and urgency and capitalizing on the dedication and expertise of staff should lead the search for better service delivery much more effectively than the previous consensus teams, where each member had the power of veto.

A planning workshop to develop a change strategy was designed. The parameters, both local and national, within which change could occur, were explored with participating senior managers by the district general manager. It was decided that a 'mission' statement would help to focus subsequent activities: 'In Mid Essex our task is to provide and promote a high standard of health care in order to improve the quality of life, within the resources available, and which are accepted by society.'

To achieve this transition change goals were felt to be vital. Those listed in Figure 19.1 were defined and subjected to review at a later workshop.

The mission statement and these goals have been approved by the district management board and the health authority.

At this stage it was recognized that in the effectiveness of individual managers lay the key to achievement of the aims expressed in the mission statement. It was vital to equip managers for what were, in many cases, new roles and also to ensure their commitment to and knowledge about necessary organizational change. Planned organizational and personal development for managers were inextricably linked. It was important to set in train activities which would recognize and develop this integration. Requirements for increased managerial effectiveness made it important to encourage managers to assess the gap between their current orientations and skills and the organizational change goals (see Figure 19.2).

We decided that a way to achieve significant reorientation both organizational and personal would be to put large numbers of managers through the same programme in a short time thus creating a 'rite of passage' from consensus to general management. One hundred and

---

1. To pursue the promotion of the corporate image of the Authority.
2. To demonstrate actively the value placed on employees.
3. To attempt to quantify current activities in terms of patient demands/needs related to outcome.
4. To provide higher quality services.
5. To ensure that staff at all levels are free to display initiative in the organization of their daily tasks.
6. To recognize and build on the organization's good practices.
7. To encourage better two-way communications both within and outside the organization.
8. To recognize more clearly areas of creative tension/potential conflict within the organization and establish clear mechanisms to resolve them.
9. To establish and maintain mutual trust throughout the organization.
10. To motivate the client group to be involved in and to take responsibilty for their own health.

Figure 19.1   Transition change goals for Mid Essex Health Authority

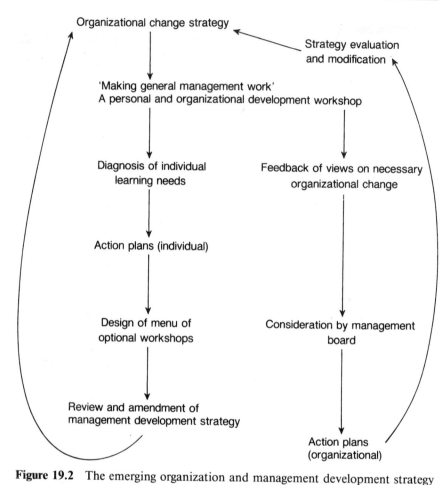

Figure 19.2 The emerging organization and management development strategy

eighty senior and middle managers were identified as participants in a series of workshops—the first stage of this process.

The workshop was designed to allow exploration of the context of managerial jobs (including the change strategy) and of change processes in organizations, building upon experiences to enhance skills. The rationale for personal effectiveness was that 'anyone who wants to improve the way they manage others must first learn to manage themselves' (Pedler and Boydell 1985). Desired outcomes from the workshop were articulated as interlinked themes of personal and organizational action planning. The former process enabled individuals, on the basis of a diagnosis of personal development needs, to opt into further workshops; the latter involved the feedback of views on the nature of, and pressures on, managerial roles and other significant aspects of the functioning of the district as part of the continual evolution and implementation of the change strategy. The latter data together with subsequent evaluation letters enabled the management board to assess the degree to which the workshops' aims were met and the goals of the change strategy were being achieved.

The outcome of the workshops were both organizational and individual. The organizational outcomes emerged from small group activities in which participants identified information about the organization which they would like to share with the board. These covered the identity of the district, its functioning, e.g. with regard to communications, managerial roles and relationships and strategies for managing change, including evaluation of these. At the individual level the workshops assisted managers to diagnose development needs to improve their effectiveness in current jobs and to enable career progression; they also enhanced identification with the district and provided a framework for decision-making about improvements in work systems and processes which participants could make.

A further series of workshops for five hundred more junior managers, using the same process as that summarized above is under way. Again, the outcomes both organizational and individual are being presented at regular intervals to the district management board, most of whose members have been involved in this second series of workshops.

Optional workshops, initially for the senior managers who attended the first workshop series, but, latterly for all managers, have been designed in response to identified needs covering a wide range of competencies needed by managers in the district. All emphasize the necessity for individual participants' objectives to be clarified prior to attendance and encourage the establishment of action plans for improved work performance after the workshops.

Since the inception of general management the NHS has adopted an individual performance review system (IPR) for managers. This involves the establishment of specific job-related objectives as relevant target areas for managers for the next year. Review of performance is based on the extent to which objectives have been met as measured by pre-determined success criteria. There is an associated performance-related pay system. An important dimension of IPR is the establishment of personal development plans which assist managers to achieve both the defined performance objectives and longer-term career goals. Hence, the link between organizational and individual performance and development is an integral part of performance appraisal as well as of organization and management development.

While the centrality of this linkage between organization development and management development had been clear to the authors and to key members of senior management since the inception of the work discussed in this chapter, it became clear as the 'journey' progressed that it would be helpful to express it more explicitly for managers as a 'learning-effectiveness bargain'. See Figure 19.3.

This came from a recognition of the need to make a statement about the district's expectations of and obligations towards its managers. Guidelines to management practice therefore were drawn up and were approved by the district management board and health authority. A copy of this document is included as an Appendix to this chapter because of its centrality to the future development of Mid Essex Health Authority as a 'learning organization'.

The responsibility of managers for their own development within the framework provided by the district has been continued through follow-up workshops and review meetings and also through support or development groups.

The former have the aim of encouraging individuals to review and revitalize their personal development plans and also provide feedback on the progress of the district in achieving the goals for transitional change

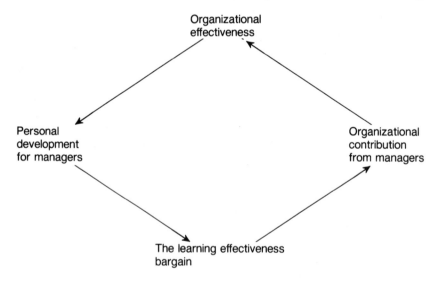

Guide to management practice

Figure 19.3 The 'learning effectiveness bargain'

outlined in Figure 19.1. (An employee attitute survey was also used as a further check on progress towards these goals.)

Support or development groups arose initially from the initiatives of individual managers, whose enthusiasm was raised by the workshops. They are used to take forward individuals' development plans. Further groups have been established as a result of follow-up sessions or other review meetings. Elsewhere (Attwood and Beer 1988) we have described the activities outlined in this chapter as concerned with *both* developing individual managers *and* developing managing by providing a framework within which individuals and managerial groups can work through a series of questions:

Personal development questions	*Organization development questions*
Who am I?	What kind of organization is this?
What stage have I reached in my life so far?	What are its current characteristics/ issues it faces?
Where do I want to go in the future?	What needs to change?
How am I going to get there?	How can change take place?

In the next section we explore our emerging definition of a learning organization which enables these questions to be both asked and answered.

A model of the learning organization

We start by proposing a general model of the learning organization.

Throughout the 'journey' there has been clarity about the sorts of processes that have been sought in moving towards the learning organization, but our view of the end product has been less clear; the definition of the learning organization is implicit rather than explicit. It emerges from our attempt to answer the question, 'How will I recognize the learning organization when I see it?' We decided that we would be able to recognize the following necessary elements of the learning organization:

1. The role of management

- The senior management team allocates time for its own development, which is pursued both collectively and as individuals.
- Senior management team decision-making always recognizes the learning which will have to occur if the change resulting from the decision is to be effective.
- Managers at all levels are aware of their responsibilities for prompting continuous and relevant learning, both for themselves and for their team members.
- Innovation is encouraged at all levels.

- There is a clearly expressed and widely supported aim of improving organizational effectiveness through individual development.
- Learning-supportive systems are in operation (e.g. performance review, succession planning).
- There is recognition by management at all levels of the freedom which individuals require in order to manage to their own self-development.

2. The role of organization development/personnel staff

- There is a training and development staff able to offer advice and expertise from a wide base of learning strategies and methods, and able to do so in response to learning initiatives from others, as well as their own.

3. The shared responsibility of staff for the learning process

- Individuals take responsibility for identifying their own learning needs and for pursuing the means of satisfying these.
- Many different learning methods are employed throughout a range of levels and locations, choice is available from among these methods, and encouragement is given to individuals and groups to exercise their choice.
- Pan-organization learning activities exist. These have originated from the initiatives of individuals and groups, as well as from formal development and training processes.
- Informal, learning networks exist, both pan-organizationally and locally, and do so with the approval of management.
- Individuals act reasonably when utilizing the freedom they come to acquire (i.e. they exercise 'responsible freedom', a notion which is referred to later in this chapter).

4. The robustness of the learning process

- When internal changes of structure and functioning occur the learning impetus continues.

5. The continuity of feedback

- Evaluation is frequent and regular, both at the individual and the collective level.

6. The rate of learning

- The organization's rate of learning is equal to, or greater than, the rate of change in its environment and thus it is likely to survive.

This notion, popularized by Revans in his use of the ecological formular $L \geqslant C$, is seen at one level in the activities of the most senior managers in looking upwards and outwards and ensuring that other senior managers are responding to, or anticipating, events in the organization's environment. However, it will also be seen from the foregoing list of characteristics of the learning organization that managers at all levels will be similarly scanning their local environments, endeavouring to match the changes with their own learning, and assisting colleagues and subordinates to do the same.

Within this model of the learning organization it follows that individuals will be exercising choice in a number of ways. They do not have a 'bill of rights' or privileges conferred upon them; what they do have is freedom to operate within the framework which management has created in accordance with its values and beliefs; what is being recommended is the normal mode of operation within this view of the learning organization, and what is normal is that individuals can:

- make proposals;
- challenge more senior management;
- be heard;
- be allowed to learn and be seen to be learning;
- have responsibility for their own learning;
- identify their own learning needs and choose the methods of meeting them;
- have differences between different parts of the organization recognized as legitimate;
- hold views which are at variance with others in the organization, have these views debated freely, and at the end of the debate continue to hold them;
- make cross function/cross department/cross unit contacts without consulting more senior line management;
- receive feedback and have an open discussion about one's own performance with one's boss;
- give direct feedback about ways in which the boss's performance assists or constrains their own performance;
- be supported in the foregoing by their managers and the organization.

Issues in progressing towards a learning organization

The foregoing describes the sort of freedom which will pertain in the learning organization. In Mid Essex Health Authority progress is being made towards this mode of operation, but at this stage there are some significant issues which are needing regular monitoring and which might soon need to be addressed with new interventions. Among these issues are those of liberating structure, organizational sub-climates and 'responsible freedom'.

Liberating structure
As managers in Mid Essex have progressed from the core workshop, through optional workshops, individual performance review interviews and other structured learning events, the 'riddle of liberating structure' (Pedler 1981) has persisted as a central issue in the attempt to create an open learning climate. In each of these learning settings the preferred and recommended learning processes are endeavours to allow the actors an opportunity for the exercise of individual choice, both in identifying and satisfying their learning needs. However, while these may be honest and diligent attempts to 'facilitate' and 'enable' self-directed learning, they are organization-led, and, within each of them, it is apparent where power, and perhaps knowledge and expertise, actually reside. So, as yet, many managers do not have ownership of their learning, despite attempts to transfer this to them. If learners are to be truly freed to self-develop, this issue requires constant monitoring, with new sorts of learning settings being made available, and with management style becoming a significant factor in the creation of an appropriate learning climate.

Organizational sub-climates
The characteristics of the learning organization and the normal mode of operation within it, which are described earlier, identify preferred end states.

To some degree they parallel Temporal's (1981) climate constituents that are considered conducive to self-development, and we find agreement with Temporal in that within the list of general constituents may be found differences which result from the existence of sub-climates. These may be identified by level, function and profession. In some cases these sub-climates pose problems in that within them are environmental blockages to learning, such as seniors' reluctance to encourage or even to allow subordinates self-development initiatives. This can occur when the approach to professional development has been highly structured and 'teacher-centred'. Some managers also have a management style which stifles the development of their subordinates by thwarting the latter's questions or requests to be able to do things differently.

Within Mid Essex there is some evidence of environmental blockages to learning. The overall picture is patchy; there are examples of excellent manager/subordinate collaboration and freedom to learn, and, at the same time some more constrained sub-climates. In general, there is more satisfaction in the higher levels of the organization, where senior managers seem to experience more freedom and choice to operate within their own styles, whereas there is more tension between levels further down the organization, reflected in constraints on two-way communication and inhibition of individual decision-making. The formulation of processes which prompt senior managers to act as models for more junior colleagues is central to the development of generally more favourable sub-climates.

The notion of responsible freedom
Within the learning organization individuals have some forms of freedom which are not commonplace in organizational life, but which would seem to us to be prerequisites for successful learning. Their full exercise becomes possible only where high levels of trust exist between different levels, functions and units, and it is therefore incumbent upon learners to act responsibly in relation to other individuals and departments and, in particular, in relation to their own managers and subordinates. Within some organizations the notion of 'responsible freedom' will seem naïve, and its introduction an invitation to anarchy, but this situation is far from universal.

Our own experience in working closely with many Mid Essex managers over the past two years had impressed upon us the high levels of responsibility, integrity and loyalty which exist and we conclude that these staff can and will act with 'responsible freedom'. This situation might not be general among health authorities, but views expressed by practitioners like Barclay (1988), who has returned to the Health Service after a period in the private sector, confirm a degree of goodwill, loyalty and idealism within a supportive atmosphere, which suggests that this could be fairly common within the National Health Service.

Future actions to promote the learning organization in MEHA

Alongside the regular monitoring of these three outstanding issues of liberating structure, organizational sub-climates and responsible freedom, the evaluation of progress in Mid Essex confirms that some of the organizational and individual outcomes which emerged from the initial workshops, and which became the basis of recommendations for action, are still requiring attention. Feedback from staff has enabled us to identify some actions which will form the basis of the development agenda in Mid Essex for the next two years. In some instances these actions require improvements to be made to existing practices, while in other cases new measures are recommended if Mid Essex is progressively to acquire the characteristics of a learning organization defined on pp. 239–241. These actions are as follows:

1. Effective operation and maintenance of the Individual Performance Review scheme (IPR) The design of IPR allows ample opportunity for managers to identify their own development needs and propose ways of meeting these, as well as allowing for a free exchange of ideas between manager and subordinate. It offers an organization-wide framework for developing skills which are relevant to the operation of the learning organization. At this stage the quality of the IPR application is patchy, and the element which particularly needs strengthening is the definition of the personal development plan and the design of appropriate learning activities contained in it.

As well as improving the IPR process it is also necessary to extend its application to more junior levels of the organization.

2. Involvement of non-managerial staff in the learning organization If the learning organization is to become fully functioning non-mangerial staff need to be drawn into learning organization thinking and practice. This is beginning to occur in some parts of the organization where managers are working to establish sub-climates conducive to organizational and personal development. In pan-organizational terms extension of the learning processes for managers described earlier in this chapter are highly desirable but will require further training/development resources including those required to further enhance managers' skills in the development of their own staff. The implementation of the Guidelines for management practice (see the Appendix) is being used to prompt debate of these issues.

3. The use of individual development methods which are consistent with the characterisitics of the learning organization The workshops described in this chapter are an attempt to move away from traditional courses. This will continue, unless courses are staged at the request of the learners and/or develop skills which are relevant in the learning organization (such as coaching, counselling and delegation for development) or they employ processes which enable managers to learn how to learn. Other preferred activities will include self-development groups, action learning, projects and assignments, understudy and mentoring, and will involve staff in designing and running learning experiences with and for their peers.

It is intended that these learning methods will be supported by a resource centre. This must be supported by competencies and experiences of managers already employed by the authority, access to which can be offered to other learners.

4. Selection and induction processes which convey the Mid Essex culture as a learning organization   Newcomers to the authority will have experienced a selection procedure in which they are well informed of the culture they will be entering. This is especially important for managers, who will need to be fully informed about the district's Guidelines for management practice (see Appendix).

After receiving this information at selection, the induction processes will reinforce the messages about the culture, and may be supported by practices like:

- senior management visits to new staff;
- counselling support;
- pairing of new recruits with a 'buddy' (an existing employee who is responsible for the new entrant's continuing induction).

5. A management style which is consistent with the district's Guidelines for management practice   The changing nature of general management in the Health Service has meant that responsibility has been increasingly devolved to junior managers. This policy has been enthusiastically pursued in Mid Essex and its articulation is found in the Guidelines for management practice. Relevant examples of this in the Guidelines are:

(a) Communication
  ... managers should create a climate where staff feel confident to make suggestions to improve services. Where appropriate, employees' views must be reflected to other members of management or relevant professionals.

(b) Decision-making
  ... It is the policy of the Authority that decisions should be made as close to the point of service delivery as possible. Managers are expected to devolve decision-making, to encourage staff to take initiatives and to ensure that they have the opportunity to develop competencies which will enable them to deliver services effectively and efficiently.

The democratic management style which has been adopted in Mid Essex, and which the Guidelines promote, is one which exists within the 'loose–tight' principles of the type described by Peters and Waterman (1982). The 'tightness' is evidenced in the framework offered by senior management in their role as custodians of the district's core values, while the looseness is the freedom for junior managers to operate within this framework.

The challenge for senior management is in continuing to devolve responsibility in a difficult managerial climate, and also in successfully intervening at lower levels when middle and junior managers are discovered not to be operating in like vein.

6. Regular and frequent evaluation of progress If there is to be continuous learning about the learning organization there is a requirement for continuous feedback from staff, with this feedback being available from all levels.

The model of organizational and individual development (Figure 19.2) indicates how feedback is received on organizational issues from workshop participants. This source of rich information continues to supply data as more members of junior management attend workshops and other organization or management development activities.

The district has also been using survey feedback interventions. An attitude survey has been conducted and the results fed back to staff together with management's decision about the areas which would be acted upon. A communications audit is to be undertaken. (An external consultant has also worked with groups of managers to identify the results of the initial workshop series for their individual development and their future needs and to check progress on organizational development. The results of this work have been assessed by the district management board.)

Other, informal ways of organization sensing are also in use; for example, members of the senior management team receive feedback from staff, particularly at lower levels, during the discussions which occur in their programme of planned visits to all parts of the organization.

The process of regularly taking stock is fundamental to the achievement of the characteristics of the learning organization defined in this chapter; apart from the usefulness of the feedback in enabling senior management to respond to identified needs, the open exchange of ideas fosters innovation and collaboration, and facilitates problem-solving, change management and resource utilization, as well as valuing and recognizing staff at all levels.

7. New and appropriate interventions Up to now senior management's responses to the flow of feedback on the progress of the district towards becoming a learning organization seem to have been appropriately chosen to stimulate this progress or remove blockages to it. This will need to continue. In the event of impediments to progress, whether in general or specific to a sub-climate, new interventions will need to be made relevant to the demands of the situation.

There are two particular matters which might call for careful choice of intervention if the feedback shows this to be needed. The first of these concerns control of the 'tight' area of the loose–tight properties of the organization. What action should be taken if managers are seen to be falling down on the maintenance of the core values? The second concerns the 'loose' area. What sorts of facilitating interventions should be made if managers are seen to be failing in the minutiae of the operation?

The notion of 'loose–tight' properties has substantial support in the feedback obtained from the organization, and it has a central place in our model of the learning organization. However there may be a dilemma to be resolved in the implicit conflict between applying 'looseness–tightness' and allowing the freedom of choice which is also recommended. At present it feels easier to police 'tight' core values than to require and encourage freedom of operation within these boundaries. Managing this paradox will be the principal challenge for the next two years.

References

Attwood, M. E. and D. B. Johnson (1987) 'Making general management work', Conference Paper, Centre for the Study of Management Learning, University of Lancaster.

Attwood, M. E. and N. F. Beer (1988) 'Development of a learning organisation: reflections on a personal and organizational workshop in a district health authority' in *Management Education and Development,* **19**(3).

Barclay, R. (1988) 'Culture contrast' in *Health Care Management,* **3**(3).

Griffiths Report (1983) *NHS Management Enquiries,* DHSS, London.

Pedler, M. (1981) 'Developing the learning community' in T. Boydell and M. Pedler (eds), *Management Self-Development: Concepts and Practices,* Gower, Aldershot.

— and T. Boydell (1985) *Managing Yourself,* Fontana, London.

Peters, T. J. and R. H. Waterman, Jr (1982) *In Search of Excellence,* Harper & Row, New York.

Revans, R. W. (1982) *The Origins and Growth of Action Learning,* Chartwell-Bratt, Bromley and Lund.

Temporal, P. (1981) 'Creating the climate for self-development, in T. Boydell, and M. Pedler (eds), *Management Self-Development: Concepts and Practices,* Gower, Aldershot.

Appendix   Mid Essex Health Authority
Guidelines for management practice

1. Introduction
In Mid Essex our task is to provide and promote a high standard of health care in order to improve the quality of life, within the resources available, and which are accepted by society.

In order to achieve this we must:

- pursue the promotion of the corporate image of the Authority
- actively demonstrate the value placed on employees
- attempt to quantify the current activities in terms of patient's demands/needs related to outcome
- provide higher quality services
- ensure that staff at all levels are free to display initiative in the organisation of their daily tasks
- recognise and build on the organisation's good practices
- encourage better two way communications both within and outside the organisation
- recognise more clearly areas of creative tension/potential conflict within the organisation and establish clear mechanisms to resolve them
- establish and maintain mutual trust throughout the organisation
- motivate the client group to be involved and to take responsibilities for their own health.

Change is part of everyday experience in the Health Service. Managers of Mid Essex Health Authority are expected to adopt a positive and initiating role, seeking to promote the District's change objectives wherever possible within the framework of Authority policies. They are expected to be concerned with the maintenance of good standards within the organisation.

2. Purpose of these guidelines
These guidelines set out the standards of conduct which are expected from managers and the responsibilities of the Authority to holders of these positions. They apply to anyone who fulfils managerial roles and responsibilities within the District.

3. The obligations of managers
The concern of managers must be the achievement of the goals of the organisation as a public service and as a social entity. Managers' primary responsibility is to the Authority for the management of the resources

both physical and human which are entrusted to them. They have obligations to patients, clients, to staff whom they manage, to professional bodies and to other colleagues within the organisation. They are the privileged recipients and guardians of personal information and confidences. Mid Essex believes firmly that the management of people is a core responsibility of every manager's job. It is only through its own staff that the Authority can deliver good services to patients and clients.

4. The obligations of Mid Essex Health Authority to its managers
The Authority recognises that its managers are central to its activities and in particular to the achievement of improvements in both organisational effectiveness and efficiency, The responsibilities placed on managers always will be onerous. The Authority supports managers in their efforts to meet the requirements of these guidelines accepting fully the personal responsibilities thus implied. The District is committed to the development of its managers in pursuit of both individual career goals and organisational development.

5. Managerial responsibilities
In carrying out their responsibilities managers are expected to adhere to the following principles:

(a)   Commitment to the organisation
Managers will at all times endeavour to enhance the good standing of Mid Essex Health Authority and of the part of the organisation in which they work, the Acute or Community Units, District services or the Essex Ambulance Service. Fostering a feeling of belonging, pride and corporate identity is part of job satisfaction.

(b)   Communication
Managers should be visible and accessible; spending time seeing and listening to staff is essential. Managers should create a climate where staff feel confident to make suggestions to improve services. Where appropriate employees' views must be reflected to other members of management or relevant professionals. Communication of information to staff about the Authority's objectives, achievements and difficulties is important even if the information has no direct impact on the staff concerned.

(c)   Staff motivation
Employees are the District's most valuable resource. Managers must do everything possible to ensure that their staff are asssisted to carry out their tasks. Clearly defined goals and targets should be established in

discussion with those concerned. Individuals should be aware of what is expected of them and constructive feedback given on a regular basis. Effective performance should be actively encouraged and recognised.

(d) Decision-making

Managers must seek to take advantage of opportunities that change brings for the benefit of patients and staff. It is the policy of the Authority that decisions should be made as close to the point of service delivery as possible. Managers are expected to devolve decision-making, to encourage staff to take initiatives and to ensure that they have the opportunity to develop competencies which will enable them to deliver services effectively and efficiently.

(e) Development of others

In conjunction with personnel specialists, managers will seek to achieve the fullest possible development of their staff to meet both individuals' career goals and the present and future requirements of the organisation.

(f) Self-development

As a basis for the encouragement of their own staff as well as to enhance their contribution to the organisation managers should continuously update their personal skills and knowledge in relevant fields.

(g) Counselling and coaching

Managers will be prepared to act in a counselling or coaching role to individual employees and the dependants of patients and clients where they have the competence to do so. Where appropriate they will refer individuals to other professionals or helping agencies.

(h) Confidentiality

Managers must respect requirements for confidentiality of information entrusted to them including the safeguarding of information about current, past and prospective employees and current past and prospective clients. They must ensure the privacy and confidentiality of personal information to which they have access or for which they are responsible, subject to any legal rights of staff or patients and clients in respect of information relating to themselves.

(i) Equal opportunities

Managers must promote fair employment practices in line with current legislation and the Authority's Equal Opportunity Policy. They must ensure that their own staff are fully aware of their personal obligations in this area.

(j) Integrity
Managers will at all times act in accordance with these guidelines and the duties that they own to the Authority and to its employees.

(k) Legality
Managers will not act in any way which would knowingly countenance, encourage or assist unlawful conduct by either the Authority or its staff.

6. Organisational responsibilites to managers
The need to support managers in their efforts to meet the requirements of these guidelines is central to the role of all members of the District Health Authority and its management Board. Managers in Mid Essex have rights in pursuit of their personal role requirements.

These are the right to:

(a) have proposals for improved organisational efficency or effectiveness treated seriously by their manager
(b) challenge more senior management
(c) have a personal development plan, the furtherance of which will be actively encouraged
(d) make cross-functional/cross-departmental/cross-unit contacts without consulting their manager
(e) receive feedback and have an open discussion about their personal performance with their manager
(f) give feedback to their own manager about ways in which improvements in the latter's performance would be of assistance.
(g) be supported, for example, by management development initiatives in their efforts to enhance their personal competencies to meet the obligations defined by these guidelines.

20
What price the learning organization in the public sector?
John Edmonstone

Introduction

The notion of the 'learning company' or 'learning organization' is finding increasing favour among people concerned with management development. This has been simulated by the Management Charter initiative, growing from the Handy and Constable reports. This chapter attempts to define what a learning organization may be, drawing on recent work in this area, before examining the current situation of organizations in the public sector. It goes on to consider whether the learning organization concept relates to the situation and problems presently facing public sector organizations, using the National Health Service as an example. It concludes with some hopeful signs, but is sanguine about the extent to which public sector organizations can become learning organizations.

What is the 'learning organization'?

The phrase 'learning organization' has been used by a number of recent writers. Pedler, for example (1987), writing in the context of self-development in organizations, describes it as being distinguished by 'attempts to apply the notion of self development more wholistically to organizations as compared with focussing on specific aspects'.

A recent Ashridge Management College report (Barham et al. 1988) saw learning organizations as those where training and development had become intrinsic to the organization; where learning was not restricted to discrete 'chunks' of training activity (either fragmented or systematic) but where it had become a continuous process; and where on-the-job learning had become a way of life. They were environments in which individuals would not only be empowered to learn new things, but also to learn about the process of learning itself.

Recognizing the difficulties in 'operationalizing' the learning organization concept, Pedler later redefined it as 'a vision of an organizational strategy to promote self development amongst the membership and to harness this development corporately by continuously transforming itself as part of the same process'.

The key words here seem to be:

- *strategy*   implying a high level of generality, being future-orientated and providing a degree of coherence and direction;
- self-development   being concerned with self-development and the values which underline it—and not with other organization/management development approaches derived from different value assumptions;
- harness   A dictionary definition suggests 'using natural forces for motive power; the implication is that self-development is an independent and autonomous 'natural' force which cannot be tightly directed and controlled;
- corporately   for the purposes or benefit of the organization;
- continuously transforming itself   the learning organization concept is not static and fixed, but rather fluid, flexible and reflexive.

Pedler goes on to describe elements of the social technology associated with the learning organization, including resource centres and associated guidance systems, open learning, self-review and appraisal, career planning, self-development and support groups. He also points out that:

- hierarchical organization structures do no easily lend themselves to people taking responsibility for their own development;
- self-development opportunities are only taken up by significant numbers if they are partially structured;
- the term 'culture' is probably a more important one than structure;
- organizations are *instrumental* in nature: they are a means to an end and learning has to be balanced against production of goods and services.

The Ashridge view overlaps considerably with Pedler. They both see the learning organization as reflected in the corporate culture, the organization strategy, the organizational structure and a focus on the individual.

The *corporate culture* is marked by a structure which embodies a lack of specific goal clarity, a lack of stability, together with a pressure from above to excel. High learning is equated with good upward communication and the learning organization tends to attract people who are 'naturally' high learning individuals.

The *organizational strategy* ensures that training and development are focused on business goals and strategy. Training is well-integrated into the planning process and as plans cascade down through the organization consideration is given to training as one more resource needed to make the plans a reality. Training and development is driven from the top, as part of a change initiative, and there is a close interplay and mutual influence between training staff and top management. Learning organizations develop mechanisms (through restructuring and changing the organizational culture) which enable them to monitor and learn from their internal and external environments. Training is just such a vital mechanism.

The *organizational structure* features the devolution of responsibility to independent business units and profit centres and the greater use of project teams and temporary task forces. Project management skills and the development of general management expertise earlier in the career are central learning needs.

The *focus on the individual* recognizes on-the-job training as the 'best' form of development. Individuals get early responsibility (with support) and mistakes are tolerated. Work problems become the basis of considering new theory and an emphasis on self-development promotes learner control, some degree of continuity and a long-term perspective.

Garratt, too, relates to the Ashridge view of the learning organization in his book of the same name (1987). He suggests a threefold division of organizational activites:

1. *Policy* Concerned with organizational *effectiveness*; with looking 'upwards and outwards' towards the issues and problems in the organization's environment which are likely to impact in the future. Focused towards change, anticipation of problems and the establishment of new directions.
2. *Operations* Concerned with organizational *efficiency*; with looking 'inwards and downwards' at issues of control and performance. Focused towards the immediate and the short-term and emphasizing maintenance of consistency and correction of deviations.
3. *Strategy* Located between policy and operations, strategy is concerned with balancing between the two other orientations; with

developing a feeling of wholeness and coherence and with fe a sense of direction and purpose.

For Garrett, the learning organization has the following characteristics:

- a three-level hierarchy of policy, strategy and operations;
- a double loop of learning which allows multiple feedback from information flows, direction-giving and the monitoring of changes in the external and internal environments;
- a means of processing and integrating these information-flows by positioning the direction-givers at the centre of the organization's learning.

There appears to be a tension between the 'self-development' and 'managerial' views of the learning organization. The former is concerned with the development of *all* organization members and tends to emphasize pay-offs to individuals. The latter tends to focus on managers (especially top managers) and emphasize pay-offs to the organization. These tensions perhaps reflect the origins and interests of key idea-formers and are hardly surprising in this emerging field. Both the 'self-development' and 'managerial' views would be agreed that:

- learning is a continuous process;
- learning is about task/content *and* the learning process;
- learning largely takes place at work;
- double-loop learning is a crucial activity;
- both a strategy and a technology for learning are needed.

Nonetheless, Pedler has noted the underlying elitist and hierarchic assumptions behind the 'managerial' view (1988). Specifically, Pedler questions whether:

- double-loop learning is to be only the preserve of senior managers, and if not, how other people can be involved in strategy-making?
- at a time when organizational structures are getting flatter, should we not be departing from the hierarchical model?
- if learning involves differences and conflict, how can the tension between performance (= stability) and disequilibrium (= first requirement for new learning) be effectively managed?
- attempts to describe the learning organization based on cybernetic models may not address feeling and doing by concentrating on thinking?

Central to all the writers mentioned are notions of first- and second-order change, single- and double-loop learning and the 'reframing' process. Watzlawick *et al.* (1974) suggest that most people restrict their frame of reference, or context, for the problems which they are facing so that little true change can occur.

Work routines limit the ways in which they view problems—generally to 'more of' or 'less of' the same. This first-order change is related to what Argyris and Schon (1978) call single-loop learning. Single-loop learning rests on an ability to detect and correct error in relation to a set of operating norms. This involves:

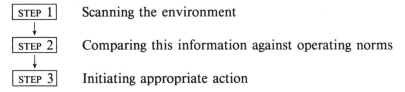

STEP 1	Scanning the environment
STEP 2	Comparing this information against operating norms
STEP 3	Initiating appropriate action

An example of single-loop learning, drawn from the manpower field in the NHS is shown in Figure 20.1.

Second-order change occurs when people are able to look away from the immediate symptoms and set the problem in a wider context. It

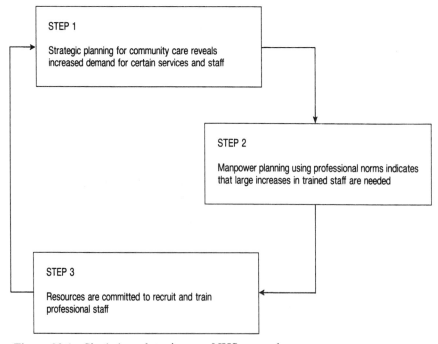

Figure 20.1   Single-loop learning: an NHS example

involves 'escaping' from the problem as initially defined. In terms of double-loop learning it involves another step (step 2a) which is the process of questioning whether the operating norms are appropriate or not. Figure 20.2 illustrates this with the same NHS example.

Crucial to the process of second-order change and double-loop learning is what is known as 'reframing'—setting the wider context or perspective and thinking about problems in a way that transcends routine thought processes. Watzlawick *et al.* (1974) suggest that to reframe means 'to change the conceptual and/or emotional setting or viewpoint in relation to which a situation is experienced and to place it in another frame which fits the "facts" of the same concrete situation equally well or even better, and thereby changes its entire meaning'. The reframing process seems to lie at the heart of creativity in the arts and sciences. Koestler (1959), for example, proposes that:

This operation of removing a problem from its traditional context and placing it into a new one, looking at it through glasses of a different colour as it were, has always seemed ... the very essence of the creative process. It leads not only to a

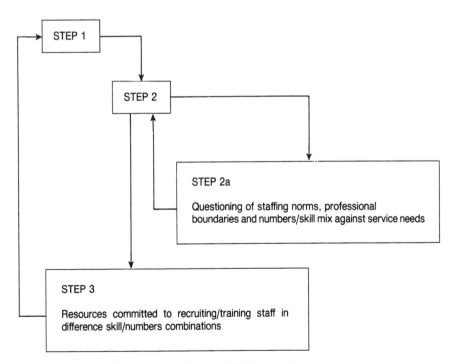

Figure 20.2 Double-loop learning: an NHS example

re-evaluation of the problem itself, but often to a synthesis of much wider consequences, brought about by a fusion of two previously unrelated frames of reference.

In summary, therefore, it seems that learning organizations:

- have general organizational strategies related to learning;
- promote second-order change/double-loop learning through reframing;
- have structures (or cultures) which both *enable* learning to happen and *harness* it towards organizational ends;
- accept that the concept of the learning organization is not yet well-defined. The tension between the self-development and managerialist views provides some evidence of this.

General inhibitors to learning

While the focus of this chapter is the application of the learning organization concept to the public sector, there are also more general inhibitors which limit the application of the approach to *all* organizations. Recognizing that many organizations display elements of the classic bureaucracy, Morgan (1986) suggests that the fundamental organizing principles of bureaucracies often operate in ways which obstruct the learning process, and in particular block the process of reframing. Three of these obstructions are worthy of special attention.

First, bureaucratic organizations impose *fragmented structures of thought* on their staff and do not encourage employess to think either for themselves or in a wholistic manner.

Organizational goals, objectives, structures and roles create defined patterns of accountability and responsibility and so fragment interest in what the organization as a whole is doing. Information and knowledge rarely flows in a free manner, and different parts of the same organization can operate on the basis of different pictures of the situation and pursue local goals as ends in themselves, unaware of, or disinterested in, the way they fit the wider picture.

Staff are usually encouraged to occupy and keep to a predefined role and activity within the organization and are rewarded for doing so. Situations in which the status quo is challenged tend to be exceptional, rather than the rule. Sophisticated single-loop learning systems (tight management information systems, rigid project management, inflexible budgets, etc.) may serve to keep the organization on the wrong course, since staff are unable or unwilling to challenge underlying assumptions. The existence of single-loop learning systems may thus prevent double-loop learning from occurring.

The second major barrier to double-loop learning is often associated with the principle of *accountability*. Staff are held responsible for their performance within a system that rewards success and punishes failure and have an incentive to engage in various forms of deception to protect themselves. Staff tend to find ways of obscuring issues and problems that may place them in a bad light. They find ways of deflecting attention and of covering up, as well as engaging in forms of 'impression management' that make the situations for which they are responsible look better than they actually are. Through the 'filtering' process there is a temptation to tell managers exactly what they want to hear.

When accountability systems foster this low level of trust an organization is rarely able to tolerate high levels of uncertainty. Managers and staff have a tendency to want to 'tie things down' and to be 'on top of the facts' which often leads them to create oversimplified interpretations of the situation. Managers and staff tend to be interested in problems only if there are solutions at hand.

Complex issues which are difficult to address are often discussed or downplayed in importance to create time for solutions to emerge or for someone else to take on the responsibility. Bearers of 'bad news' are rarely made welcome and operating assumptions are rarely challenged in an effective way.

The third barrier to double-loop learning stems from the gap between what people say and what they do, between what Argyris and Schon call *'espoused theory'* and *'theory-in-use'*. Many managers and professionals attempt to meet problems with rationalizations that give the impression that they know what they are doing. This may not be just to impress others, but also to convince *themselves* that all is well and that they have the ability to cope. They also often engage in diversionary behaviour, as when threats to a central activity lead an individual or profession to deflect blame elsewhere and to tighten up on that activity intensifying rather than questioning its nature and effects.

It becomes increasingly difficult for the manager or professional to confront and deal with realities of a situation. Developments here are reinforced by social processes such as 'groupthink' which are very difficult to break. Individual managers and whole professions may develop espoused theories which effectively prevent them from understanding and dealing with their problems. Double-loop learning requires that the gulf between theory and reality is bridged so that it becomes possible to challenge the values and norms embedded in the theories-in-use, as well as those that are espoused.

One further inhibitor may be revealed by recent studies of the nature of managerial work. For some time the notion of management as a systematic and rationalistic activity has been under challenge. Mintzberg (1973), Stewart (1982) and Kotter (1982) have all identified that this representation of management is a form of espoused theory. The nature of the theory-in-use is very different, as recent work by Mumford and Stradling (1987) has made clear. The reality of management, particularly at top levels, is marked by a hectic pace, with a constant flow of work and few opportunities to pause. Activities are fragmented, with no single-minded concentration on one theme at a time. Behaviour is more intuitive than rational; responsive rather than reflective; unaware rather than sensitive and unplanned rather than proactive. Such managers receive and process information in a number of forms, often in an unplanned or unstructured way. They use informal networks to get things done without following the organizational chart.

They are interactive, working with and through other people, often through unconscious offers and trade-offs to get things done. They deal with many issues at once and have to recognize the relationships between them. They tend to be constrained rather than innovative, more often aware of what prevents action rather than active in reframing problems and solutions.

Roger Harrison (1987) notes a conflict related to how managers see the world. Managers learn to be competitive, action-orientated and autonomous and to think in 'left-brained' ways: analytically, concretely and rationally. These are qualities of behaviour and thought which lend themselves to dealing with the physical world. Dealing effectively with organizations requires different habits of thought, such as co-operation, nurturing relationships and appreciating interdependency. Alternative modes of thought and feeling are 'right-brained', intuitive, open to feelings as well as facts and generally wholistic. The general 'busy-ness' associated with top management jobs seems to limit the capacity to stand back, reflect and get in touch with personal feelings and thoughts. Apart from the more general inhibitors associated with the bureaucratic process in all organizations, senior managers who might be expected to recognize this situation seem trapped by the nature of managerial work and unable to recognize this state of affairs. They are faced with a powerful espoused theory (or managerial ideology) which represents a collection of 'shoulds' and 'oughts' related to a rationalistic and systematic view of management, the world and themselves.

Understanding the public sector

Attempting to understand the problems faced by the public sector, one is faced by an immediate difficulty of definition. What is the public sector? It is important to be specific over which *part* of the public sector is being addressed at any one time. Currently it includes the Civil Service, local government and the National Health Service, together with those public corporations not yet targeted for privatization. The example which will be pursued in this chapter relates to the NHS, which is provided by over 200 regional and district health authorities in England and Wales. Health authorities are headed by general managers, who relate to health authority members, largely appointed by the Secretary of State for Health.

Thus, although there is a management process in operation, managers are accountable to their members, particularly the health authority chair, and through him or her to the Secretary of State and ultimately to Parliament.

Flynn (1986) has noted that the current political arena is characterized by 'belief in financial incentives, the admiration of the Private Sector, the desire to cut public expenditure, and the desire of central government to control local services'. Any attempt to understand what has been happening in the public sector needs to be seen against the influence of 'New Right' political, social and economic ideas (King 1987). The term 'New Right' refers to the combination of two sets of economic and political theories and ideas—that of economic *liberalism* (founded upon free market and individualistic approaches), and that of social and moral *conservatism* which arises from the pursuit of liberal economic policy. Especially important is the notion that the welfare state reduces freedom. It is claimed that this happens because the welfare state:

- encroaches upon property rights through imposing an increased tax burden;
- tends towards uniformity and standardization by limiting the range of services available;
- is intrinsically paternalistic through deliberate directing of citizens towards defined choices;
- imposes bureaucratic and legal restrictions upon individuals;
- results in dependency amongst recipients, and militates against their pursuit of alternative options;
- creates its own supporting interest groups amongst bureaucrats and beneficiaries who undermine any efforts to reduce the public welfare sector.

The welfare state, the mixed economy, and Keynesian economic techniques designed to maintain full employment, constituted the basis of the post-war consensus in Britain. Attacks on the functioning of nationalized industries; the supposed expense of the welfare state; the alleged inefficiency of state provision and control of industries and social services; the supposed ineffectiveness of Keynesian economics in the long run; the inexorable propensity of voters to demand more services, politicians to accommodate these demands and bureaucrats to share in these expansionary interests—all these formed the context within which New Right ideas were formulated, promoting alternative economic, political and social policies and evaluative criteria. The New Right is now the new orthodoxy and forms the context against which all debates over management, management development and considerations of the learning organisation take place.

Understanding the public sector also implies understanding the evolving relationships between professionals and managers in the larger context of changes in the national and international economy. The 1974 reorganization of the NHS, for example, was seen as a managerial exercise. On reflection, it is possible to see that change, as reflecting a much deeper and longer-term trend that affected all the social services during the twentieth century, that of the growth of professional autonomy and responsibility within the statutory services.

The traditional professions had gained independent, self-governing status by the nineteenth century, but operated in a market environment as independent contractors, constrained by the need to sell their services in the marketplace. Other groups (like teachers and social workers) were also developing professional characteristics, but had not achieved them by the time the new comprehensive state services were created. After 1948, the caring professions came to work within a statutory, non-market sector. The removal of the market in the welfare sector and the much broader trends to professionalization in society continued in the first 25 years of the welfare state to give the professions previously unequalled influence. Thus, the 1974 NHS reorganization marks the high point of the influence of professional values.

Professional values begin with patient's needs, viewed from the perspective of the particular profession's own body of knowledge and experience. Demands on resources are viewed as infinite, or loosely constrained, because the focus of professional training and ethics are of service to the individual patient. In every welfare organization professional values are in conflict with organizational values. These latter relate to giving the organization direction and coherence; resolving conflicts of professional interest and setting priorities within limited resources. In the expansionary period of the 1950s and 1960s professional values and interests held sway.

Nevertheless, just as the 'Grey Book' (DHSS 1972) was published two new trends were rapidly emerging. First, resource constraints tightened sharply, a move sparked off initially by the 1973 oil crisis and the deeper reassessment of the public sector that this eventually produced. Second, was the reassertion by politicians of their right to determine overall resource priorities and to hold the NHS to account for the effective use of resources. These trends were not confirmed to the health care system, nor to any one political party, nor indeed to Britain alone. The strains this imposed on consensus decision-making between professional groups proved intolerable, although it took some time for this to become obvious.

Major shifts in service provision needed to be achieved and it needed a shift in emphasis in management style from consensus to 'conflict resolution'. The 'Griffiths' introduction of general management into the NHS represented one attempt to achieve a shift in the balance between professional and organizational values and to provide a means of resolving that tension.

In order to counter the historical professional orientation within the NHS many of the new general managers have initiated searches for 'core purposes' to which both professionals and managers can subscribe. Strenuous efforts are made to incorporate professionals into managerial decision-making and 'fast-track' development programmes seek to identify 'high fliers' within professions and socialize them into the organizational values of general management via such processes as exposure to educational programmes at university centres, mentoring by existing general managers and entry to the fast track by 'rites of passage' such as assessment centres.

The strengthening of organizational values and the parallel weakening of professional values requires an 'official' ideology to act as a raison d'être and a reference point. This was provided by the NHS Training Authority through a review of management development requirements (NHSTA 1986a) which expressed the view that management has a proper responsibility for the direction, quantity and quality, as well as the cost of care and challenged the 'tribalism' of the health care professions.

This emergence of general management as a counterweight to professional values is largely an NHS phenomenon. It can also be seen as part of a larger 'vocationalist' movement in the labour market which aims to make employer's needs paramount. Invidious comparisons have been made between the vocational training systems of the UK and our economic competitors (Hayes *et al.* 1984) and from this has flowed a range of initiatives aimed at increased efficiency and competitiveness. The NHS is therefore being exposed to the same challenges as other organizations, but the challenge may be more powerful as it runs counter to professional values which have held sway over the internal NHS labour market for over forty years.

Understanding the public sector begins with acceptance that New Right ideas form the backcloth to all considerations of management and management development. Also crucial is the changing nature of professionals to managers. Professionals abound in public sector organizations and their values often run counter to those of the organization. Exposure of the NHS and the entire public sector to a view which considers the needs of employers to be paramount over all other interests is particularly challenging to a sector which has traditionally regarded itself as 'different' and where the circumstances which held for other organizations simply did not apply.

Management in the public sector

Although the current orthodoxy is that management in the public sector is no different from that in the private sector there is some evidence to the contrary (Edmonstone 1982). However, when it comes to the impact of management thought on theory and practice in private and public sectors there are some obvious differences. Figures 20.3 and 20.4 reveal the principal influence in each sphere.

In the private sector the dominant managerial ideology was Taylorian 'scientific management' but this came to be seen as less than relevant, partly due to the influence of the organizational development 'movement' in the 1960s and 1970s, which in turn was a reflection of the humanistic values of those decades. The late 1970s and 1980s have been marked by the impact of New Right values, together with an emphasis on 'consumerism' and 'excellence'. By contrast, the public sector embodies a continuation of scientific management ideas, to which were added professional values at their apogee in a kind of 'unholy alliance' reflected in the 1974 changes. There were also OD experiments in the public sector (later and less wholeheartedly than in the private sphere) and also a critique of 'professionalism' by Illich, who sought to 'demystify' professional work. More recently, management has been significantly affected by New Right values and also by consumerism, the excellence studies and an emphasis on equal opportunities, exemplified by the 'public service orientation' in local government (see below).

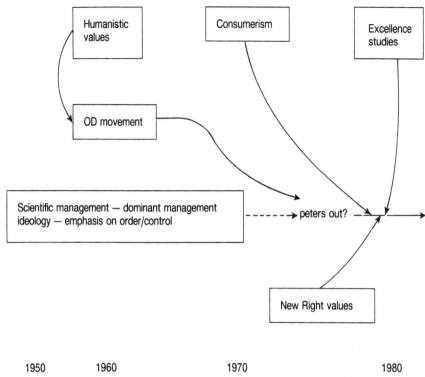

1950   1960   1970   1980

Figure 20.3 Influences on management thought in the private sector

Faced with this situation general management in the public sector can be examined using Garratt's earlier model of policy, operations and strategy. Seen within this framework, the policy sphere is often characterized as 'feeding the beast', that is coping with political masters (both national and local); relating to the various professional bodies and being almost obsessive about the external environment. The operations field is most seductive to those who are required to take on a strategic emphasis. It is where many of them emerged from and is exemplified by the 'administrative ethic'. The danger is of being sucked into detail and of being concerned with process rather than outcome. The strategy area comes to be seen as striving for a unifying vision or mission and primarily with the management of change.

What price the learning organization in the public sector?

It is clear that public sector organizations face exactly the same general inhibitors to learning as their private sector counterparts. The problem is,

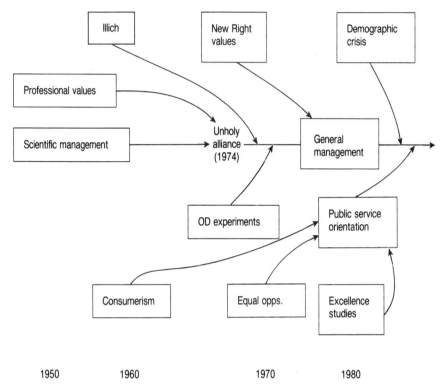

1950   1960   1970   1980

Figure 20.4 Influences on management thought in the public sector

however, exacerbated because most public sector organizations are both bureaucracies *and* contain many professionals. The scope for fragmentation, goal displacement, etc., is therefore very great indeed.

Moreover, public sector organizations are typically subject to public accountability, which means that there is also parliamentary scrutiny of their affairs through parliamentary questions, the select committee system of the House of Commons, the Ombudsman, etc. This emphasis on public accountability has led to proliferation of management control systems which emphasize only single-loop learning.

In addition to these general inhibitors, there are particular problems which public sector organizations face. These include the following.

Ambiguity over core purpose
Although attempts are being made to define and agree statements of core purpose this is a difficult process given the ambiguity within the NHS, for example, over what constitutes 'health'. Similarly, in local government

the services which are provided have grown incrementally and purpose is difficult to define. In the NHS there is further ambiguity over the precise influences which improve the health of the population. This ambiguity opens up the opportunity for many points of view to be expressed about the relative importance of certain services, certain resources and their organization. Thus individual professional perspectives vie to influence the way in which services should be delivered.

Task-obsession

Most public sector organizations seem marked by an obsessive concern for task accomplishment, with *what* is to be done, at the expense of concern for process, or *how* it is to be done. The raison d'être for management resides in the achievement of task, while the effectiveness of management often depends on process. Managers are paid to cajole, persuade, build commitment and foster acceptance *only* as a means to achieving certain (task-oriented) ends. While systems of managerial accountability are often task-based, a manager's performance, however, frequently depends upon attention to process. As a consequence, there is often a counter-productive tension between mechanisms for managerial accountability and the strategic time horizon. Managers are encouraged to focus on producing 'visible' short-term results at the expense of developing their organization's capacity to deliver results over the longer term.

This over-emphasis on task can also lead to a growing gap between statements or aspirations of strategic intent (*what* change is required) and the organization's ability actually to implement and deliver change. In the NHS, this gap between strategic intent and operational reality is often revealed by aspirational strategic plans disconnected from the day-to-day concerns of most managers and staff. In local government this has led to abandonment of longer-term planning in favour of a form of 'opportunistic incrementalism'.

The task-obsession is derived from centralist pressure from ministers and civil servants for greater throughput and efficiency. As a result, many highly-paid managers are driven to undertaking operational 'fire-fighting' activities. A recent survey of the work of unit general managers in the NHS (Smith 1987) indicated that most of their actions were within their own unit and focused on 'inward and downward' activities. Those activities least done were of the 'upward and outward' variety.

No rewards for risk-taking

The delivery of heatlh care is inherently a vague and ambiguous task which makes it difficult to set meaningful and measurable goals. Revans described hospitals as 'institutions cradled in anxiety' (1964) and implied that the sources of this centre on the feelings of both patients and staff. Many hundreds of patients may be grouped together, each concerned with their own problems, inevitably influenced by those others around them with similar or different difficulties. The staff's contribution to the anxiety seems to have three sources. Firstly, the tremendous weight of responsibility carried by those in the clinical situation; secondly, the combination of a student role with a fairly gruelling employee role, and finally, those anxieties which all members of a work group are prone to—poor health, domestic difficulties, financial problems and interpersonal issues.

Health care organizations deal with life-and-death' issues and this adds anxiety and stress to the basic frustration created by not being able to know with any certainty if and when you are succeeding. Menzies (1967), using a psychodynamic perspective, illustrated the effects of anxiety on the social structure of the hospital. Under such conditions it is difficult for health care organizations to develop a climate of experimentation and innovation.

Moreover, from a situation where staff were recruited as part of a 'psychological contract' which offered them adequate remuneration but high job security in return for undertaking work which most of the population finds distasteful, anxiety-provoking and tiring, there has been a move (paralleled by developments in the private sector) towards no security of tenure, fixed-term contracts and performance-related pay, which all tend to engender a focus on the short-term and a fear of failure.

No training culture
Curiously, in an organization as labour-intensive as the NHS there is no training culture which might provide the foundation for the development of the learning organization. A recent examination of the problem (NHSTA 1986b) identified twelve 'problems in search of a remedy':

- Training was perceived as a cost to the enterprise, rather than as an investment in its effectiveness.
- Training aims were imposed on a sectional, unco-ordinated basis with the assumption that training was an occasional activity, not a cumulative and continuous one.
- Training plans rarely related training to the business context.
- Training targets were foreign to NHS thinking.
- The potential contribution of training strategies to wider manpower strategies were not routinely considered.

- There were no coherent means of allocating finite resources to priority training needs.
- The prevailing view was that 'training equals courses' and other important forms of training went unrecognized.
- 'Competence' was mainly identified within narrow, technical skills.
- Resources were sketchy while the NHS faced fundamental changes with massive training implications.
- There were many providers of training, but no single focus.
- There was no sound training information base.
- The efficiency and effectiveness of the training process was not debated.

What might be done?

Faced with this state of affairs what might be done to foster the development of the learning organization within the public sector? What actions are needed to ensure that health care organizations, for example, make the concept a reality rather than an aspiration?

It is possible, as a first step, to indicate the required direction of movement, under such headings as organizational culture, organizational strategy and the nature of education and training:

Table 20.1   Towards a learning organization for the NHS

	From	*To*
Organizational culture	Rigid and hierarchical structure and roles	Loose, flexible and fluid structures and roles
	Emphasis on public accountability and short-term goals	Emphasis on broad and general goals, performance and allowable risk
	External pressure to excel	Internal drive to excel
	Primary emphasis on 'professional' values	'Organizational' values as the context for 'professional' values
	Fragmented professional/ bureaucratic 'tribal' thinking with low trust levels and associated filtering and screening of information	Wholistic thinking and associated high trust levels with good vertical and lateral communication

Table 20.1 *continued*

	From	To
	Preference for the status quo, stability, over-simplification and resistance to change	Acceptance of complexity, ambiguity, instability, continous change and challenging of underlying assumptions
Organizational strategy	Fragmented, incoherent and inchoate	Integrated, coherent and comprehensive
	Operational decisions typically drawn up to 'higher' levels	Devolution of responsbility to lowest possible levels
	Seniority and experience rewarded	Early responsibility and success rewarded
Nature of education and training	Training disconnected from business goals and strategy	Training focused on business goals and strategy
	Either a 'free market' (*laissez-faire*) or 'command economy' (highly structured) approach to training	A 'mixed economy' approach, featuring both structure and choice
Nature of education and training	Training as an 'optional' extra	Training as both a resource and a means of mobilizing other resources
	Spurious distinctions between 'education' and 'training'	Focus on 'learning'
	Training owned by professional and educational interests	Training owned by the organization
	Training as off-the-job and teacher-centred	Training as on-the-job and learner centred
	Training as advancement of knowledge and fostering dependent relationships	Training as development of competence and fostering self-employment
	Training resources in short supply and owned by particular interests	Training resources more widely available and targeted at problems

This only takes us so far. What does this actually *mean* in terms of actions, activities, roles? What needs to change, and more particularly, *who* needs to change and in which directions? The movement indicated here is nothing less than a fairly radical culture change for the public sector, involving the challenging of many sacred cows. It is challenging also to the public sector's political masters who have typically sent 'mixed messages' with regards to their expectations—be as effective and efficient as the private sector purportedly is, but to maintain the public service ethic and public accountability, for example.

There is some evidence of movement towards the preconditions for the learning organization in the public sector. The development of general management in the NHS, the work of the NHS Training Authority and the Local Government Training Board and the increased willingness to use consultancy/advisory help all indicate a move away from seeing public sector organizations as closed systems.

But a number of other developments are needed. The main possibilities are outlined here:

Development of the 'public service' orientation
Stewart and Clarke (1987) have developed the notion of the 'public service' orientation within local government. This recognizes that:

- a public service organization's activities exist to provide service for the public;
- a public service organization will be judged by the quality of service provided within the resources available;
- the service provided is only of real value if it is of value to those for whom it is provided;
- those for whom services are provided are customers demanding high quality service;
- quality of service demands closeness to the customer.

They note that this means service *for* not *to* the public and that this implies a focus on the customer and the citizen. It is this latter point which distinguishes the public service orientation from that concern for the customer that should mark any service organization. It raised issues of participation and public accountability and is not, therefore, merely consumerism.

The public service orientation has made some impact on local government but very little within the NHS. Nevertheless, it offers a conceptual foundation from which to build new possibilities of what public sector organizations are in business for.

Greater structural flexibility

For public sector organizations to take on some of the features of the learning organization implies greater flexibility in such matters as pay, grading, reward and career advancement systems. Nationally negotiated agreements in these areas limit the ability of local managers to reward 'natural' learners, position such people in appropriate roles and assist movement within and across professional domains. A related matter is that of job design and redesign. Professional boundaries demarcate between professions and occupations and restrict the possibility of mixing and matching tasks, jobs and individuals.

Management development

From the foregoing is it possible to identify those areas of managerial competence which would form the basis of selection and management development for the future. They include such areas as:

- flexibility and adaptability;
- emotional resilience;
- ability to manage change;
- coping with complexity and ambiguity;
- wholistic thinking;
- a willingness to 'turn the world upside down'.

It is also possible to postulate, form Mumford and Stradling, that the appropriate model for management development would be what they call the 'Type 2' or 'integrated managerial' approach which uses opportunistic processes. Its characteristics include:

- it occurs within normal managerial activities;
- it is marked by the explicit intention of focusing on both task performance *and* development;
- it has clear development objectives;
- it is structured for development by the boss and the surbordinate;
- activities are planned beforehand or reviewed subsequently as learning experiences;
- it is owned by managers.

As a result, the learning is real, direct, conscious and more substantial.

On its own this may not be enough. It is a characteristic of many managers in the public sector that their sources of personal self-identity are external. They derive from their earlier professional socialization. Managers often seem outer-directed and powerless and may 'withdraw' from interactions which they find distasteful or harrowing. A learning organization, it is assumed, would prefer managers whose source of self-identity is internal. Such individuals would be marked by a greater degree of self-awareness and understanding. They would be inner-directed, assertive, creative and powerful people.

Pedler (1986) notes that development is both an inner and an outer process. It involves a continuous passing from outer actions (experience) to inner processes (reflection), back to action and so on. Professional socialization encourages managers to look outward to their peer group as a prime source of identity and it is in the very nature of many management pressures (urgency, deadlines, time management, etc.) to be outer-directed. The implications of this are that professionals becoming managers must create order within themselves first, before they can do so in external situations. It means learning to manage the self first. It implies managing from the inside out. Development becomes whole-person transformation. It is impossible to deal solely with the 'role person'. The role of the management developer is one of facilitator and the approaches used focus on the whole person.

The training and development function

In the learning organization training is clearly something too important to be left only to the trainers. In many public sector organizations, however, the expectations which managers have of trainers are typically low-level. A recent study of Health Service trainers (Edmonstone 1988) confirmed that the self-perceptions of trainers limited their role to direct training or instructing through the medium of 'courses', rather than a problem-centred organizational or a strategic and anticipative approach. Pettigrew *et al.* (1982) describe this as the phenomenon of 'role-locking', whereby the beliefs and actions of the trainer's role-set provide the conditions for locking into a limiting role. Among the immediate causes of role-locking are the client's perception of the 'legitimate' activities of the trainer (in the public sector significantly based on an academic model); the denying of any significance to a service function; a limited conception of the trainer role and little clear expectation of trainers. These causes are supported by broader mechanisms such as the personal background, experience and aspirations of the trainer, historical factors and such structural factors as location in the organization and relationship to key organizational activities.

A changed expectation of the part of managers and the development of facilitator skills and a strategic orientation on the part of trainers is clearly called for.

The professional construction of reality

Ultimately, however, and lying beyond these measures, lies the need for managers (and national and local politicians) to challenge the power of professions to set the agenda in the public sector and to define social reality. The powerful influence of professional socialization through a learning process controlled by a profession itself (another closed system) is now recognized (Melia 1987). The need may be to develop alternative models of what it means to be a professional. In his book *The Reflective Practitioner* Donald Schon (1983) sets out two opposing models of professional practice. In the 'technical-rationality' model, professional practice is seen as the application of a body of knowledge to the solution of problems.

The model assumes that problems come clearly defined, and that professional knowledge is directly applicable to those problems without the need for further reworking.

Schon suggests that practice cannot be separated from theory and that professionals use 'reflection-in-action' as a way of developing new understandings. The impetus for 'reflection-in-action' arises from the real-life problems to which a professional has to respond. These are complex and difficult to define and so the professional will construct his or her own new theory out of reflective consideration of action.

These models have implications for the relationship between professional and client. The traditional professional–client relationship carries implications of autonomy and authority on the part of the professional and of defence and compliance on the part of the client. Clients render their problems to the ministrations of professionals who do not exceed the limits of their competence. They safeguard as confidential the private information about clients that comes their way and do not abuse the powers vested in them for their benefit.

Not all clients are happy to hand over responsibility for their own affairs nor to be placed in a role that is essentially childlike in the face of a beneficient authority. Professionals also make things worse, unintentionally, as well as some of their number doing things wrongly, in the sense of witting malpractice. The former situation may lead to secret non-compliance with the professionals' recommendations. The latter is at the heart of the critique of professions and of calls for deprofessionalization (Illich 1975). Neither of these responses solves the problem. The one leaves clients in an adversarial relationship with professionals; the other leaves them in the hands of lay persons whose 'practice' is based on ignorance and lacks even the protection of the professional code.

The relationship between the reflective professional and client is different. Instead of being the object of another's practice, the client is involved in a reciprocal process of enquiry alongside the professional. Rather than the client's questions and comments on the professional's practice being ignored, or worse, punished in some way, they become a legitimate part of testing the appropriateness to this case of the expert's knowledge.

Grasping the political nettle
Current evidence does not suggest that professions within the public sector find the 'reflective practitioner' notion an attractive one. History, tradition and self-interest militate against such a change. The only people who might be able to mount a constructive challenge to professional hegemony are national and local politicians. Unfortunately the level of debate on matters of this nature among politicians is disappointingly low. Politicians typically send out 'mixed messages' with regard to the public sector. Yet it is they who could do so much to create the climate within which public sector organizations operate. They could, for example, be more tolerant of risk-taking (which implies 'failure' sometimes); could loosen parliamentary controls or could 'deregulate' aspects of the public sector labour market. What is clear is that further developments in making public sector organizations 'learning organizations' are conditional upon political will and resilience.

Conclusion

The learning organization concept, while not yet well-defined, seems to imply that organizations have strategies related to learning; that these strategies promote challenge to the status quo through the reframing process, and that this orientation is embedded in the cultures and structures of such organizations.

While there are general inhibitors to the development of learning in all organizations, they may be particularly acute in public-sector organizations. In addition, the public sector now exists within a context of 'New Right' thinking and within a tension between 'professional' and 'organizational' values. The creation of learning organizations in the public sector is problematic because of such difficulties as ambiguity over core purpose, task obsession, lack of rewards for risk-taking and the absence of a training culture.

It is possible to identify the desired direction of movement, but this could be further enhanced by the development of a 'public-service' orientation; greater structural flexibility; a focus on certain management competences and management development methods; changed expectations by managers of the training and development function; but above all by changes in the meaning of 'professions' and 'professionalism' which is unlikely to come about without a significant degree of political support.

A postscript

As this chapter was completed the Government published its proposals for the future of the NHS, following a year-long review (Department of Health 1989). Among the significant features are:

- the development of an 'internal market' to allow different parts of the health care system to trade with each other;
- the creation of self-governing trusts to run the larger hospitals outside central control, and setting their own pay and conditions of service levels;
- health authorities modelled on company boards of directors, with executive and non-executive directors;
- the 'hiving-off' of activities which are not central to organizational functioning to separate agencies or the private sector;
- the separation of the financing and regulation of health care from the provision of the same.

While it appears that such proposals go a significant way towards creating a framework for the learning organization in health care, especially in terms of greater structural flexibility, it remains to be seen how matters will work out in practice.

References

Argyris, C. and D. Schon (1978) *Organizational Learning: A Theory of Action Perspective*, Addison-Wesley, Redding, Mass.

Barham, K., J. Fraser and L. Heath (1988) *Management for the Future —* Foundation for Management Education/Ashridge Management College, Berkhamsted.

Department of Health and Social Security (1972) *Management Arrangements for the Reorganized Health Service*, HMSO, London.

Department of Health (1989) *Working for patients*, HMSO, London.

Edmonstone, J. D. (1982) 'Human service organizations: implications for management and organization development', *Management Education and Development*, **13**(3), Autumn, 163–73.

—— (1988) *Trainer development in Wales: A Review — Manpower, Training and Development Services*, for Welsh Health Common Services Authority/ Manpower Consultancy Service, April, Cardiff.

Flynn, N. (1986) 'Performance measurement in public sector services, *Policy and Politics*, **14**(3), July.

Garratt, B. (1987) *The Learning Organization*, Fontana/Collins, London, pp. 71–82.

Harrison, R. (1987) *Organization Culture and the Quality of Service: A Strategy for Releasing Love in the Workplace*, Association for Management Education and Development Focus Paper, London, pp. 2–3.

Hayes, C., A. Anderson and N. Fonda (1984) *Competence and Competition: Training and Education in the Federal Republic of Germany, the United States and Japan*, National Economic Development Council/Manpower Services Commission, London.

Illich, I. (1975) *Medical Nemesis: The Expropriation of Health*, Calder and Boyars, London.

King, D. S. (1987) *The New Right: Politics, Markets and Citizenship*, Macmillan Education, Basingstoke.

Koestler, A. (1959) *The Sleepwalkers*, Hutchinson, London, p. 341.

Kotter, J. (1982) *The General Managers*, The Free Press, New York.

Melia, K. (1987) *Learning and Working: The Occupational Socialization of Nurses*, Tavistock, London.

Menzies, I. E. P. (1967) *The Functioning of Social Systems as a Defence Against Anxiety: A Report on a Study of the Nursing Service of a General Hospital*, Tavistock Institute of Human Relations, London.

Mintzberg, H. (1973) *The Nature of Managerial Work*, Harper & Row, New York.

Morgan, G. (1986) *Images of Organization*, Sage, London, pp. 89–91.

Mumford, A. and D. Stradling (1987) *Developing Directors: The Learning Processes*, Manpower Services Commision, Sheffield, p. 27.

National Health Service Training Authority (1986a)—*Better Management, Better Health*, August, Bristol.

— (1986b) *Challenging Complacency in N.H.S. Training*, Occasional Paper No. 3, July, Bristol.

Pedler, M. (1986) 'Developing within the organization: experiences of management self-development groups,' *Management Education and Development*, **17**(1), Spring, 5–21.

— (1987) *Applying Self-Development in Organizations*, Manpower Services Commission, Sheffield.

— (1988) 'Review of *The Learning Organization*', *Management Education and Development*, **19**(2), Summer, 158–60.

Pettigrew, A. M., G. R. Jones and P. W. Reason (1982) *Training and Development Roles in Their Organizational Setting*, Manpower Services Commission-Training Studies Paper, October, Sheffield.

Revans, R. W. (1964) *Standards for Morale: Cause and Effect in Hospitals*, McGraw-Hill, Maidenhead.

Schon, D. (1983) *The Reflective Practitioner*, Maurice Temple Smith, London.

Smith, P. (1987) 'Appraising your progress as the unit general manager', *Hospital and Health Services Review*, **83**(6), November.

Stewart, J. and M. Clarke (1987) 'The public service orientation: issues and dilemmas', *Public Administration*, **65**, Summer.

Stewart, R. (1982) *Choices for the Manager: A Guide to Managerial Work and Behaviour*, McGraw-Hill, Maidenhead.

Watzlawick, P., J. Weakland and R. Fisch (1974) *Change: Problem Formulation and Problem Resolution*, W. W. Norton, New York.

Name Index

Allen, B.J., 129
Ambrose, K., 208
Anderson, A., 277
Anselm, St, 25
Aquinas, St Thomas, 29
Argyris, C., xii, 14, 165, 256, 259
Arroba, T., 179
Assagioli, R., 83, 177
Athos, A.G., 232
Attwood, M.E., 54, 234

Bacon, F., 26–27, 30
Bandler, R., 186
Bannister, D., 83, 149, 155
Barclay, R., 243
Barham, K., 252
Barrett, P., 208
Bartunek, J., 210
Bateson, G., 6, 14, 210
Beethoven, L. van, 23
Belbin, (R.)M., 74, 188
Boak, G., 136
Bolen, J.S., 179
Boot, R., 97
Bowen, H., 55
Boyatzis, R., 144
Boyd, W., 25
Boydell, T.H., xii, 6, 7, 11, 12, 21,
    164, 236
Bradford, D.L., 174
Brown, M., 86
Burgoyne, J.G., 6, 15, 21, 87, 164,
    207
Burrell, G., 16
Buzan, T., 73, 83

Calvin, J., 25, 29
Carnegie, D., 8
Casey, D., 151
Clarke, D., 209, 210
Clarke, M., 271
Cohen, A.E., 174

Constable, J., 86, 88, 252
Cooper, R., 32
Cooper, S., 109
Critchley, W., 151

Deal, T., 94
Derrida, J., 21, 29, 30, 31, 32
Dunnett, G., 83

Edmonstone, J.D., 264, 273
Egan, G., 170, 173
Einstein, A., 23

Ferrucci, P., 83
Fisch, R., 277
Flynn, N., 261
Fonda, N., 277
Fransella, F., 83, 149, 155
Fraser, J., 276
Freire, P., 18
Freud, S., 17
Fricker, J., 96

Gaitskell, H., 6
Galilei (Galileo), 26
Garratt, R., 164, 254, 255, 265
Gawain, S., 83
Gendlin, E., 83
Germain, C., 9
Griffiths, P., 129
Grinder, J., 186
Guzie, N.M., 179
Guzie, T., 179

Habermas, J., 17, 24, 211
Hackney, R., 212
Handy, C., 86, 88, 94, 101, 179, 252
Harrison, R., 9, 174, 260
Harvey-Jones, J., xi, 85
Hayes, C., 264
Heath, L., 276
Heron, J., 163, 165

Hill, C., 24
Hodgson, V., 97
Holland, R., 4–5
Honey, P., 137
Huxley, A., 13
Huxley, J., 8–9, 14

Illich, I., 264, 274

James, K., 179
Johnson, D.B., 234
Joinnes, V., 177
Jones, G.R., 277
Jung, C.G., 83, 179

Kahn, R.L., 160
Katz, D., 160
Kelly, G.A., 146, 148, 149, 151, 156
Kelly, O., 210
Kemp, N., 61, 62
Kennedy, A., 94
Kidd, P., 191
King, D.S., 261
Klemp, G.O., 144
Knevitt, C., 220
Knowles, M., 136
Koestler, A., 12, 257
Kolb, D., 72, 137, 139
Kotter, J., 260
Kuhn, T., 23

Lao Tzu, 32–33
Lawrence, P.R., 12
Lévi-Strauss, C., 28
Lorsch, J.W., 12
Lukes, S., 8
Luther, M., 25, 27, 29
Lyons, G., 171

Mann, S.J., 9
Marx, K., 17
Maslow, A., 6
McClelland, D., 144
Megginson, D., 6
Melia, K., 274
Menzies, I.E.P., 268
Mintzberg, H., 260
Moch, M., 210–211
Morgan, G., 258
Morris, J., 16

Morris, W., 23, 28
Mossman, A., 54
Mumford, A., 137, 260, 272

Nencini, M., 54–55, 57, 58, 64
Newton, Sir I., 26
Nietzsche, F., 28, 32
Norris, C., 29, 30

Ornstein, R., 83

Panos Institute, 18
Pascale, R.T., 232
Pedler, M.J., xii, xiii, 5, 6, 7, 10, 12,
    15, 21, 27, 55, 61, 62, 164,
    165, 208, 236, 242, 252, 253,
    255, 273
Perlmutter, H., 212
Peters, T.J., 4, 14, 86, 232, 245
Pettigrew, A.M., 273
Piaget, J., 6
Plato, 30, 31
Porter, E., 74
Pritchard, S., 54, 55, 58, 59, 60, 61
Progoff, I., 83

Quintilian, 25–26

Reason, P.W., 277
Revans, R.W., 14, 17, 137, 241,
    267–268
Rogers, C., 4, 6, 173, 207
Roscellinus, 25
Rousseau, J.-J., 22, 23, 28, 30
Ruskin, J., 28
Russell, B., 26
Russell, P., 83

Saussure, F. de, 29
Schein, E.H., 156, 165, 174
Schon, D., 14, 256, 259, 274
Shone, R., 83
Smiles, S., 8
Smith, M.J., 179
Steiner, R., 6
Stephenson, M., 136
Stewart, I., 177
Stewart, J., 271
Stewart, R., 178, 260
Stradling, D., 260, 272

Stuart, R., 6

Taylor, B., 208
Temporal, P., 242
Trist, E., 212
Tschudi, F., 156

Ure, A., 17

Vergerio, 25–26
Vittorino de Feltre, 26

Wales, N., 220
Waterman, R.H., 4, 14, 232, 245
Watson, S., 191
Watzlawick, P., 256, 257
Weakland, J., 277
Wilhelm, R., 83
Wordsworth, W., 23

Zwingli, U., 25

Subject Index

Accountability, 259, 263–264, 266
Action Learning, 17, 137, 145
Appraisal (*see* Performance assessment)
Ashridge Management College, 252, 253, 254
Assessment (*see* Performance assessment)
ASSET (Acquire Skills by Self Education of Texaco), 109
Astrology, 71

British Institute of Management, 86

Charter Group Initiative, 104, 174, 252
Chinese philosophy, 69, 71, 74–75
Christianity, 24–28
Civil Service College, 11
Communication, 245, 249 (*see also* Feedback)
Community (*see* Learning community)
Companies (*see* Learning organization; Organizations)
Competences (*see* Skills)
Competitive tendering, 224, 229
Confidentiality, 250
Conflict (*see* Internal conflict)
Conservatism, 261
Consumerism, 264
Constructs (*see* Personal construct psychology)
Consultants:
  management development programmes, 221–224
    design and implementation, 228–230
    familiarization and investigation, 224–227
    final report, 230–231
    identification of issues, 227–228

    initial contact, 224
Consumer Credit Act 1984, 108
Contracts (*see* Management learning contracts)
Corporate training events, 127–128 (*see also* Residential courses)
Counselling, 250
Cultural dominants, 22–24
Culture change, 50–52, 80
  group dynamics, 158
  management training, 60
  Prudential Insurance Company, 93–95
  response of training function, 96

Databases, 132
Decision-making, 245, 250
Deconstruction, 20, 21, 22, 27–34
Deprofessionalization, 274
Development, definition of, 6–7, 222
Development workshops, 129–131
Distance learning, 9–10, 111–112
Double-loop learning, 255, 257, 259

Education (*see also* Learning):
  humanistic, 25–26
Effective Manager programme, 94, 97–99
  application of new learning, 103
  company involvement, 100–101, 102
  content, 102
  enrolment profile, 100
  integration with other training, 103
  learning style, 102
  management support, 103
  marketing the course, 99–100
  student response, 101–102
  trainees, 99
Employees:
  dissatisfaction, 41
  needs recognized by organizations, 50–51, 68–69

Enlightenment, 24, 27
Equal opportunities, 264
  emotions underlying discriminatory
    practices, 198–199
  legislation, 198
  Mid Essex Health Authority, 250
  workshop exercises
    design, 199
    evaluation, 205–207
    exploring assumptions, 200–201
    reactions influenced by new
      information, 203–204
    reactions to physical differences,
      201–202
    use of creativity and intuition,
      202–203
Espoused theory, 259
Excellence, 264
Existentialism, 31
Experiential learning, 10, 13
Experiential learning, 10, 13

Facilitators, 62–63, 68, 70, 166–167,
    184, 185, 206, 221
Fantasy (see Guided affective
    imagery)
Feedback, 240, 246, 255
First-order change, 255, 256
Fit for the Future, 67–69
  course content, 73–76
  critical success factors, 69–71
  design considerations, 71–73
  measurement and evaluation,
    76–81
  overcoming specific problems,
    81–82
Forward Trust Group, 106, 108–111
Functionalism, 23

Gestalt, 69, 166, 186
Grey Book, 263
Grids (see Repertory grid
    construction)
Griffiths Report, 234, 263
Group dynamics, 158
Groups (see also Facilitators; Quality
    circles; T-groups):
  Life Business Workshop, 39–52
Guided affective imagery, 69, 74–5,
    167

sub-personalities, 182–186

Health Authorities (see NHS)
Hewlett Packard, 223
Hoechst UK, 121–124
  competences
    development, 124–126
    job analysis, 127
    performance assessment, training
      and development needs,
      126–127
    training events, 127–128
  development workshops, 129–131
  identification of potential, 128–129
  internal and external recruitment,
    131–132
  manpower planning systems,
    132–133
  people broking, 132
Humanism, 20, 21, 22, 25–28, 29–30

IBM, 67–68, 69, 70, 72, 76, 79, 80,
    81, 82–83, 223
I Ching, 71, 74–75, 82
Independent individuals, 86
Individual development (see
    Self-development)
Individualism, 8, 16, 171
Individual performance review (see
    Performance assessment)
Induction processes, 245
Industrial Training Act 1964, 7
Inhibitors to learning, 258–260
Interactive video, 112
Internal conflict, 176–177
  releasing 'negative' energies,
    180–182
  sub-personalities, 177–179
    guided imagery, 182–186
    harnessing, 186–189
Interpersonal skills, 117, 173

JLD Associates, 106
Job analysis, 115–116, 124–127, 229

Key jobs, 131
Keynesian economics, 262
Key staff, 131
Knowledge workers, 86

Learning, 3–5
    action learning, 17, 137, 145
    contracts (see Management learning
        contracts)
    definition, 210–211
    distance learning, 9–10, 111–112
    double-loop, 255, 257, 259
    inhibitors, 258–260
    open learning, 9–10
        confirming performance
            standards, 118–120
        definition, 114
        targets and deadlines, 117–118
    self-managed, 5–6, 61–62
    single-loop, 255, 256
    student-centred, 5–6, 7, 216, 217
Learning Community, 10, 208–209
    community defined, 209–210
    designing the learning event,
        214–217
    experience of managers, 218
    independence and interdependence,
        212
    learning defined, 210–211
    resourcing, 219
    reviewing process, 218–219
    role of the professional, 212–213
    role of the trainer, 217
Learning company (*see* Learning
    organization)
Learning cycle, 137
Learning organization, 12, 14–16, 41,
    87, 88
    inhibitors to learning, 258–260
    Mid Essex Health Authority
        feedback, 246
        guidelines for management
            practice, 248–251
    individual development methods,
        244–245
    Individual Performance Review
        scheme (IPR), 237–244
    involvement of non-managerial staff,
        244
    liberating structure, 242
    management style, 245–246
    new and appropriate interventions,
        246–247
    organizational sub-climates, 242–243
    responsible freedom, 243

    selection and induction processes,
        245
    transition change goals, 234–239
        model, 252–258
        continuity of feedback, 240
        rate of learning, 240–241
        robustness of learning process,
            240
        role of management, 239–240
        role of training and development
            staff, 240
        shared responsibility for learning
            process, 240
    public sector inhibitors
        ambiguity over core purpose,
            266–267
        no rewards for risk-taking,
            267–268
        no training culture, 268–269
        task-obsession, 267
    public sector potential, 269–271
        development of public service
            orientation, 271
        greater structural flexibility,
            271–272
        management development,
            272–273
        professional construction of
            reality, 273–275
        training and development
            function, 273
    public sector values, 261–264
        management, 264–265
Learning resources centres, 106–107
    benefits of self- and continuous
        development, 108–109
    disadvantages, 108
    distance learning, 111–112
    Forward Trust's TALENT scheme,
        108–111
Learning sets, 61–66
Left brain, 44–45, 73, 74, 75, 260
Liberalism, 261
Life Business Workshop, 39–52
Local authorities
    ambiguity over core purpose,
        266–267
    management development
        programmes, 224
    task-obsession, 267

'Loose-tight' management, 245–246, 247

Mail order systems, 111–112
Management's role in the learning organization, 239–240
Management Charter Initiative, 104, 173, 252
Management consultants (*see* Consultants)
Management learning contracts, 135–137
  assessment, 143–144
  contracts and projects, 137–138
  diagnosis, 139–140
  drafting, 140–141
    dependencies, 142
    explicitness, 142–143
    ownership of the contract, 141–142
    setting the target, 141
  priming, 138–139
Management skills, 117
Management style:
  Mid Essex Health Authority, 245–6, 248–251
Management training, 7, 114–115
  consultancy designed programmes (*see* Consultants)
  public sector, 272–273
  Radio Rentals, 57–61, 63–66
  self-managed learning groups, 61–62
  set advisers, 62–63
  single-sex (*see under* Women)
  W H Smith
    confirming performance standards, 118–120
    identifying individual needs, 115–116
    providing training responses, 116–118
  learning community (*see* Learning community)
Manpower planning, 124, 131, 132–133
McDonald's, 17
Mercedes Benz, 222
Mid Essex Health Authority (*see under* Learning Organization)

Mindmapping, 73
Mixed economy, 262
Modernism, 20, 22, 24, 27
Motivation, 136, 249–250
Myers Briggs Type Indicator, 179

National Examinations Board for Supervisory Management, 105
National Health Service, (*see* NHS)
NCVQ (National Council for Vocational Qualifications), 104
Neuro-Linguistic Programming, 186
New Order, 86
New Right, 261, 262, 264, 275
NHS, 261
  accountability, 263–264
  ambiguity over core purpose, 266–267
  double-loop learning, 257
  Government proposals, 276
  Individual Performance Review (IPR), 237, 244
  lack of training culture, 268–269
  Mid Essex Health Authority (*see under* Learning organization)
  public service orientation, 271
  reorganization, 262
  single-loop learning, 256
  task-obsession, 267
NHS Training Authority, 263, 271
North East London Polytechnic, 54

Open learning, 9–10, 114
  confirming performance standards, 118–120
  Prudential (*see* Prudential Insurance Company)
  targets and deadlines, 117–118
Open University, 86, 88
  Effective Manager (*see* Effective Manager programme)
Organizational effectiveness:
  compatibility with self-development (*see under* Self-development)
Organizations:
  culture change (*see* Culture change)
  learning (*see* Learning organization)

Participative management, 59, 245–246

Performance assessment, 118–120, 126–127, 128
management learning contracts, 143–4
NHS, 237, 244
Persona (*see* Sub-personalities)
Personal conflict (*see* Internal conflict)
Personal construct psychology, 69, 73, 146–147
alternative perspectives, 147–148
qualitative assessment of construing, 148–150
quantification of construing with analysis of data, 154–159
exchange grids, 152, 154
repertory grids, 150–152, 153
Personal development (*see* Self-development)
Personal growth, 6, 173 (*see also* Fit for the Future; Life Business Workshop)
spirituality, 12–13
Personal pensions, 86
Personnel (*see* Manpower planning; Recruitment; Trainers; Training)
Planning applications, 226
Porsche, 222
Post-modernism, 20, 21, 22, 28
Private medicine, 86
Private sector, 261, 264
Privatization, 224, 229
Process culture, 94
Product life-cycle, 23
Professionals, 212–213
Professional socialization, 273–274
Profiling centres, 116
Prudential Insurance Company, 93–94
culture change, 93–95
response of training function, 96
Effective Manager (*see* Effective Manager programme)
open learning, 96–97, 103–105
Psychosynthesis, 69, 177–178
Public sector, 261–264
ambiguity over core purpose, 266–267

fostering a learning organization, 269–271
development of the public service orientation, 271
greater structural flexibility, 271–272
management development, 272–273
political action, 275
professional construction of reality, 273–275
training and development function, 273
lack of training culture, 268–269
management, 264–265
no rewards for risk-taking, 267–268
task-obsession, 267

Quality circles, 10

Racism (*see* Equal opportunities)
Radio Rentals, 54, 55
changes in training and development, 57–61
history, 56–57
self-managed learning, 61–62
set advisers, 62–63
Recruitment, 122, 124, 128–129, 131–132, 227
selection and induction processes, 245
Reframing, 255–256, 257
Renaissance, 25
Repertory grid construction, 124, 148, 150–152, 153
analysis of data, 154–159
exchange grids, 152, 154
Replacement planning, 131
Residential courses, 114, 117, 119
Resourcing, 219
Right brain, 44–45, 69, 73, 75, 202, 260
Risk-taking, 267–268
Roffey Park, 214
Role culture, 94
Role structure, 151 (*see also* Sub-personalities)
Rolls-Royce, 222
Romanticism, 22–23, 31

Second-order change, 256–257
Selection of staff (*see* Recruitment)
Self-actualization (*see* Personal
    growth)
Self-characterization, 148–150
Self-development, 91–92
    compatibility with organizational
        effectiveness, 163–164, 255
    appropriate workshop design,
        164–166, 172
    enablement versus coercion,
        172–173
    group exercises, 166–169
    interpersonal skills programmes,
        173
    personal growth experiences, 173
    responsibility of the
        self-developer, 170–171
    skills required of trainers and
        counsellors, 170, 171–172
    support mechanisms, 167–168,
        170, 174
    definition, 84–85
    for management developers, 90–91
    individualism (*see* Individualism)
    internal conflict (*see* Internal
        conflict)
    learning (*see* Learning)
    learning organization (*see* Learning
        organization)
    Life Business Workshop, 39–52
    organizational climate, 85–86
    organization of programmes, 88–90
    purpose, 86–87
    social categories, 10–11
    sponsorship, 70, 87–88
Selfhood, 20–22
    deconstruction (*see* Deconstruction)
Self-managed learning, 5–6, 61–62
Self-theorists, 4–5
Set advisers, 62–63
Seven S model, 232
Sexism (*see* Equal opportunities)
'Shamrock' organization, 86
Single-loop learning, 255, 256, 258
Single-sex management training (*see*
        under Women)
Skills
    interpersonal, 117, 173
    job analysis, 115–116, 124-127

learning cycle, 137
    management, 117
    transfer (*see* Transfer of training)
Skill shortages, 7
Social categories, 10–11
Specialists, 86, 88
Spirituality, 12–13
Sponsorship, 70, 87–88
Staff appraisal (*see* Performance
        assessment)
Staffing (*see* Manpower planning;
        Recruitment)
Strengths deployment inventory, 74
Stress, 229
Student-centred learning, 5–6, 7, 216,
        217
Sub-personalities, 177–179
    guided imagery, 182–186
    harnessing, 186–188
    releasing 'negative' energies,
        180–182
Succession plans, 131
Support mechanisms, 167–168, 170,
        174
Systematic training, 7
Systems Approach to Education, 76
Systems engineering, 70

TALENT (Total Approach to
        Learning Employing New
        Technologies), 108–111
Taoism, 32
Teamwork inventory, 74
Texaco, 109
T-groups, 10, 89, 209
Theory-in-use, 259
Thorn EMI, 55, 56, 61, 65
Trainers, 217
    role in the learning organization,
        240
Training:
    corporate training events, 127–128
        (*see also* Residential courses)
    job analysis, 126–127
    management (*see* Management
        training)
    NHS, 268–269
    public sector, 273
    transfer (*see* Transfer of training)
Transactional analysis, 177–178, 181

Transfer of training, 7, 60

Unconditional positive regard, 207

Video, interactive, 112

Welfare state, 261–262
WH Smith, 114–120
Women (*see also* Equal
  opportunities):
  career development at IBM, 80–81
  participation in Fit for the Future
    courses, 82
  single-sex management training,
    190–192

benefits and negative issues, 194
criteria for authentic
  self-development, 195–196
emergence from traditional
  models, 192–193
evaluation, 196
Workers Educational Association
  (WEA), 5–6
Workshops (*see also* Facilitators;
    Learning Community; Life
    Business Workshops; Quality
    circles; T-groups):
  definition, 215

Zen, 71